Home Business

◆

Big Business

Home Business

◆

Big Business

Revised Edition

The Definitive Guide to
Starting and Operating On-Line
and Traditional Home-Based Ventures

MEL COOK

MACMILLAN ◆ USA

MACMILLAN
A Simon & Schuster Macmillan Company
1633 Broadway
New York, NY 10019-6785

Macmillan Publishing books may be purchased for business or sales promotional
use. For information please write: Special Markets Department, Macmillan
Publishing USA, 1633 Broadway, New York, NY 10019.

Revised edition, Copyright © 1998 by Mel Cook.

Photo on p.6 of Stephen and Susan Schutz by Jared.
Photo on p.19 of Bill Zanker © 1988 by Donna Fields Photography.

Library of Congress Cataloging-in-Publication Data
Cook, Mel.
    Home business, big business / Mel Cook. — Rev. ed.
       p.   cm.
    Includes index.
    ISBN 0-02-862252-9 (pbk.)
    1. New business enterprises—Management. 2. Home-based businesses—
Management. I. Title.
    HD62.5.C657 1998
    65.1'141—dc21   98-13889
                                                                        CIP

0-02-862252-9
Printed in the United States of America
10 9 8 7 6 5 4 3 2 1

CONTENTS

<u>P A R T   O N E</u>

HOME-GROWN MILLION-DOLLAR BUSINESSES

   Case histories of entrepreneurs who turned ideas for
   products and services into profitable businesses—some
   achieving wealth beyond their wildest dreams.

   Eight tips on fast-tracking a home venture. Learn the
   reasons why some businesses take off while others remain
   at the starting gate.

LISTING OF MEGASUCCESSFUL HOME-STARTED FIRMS PROFILED IN *HOME BUSINESS* ♦ *BIG BUSINESS*

INTRODUCTION

I f you're skeptical about getting rich from a work-from-home business, take a minute or so to flip through the pages of the first chapter of this book. Recognize the names of some of the companies profiled?—Lillian Vernon, Borland International, Discovery Toys. What may come as a surprise is that these multimillion-dollar firms started from home—spare rooms or in apartments—and by people with little experience in the business world. How these companies and others went from small sidelines to megasuccessful corporate giants is the primary focus of this book.

Home Business ◆ *Big Business* integrates all the steps needed to start an income-generating home business. None of it is theory. All the information is based on the "what works and what doesn't" experiences of entrepreneurs who made it to the top. Their advice is pulled together into a success formula that can easily be followed. If you are thinking about going into business for yourself, and want to hit the ground running, this book is essential reading.

◆ ◆ ◆

This revised and updated *Home Business* ◆ *Big Business* is divided into six sections. Part One profiles home-started ventures that grew into million-dollar companies and spells out the growth paths they took. It makes for fascinating and inspirational reading. The details of launching, managing, and expanding a home business are covered in Part Two. Everything you need to know to get going is right there, along with a chapter on turning your home into an electronic cottage. It contains information on computers and other technology essential to operating a home office. Descriptions of over one hundred work-from-home opportunities, with proven track records, are included in Part Three. There's a business for everyone. Part Four is an exciting new section, and covers operating a home business on the Internet. The focus is on on-line businesses that make money. Information on turnkey business opportunity packages is contained in Part Five, plus chapters on the legal considerations, and home-based ventures for retirees and the disabled. Finally, an extensive Resource Guide provides indispensable reference data, making this the most comprehensive, useful, and up-to-date book on working from home.

PART ONE

Home-Grown
Million-Dollar Businesses

MAKING IT BIG

Profiles of Home-Based Ventures That Became Million-Dollar Companies

1

The central theme of the first part of this book is success—real success. It contains snapshots of ventures started in kitchens, basements, and garages by entrepreneurs who, at the beginning, would have settled for a few thousand dollars a year in extra income. The chain of events that catapulted these firms into the corporate big leagues makes for fascinating reading. More important, the stories tell us something about fast-tracking a home business.

There is nothing more inspirational than a good success story. That's why forty sketches of megasuccessful companies are included in this book, twenty-four of them in the first chapter. Each firm profiled was started by home-based entrepreneurs, typically "average" people, who launched their venture with little capital or business-world experience You may be surprised that the products and services represented are, in many instances, ordinary—women's accessories, bread, stamp packets, wax candles, pies, toys, sewn products, candy, and so forth—items you, no doubt, could have thought of if you put your mind to it. More often than not, million-dollar ideas are simply creative variations on things that already exist.

LILLIAN VERNON

Lillian Vernon

If there is one case history that can dispel any doubts about a neophyte entrepreneur going from a kitchen table–operated sideline to the top of a major American corporation, it's the experiences of Lillian Vernon.

Like many expectant mothers, Lillian had to find a way of meshing the raising of a family with some money-making activity that would add to her husband's modest income. A mail-order business seemed practical to run from her small apartment, located in a New York suburb, and, in 1951, she used $2,000 of wedding gift money and placed an ad costing $495 in *Seventeen* magazine. The products she pinned her hopes on were a monogrammed shoulder bag and belt.

At first there was a trickle of orders and Lillian wondered whether her venture would make it. But then the letters began to pour in, each

Lillian Vernon's first mail-order ad. It started an entrepreneurial career that took her to the top of a $160-million company listed on the American Stock Exchange.

containing a check or money order—money that enabled her to buy the merchandise. A one-person operation, Lillian made the bank deposits, personalized the bags and belts, typed address labels, packed the orders, and made the drops at the post office. The initial ad brought in $32,000 and Lillian's home business was off and running.

Over the years, Lillian Vernon added other products. "Get paid first, then send out the merchandise" was the way the firm bank-rolled growth. Eventually mail-order catalogs, mailed to people who had previously ordered merchandise, replaced magazine advertising as the major sales-generating source. The firm today has annual revenues of over $200 million and is listed on the American Stock Exchange. What made Lillian Vernon such a big winner? There were a number of factors, such as exceptional market sensitivity and a sound, realistic business strategy. But possibly the most important ingredient was a determined, hardworking entrepreneur who believed in the American dream.

BORLAND INTERNATIONAL

French-born Philippe Kahn started his company in true Silicon Valley, California, fashion: in a garage. Recognizing that there was a need for better software to convert programming instructions into codes a computer could understand, Philippe refined a program he was familiar with, known as Pascal. When the larger companies refused to buy it, he decided to market it himself by mail at a much lower price—$49.95—than similar software was going for in retail stores. He named the firm Borland International because, Philippe said, "It sounded like some subsidiary of a multinational company, when really we were just two guys on top of a garage." Convincing *Byte* magazine to provide credit, he ran a full-page ad. Thirty days after the ad appeared Borland had 100,000 orders. That was in 1983.

Philippe Kahn, Borland International

Philippe Kahn's shoestring venture grew quickly after that, but he continued to follow the same business strategy that he used to launch the business, namely, providing general-application software that outperformed the competition and selling it through the mail at eye-catching prices. The firm became a major supplier of database, spreadsheet, and programming software to corporations worldwide.

BLUE MOUNTAIN ARTS

Stephen and Susan Schutz, Blue Mountain Arts

I am always here
to understand you
I am always here
to laugh with you
I am always here
to cry with you
I am always here
to talk to you
I am always here
to think with you
I am always here
to play with you
Even though we
might not always
be together
please know that
I am always
here to
love
you

—Susan Polis Schutz*

Blue Mountain Arts creates beauty with words.

In 1969 Susan Polis Schutz and her physicist husband, Stephen, blended poetry and art on posters that they silk-screened in the basement of their Boulder, Colorado, home and sold from the back of a pickup truck. This effort led to the 1971 founding of Blue Mountain Arts to create a unique line of greeting cards that combined emotional poetry with natural, peaceful artwork. The all-occasion, personal relationship cards, distributed by independent sales representatives, met with phenomenal success and the firm grew. Over 300 million Blue Mountain Arts cards have been sold through 20,000 retail outlets.

DISCOVERY TOYS

Some of the best ideas for business come about by accident. When Lane Nemeth couldn't find the right educational toys for her two-year-old daughter in retail stores, she came to the conclusion other parents might be having the same problem. So she sketched out a business plan and, in 1977, using her Martinez, California, garage as a warehouse, launched Discovery Toys.

Lane Nemeth, Discovery Toys

While Lane had nothing in her background that qualified her as an entrepreneur, she had a master's degree in education and was director of a day-care center. That provided her with a pretty good knowledge of kids and toys. Borrowing $5,000, she purchased a carefully chosen selection of educational merchandise from existing suppliers and convinced three friends to demonstrate the products at Tupperware-like home "parties." Lane provided her sales force with the impressive title "educational consultants" and paid them a percentage of the sales. The marketing technique worked. Discovery Toys representatives were able to explain to parents the skill the child would develop with the toys, something retail clerks rarely have the time to do.

Discovery Toys grossed $20,000 the first year and only then did Lane quit her job. A year later sales reached a quarter of a million, and they have kept growing ever since. In addition to toys, the product line now includes games, books, and videotapes, and revenues are almost $100 million. Direct-sales representatives total 20,000.

ASK COMPUTER SYSTEMS

Like many women, Sandra Kurtzig believed that a business career had to be balanced with family. So in 1972, at the age of twenty-four, she quit her job as marketing specialist of time-sharing services for General Electric to devote more time to her children. But unwilling to totally give up on the business world, she invested $2,000 to start an apartment-based computer contract programming company and named it ASK.

Sandra Kurtzig, ASK Computer Systems

Her first assignment, setting up programs that kept track of newspaper delivery accounts, was very successful. This led to developing software for a variety of businesses. ASK quickly outgrew the apartment and employees were added to handle the increased volume. The big break came in 1976 when she came up with a program that ran on Hewlett-Packard minicomputers. It was universal-type software that could be used by most manufacturing companies. ASK's sales and profits soared, and in 1981 the firm went public. By 1983, Sandra's share in ASK was worth $67 million.

In 1991, Sandra coauthored an autobiography on her spectacular success, appropriately titled *CEO—Building a 400 Million Dollar Company from the Ground Up.*

WELL-BRED LOAF, INC.

Steve Caccavo and Judy Glicken, once part of the 1960s antiestablishment culture, would seem the individuals least likely to achieve entrepreneurial stardom. Yet they turned an apartment sideline into a multimillion-dollar bakery business.

In 1974, Steve was a guitar teacher and Judy was a social worker. Underpaid in their chosen careers, they started baking a variety of natural-ingredient products—brownies, Jewish challah, Irish soda bread, pound cake—in Judy's fourth-floor Manhattan walkup. On weekends they carted their inventory downtown to the South Street Seaport, a historic area that attracted tens of thousands of visitors, and sold the products off a card table.

Enough people appreciated the homemade taste and business thrived. A year later the two owners moved to larger quarters and began wholesaling to gourmet shops, delis, and other retailers. Annual sales grew in double digits, and in 1985 the bakery was moved into a 41,000-square-foot plant located in Congers, New York—about twenty-five miles north of New York City. The firm now employs more than one hundred workers and has annual revenues of $11 million from sales of a variety of cookies and cakes, and, of course, the brownies that gave them their start.

Steve Caccavo and Judy Glicken, Well-Bred Loaf, Inc.

SIERRA ON-LINE

Dissatisfied with the simplicity of the computer games available for their Apple computer in 1979, Ken and Roberta Williams decided they could come up with something better. Roberta, wife and mother, designed the first computer game on her kitchen table, while husband Ken, an experienced programmer, translated it into computer language. They called their game, a whodunit, Mystery House, and it was the first to include graphics.

Then they had to sell it. Roberta pasted together an ad using text and graphics clipped from magazines to save the cost of typesetting. A $200 ad in a computer magazine brought in $8,000 the first month, $20,000 the second. Disks were first packaged in resealable plastic bags, and then automated to Seal-A-Meal, a kitchen appliance that melted the plastic bags closed.

That was the humble beginning of Sierra On-Line. One game led to another, each selling better than the last because of the rapidly growing market and increasingly innovative talents of the Williamses. The firm acquired "a few million bucks" in venture capital in 1982, and six years later went public.

Sierra On-Line, located in Oakhurst, California, continues to develop entertainment products for home computers, but is now beginning to branch into the educational market. Annual sales total approximately $80 million.

Ken and Roberta Williams, Sierra On-Line

MOTHERS WORK

As is the case with so many successful entrepreneurs, Rebecca Matthias's idea for a business came while she was seeking a solution to her own personal problem. She was pregnant but could find only casual maternity clothes in the stores. Few items had the professional look she needed to remain active in her husband's computer business. Coming to the conclusion that other pregnant career women were faced with the same situation, Rebecca, in 1982, launched a mail-order business from her Boston home shortly after giving birth. She named the company Mothers Work.

Rebecca traveled to New York's Seventh Avenue, the nation's fashion center, to locate sophisticated-look maternity wear for her catalog. Using $10,000 in savings, she purchased an inventory of merchandise, printed 3,000 copies of a black-and-white catalog, and ran small ads in *The Wall Street Journal* and *The New Yorker*. Inquiries were received but sales turned out to be dismal. Her timing was off—the catalog came out too late in the season—and customers preferred color catalogs. It was a costly mistake,

Rebecca Matthias, Mothers Work

but not a fatal one. Rebecca made adjustments and bounced back. First-year sales totaled $60,000.

For the first several years, Mothers Work sold only through mail order. In 1984, Rebecca made a decision that later proved to be significant in the firm's success. She decided to grow by franchising retail stores, and revenues hit seven figures. A year later $250,000 was raised from private sources and Mothers Work started to manufacture its own clothing by jobbing out designs to independent contractors. Additional investment capital enabled it to open company-owned retail stores and profits multiplied. Philadelphia-based Mothers Work (the firm moved from Boston in 1983) is now a $100-million manufacturing and retail organization.

JBI, INC.

Lisa Lindahl (left) and Hinda Miller, JBI, Inc.

Question. Put two women joggers together with two men's jockstraps and what do you have? Answer. A product called Jogbra and the beginnings of a multimillion-dollar sports underwear firm.

Two Vermont women, Lisa Lindahl and Hinda Miller, both in their twenties, thought they needed a firmer bra support when running. Their prototype, two men's jockstraps sewn together by a friend, worked so well they decided to market it nationally. A partnership named Jogbra was formed, and with $5,000 in borrowed money they went into business for themselves using Lisa's five-room apartment. The dining-room set served as office furniture and warehousing was carried out in the living room. They manufactured a few hundred Jogbras, which were sold to area sports stores and through an ad in *Running Times* magazine. At eight dollars each, the entire batch of homemade bras quickly sold out and in 1978 profits totaled $3,000. The company was off and running.

The product's marketplace acceptance convinced bankers that Jogbra had a future and the two partners were able to negotiate a $50,000 loan guaranteed by the Small Business Administration (SBA). By 1982, sales had reached $1 million. Over the years other women's and men's sportswear items were added. In 1990, Jogbra was sold by the joggers-turned-entrepreneurs to Playtex Apparel of Stamford, Connecticut. The price was reportedly in the multimillions.

DELL COMPUTER CORPORATION

Dell Computer was started by nineteen-year-old Michael Dell in a University of Texas dormitory with $1,000 in savings. Seven years later company revenues were more than half a billion dollars a year.

In 1984, sales of personal computers were skyrocketing. College freshman Michael bought components and built systems in his room that were better than what was available off the shelf. The experience helped him recognize that retailers were making a great deal of money—markups of as much as 40 percent—for doing very little. Why should they make $1,500 on a $4,000 computer for putting a box in a car trunk? Many customers didn't need the help retailers provided, Michael reasoned, and would buy direct from someone offering equivalent value at much lower prices. He was proven right.

Initially, Dell Computer Corporation marketed only component kits through trade-magazine ads. Then a toll-free number was added and the firm began to sell IBM-compatible personal computers. First-year sales were an astounding $6 million. In 1985 Dell expanded into manufacturing its own computers and three years later the in-house sales force tailored its direct-marketing methods to meet the needs of larger corporate customers. In 1990, Dell began selling through a computer superstore chain. International sales, which were initiated in 1987, now account for a large part of revenues.

The meteoric growth of Dell Computer, from college dorm to $12 billion company, was accomplished not with gimmick, but the old-fashioned way—by satisfying consumer demand. Founder Michael Dell is now worth more than $4 billion—not bad for someone in his thirties.

Michael Dell, Dell Computer Corporation

THE AUSTAD COMPANY

Oscar Austad didn't know it at the time but being terminated from his insurance claims adjuster job was the best thing that ever happened to him. Even though he found another position in a few days, the experience made him seek something to fall back on in the event it ever happened again. He knew about the golf-supply business from family relationships and believed that it was overstuffed with middlemen, deliveries were too slow,

Oscar Austad, The Austad Company

and prices were too high. In 1963 Oscar began a sideline selling golf tubes (club grip protectors) from the trunk of his car, and shortly afterward set up a mail-order operation from his garage and basement.

In the beginning the Austad Company distributed golf equipment only to dealers. The first "catalog" consisted of a single mimeographed sheet typed by Oscar's wife, which was mailed to an area within 200 miles of their Sioux Falls, South Dakota, home. Orders were processed immediately and dealers received merchandise within a day or two. Revenues the first year were $80,000, and profit, $2,000.

Within a short time the Austad Company outgrew Oscar's basement and commercial space was rented. Selling emphasis was also shifted from dealers to consumers and a mailing list of professional people—bankers, doctors, lawyers, and so forth—was developed using the Yellow Page telephone directories from all over the country. The firm's selling theme was lower prices, speedy delivery, and an honest guarantee. Timing was right—growth was fueled by the rapid increase in the number of golfers. The Austad Company now operates retail stores, mails 32 million catalogs every year, and has annual sales of approximately $50 million.

PAUL SEBASTIAN, INC.

Leonard Paul Cuozzo (left) and Alan Sebastian Greco, Paul Sebastian, Inc.

Leonard Paul Cuozzo, an automobile salesman, lived near a fragrance plant in New Jersey and knew something about the product from friends who worked there. Alan Sebastian Greco was an office-products sales manager. In 1979 the two formed a partnership that was able to carve a multi-million-dollar sales niche in the intensely competitive fragrance industry.

Leonard and Alan pooled $1,000 each and operated out of Cuozzo's home, concocting and bottling fragrances for men. The first patch of Paul Sebastian (a combination of the owners' middle names) fragrance (now referred to as PS FINE cologne) went to men's clothing retailers, a market essentially ignored by the larger firms because they thought the volume was too small. But it turned out to be a good opening for a fledgling firm trying to gain a toehold in the marketplace. Alan's regular job required traveling, and in each city he made evening sales calls on haberdashers. In the first year, Paul Sebastian, Inc., had $25,000 in sales.

With the hiring of a fashion representative the following year, distribution expanded to 300 stores and volume hit $200,000. They then talked a Bamberger's buyer into a two-store test. Promoting their products from a table, they sold out five straight weeks. Macy's then took on the line and sales for the firm began to grow in double digits.

Paul Sebastian, Inc., is now headquartered in Tinton Falls, New Jersey, and has over 100 employees and revenues of over $50 million a year.

YANKEE CANDLE

Mike Kittredge, Yankee Candle

Unexpected events frequently shape the future. The time—a few days before Christmas 1969. Mike Kittredge, a high-school senior from a small town in western Massachusetts, had little money for holiday gifts. Raiding the pantry for canning wax, he added some colored crayons, melted the concoction on his mother's kitchen stove and used empty milk cartons as molds. Mike didn't know it at the time, but that Christmas situation started him on a successful entrepreneurial career.

The homemade candles impressed both family and friends. Word of mouth kept demand building and in a short time the business had to relocate—from the kitchen to the basement. Mike split his schedule between taking business courses at the local college and keeping the candle business growing. He started selling at craft fairs and to area gift stores.

In 1971, Mike rented a space in an old paper mill and hired some people to help. In 1978 he received a Small Business Administration loan. Yankee Candle was no longer a home sideline, but a full-time business with a future. Four years later, annual sales hit $1 million and the company moved to a new plant and retail store in South Deerfield. Today Yankee Candle is the world's largest producer of hand-crafted candles, with revenues of over $30 million and a workforce of 400. That's quite an achievement for a man who began as a seventeen-year-old kid cooking wax on his mother's stove.

DIET CENTER

Sometimes it pays to be a little chubby. In 1968 Sybil Ferguson, Idaho homemaker, weighed 185 pounds—about 50 more than she should have. But because of her diet, she was considered too malnourished for surgery. Researching in the local college library, she came up with a high-nutrition,

Sybil Ferguson, Diet Center

low-calorie diet that was both healthy and well-balanced. "I quit counting calories and focused on nutrition," she said.

Sybil's success in weight reduction attracted the attention of friends and neighbors, whom she counseled free. But when doctors started to refer patients, Sybil set up a weighing station in a spare room and initiated a weekly fee of ten dollars. As the kitchen drawer began to overflow with money, it became apparent that weight-control advice could be more than a sideline activity, and the Diet Center was born.

Sybil's husband, Roger, was a company executive who recognized the potential of franchising weight-loss centers. In 1970, the first Diet Center franchise was sold and within four years the number had grown to 120 nationwide. Through the 1970s and 1980s Diet Center continued to grow, adding franchises worldwide—2,000 at present—and a pharmaceutical laboratory to manufacture vitamin and mineral supplements. In 1985 the company was sold for $50 million to a New York investment firm, which a few years later sold it for $160 million.

HARBOR SWEETS

Ben Strohecker, Harbor Sweets

In 1975, when Schrafft's marketing director Ben Strohecker lost his job in a management shakeup, he decided it was time to go into business for himself. He had been cooking candy as a hobby in his Marblehead, Massachusetts, basement for a number of years, so he knew the art of chocolate making.

His first product came about as a result of a poll of consultants and colleagues at Schrafft's. He simply asked them, "If you could eat only one piece of candy before you died, which would it be?" It turned out to be chocolate-covered almond butter crunch—and a winner. Subsequent items were market-tested at church fairs and bake sales. All of the candy designs were related to nautical themes, such as the best-selling Sweet Sloops.

Growth quickly forced Harbor Sweets out of the basement into a Salem factory. The firm employs 150 during the seasonal peaks, most of them part-time employees who work flexible hours and share in the company's profits. Sales from mail-order catalogs, custom orders, and retail stores are now $3 million.

INTUIT

Scott Cook, a Harvard Business School graduate, was twenty-nine years old when he founded a computer software company on a single product, Quicken. Not a computer whiz himself, he joined forces with a Stanford University undergraduate named Tom Proulx in 1983 to translate the idea into prototype software. Working out of Tom's living room and funded by loans from relatives and friends, plus whatever could be bought on credit cards, they barely got by until 1986 when a major distributor began carrying the product. Then sales began to multiply.

Scott Cook, Intuit

Quicken is a program that allows consumers and small businesses to write checks and keep track of their finances on personal computers. It's considered the easiest-to-use personal-finance software available—anyone who has written a check can master it. It dominates the market, with over 2 million units having been sold. Intuit recently introduced a feature called CheckFree that links the PC to the bank for electronic transfer of funds. Obviously, Scott Cook has his eye on the future.

Intuit, located in Menlo Park, California, now has sales of almost $400 million.

AROMATIQUE

This company was built on a mélange of botanicals found just about everywhere—acorns, pinecones, hickory nuts, and so forth. In 1982, creator Patti Upton began mixing her backyard harvest with green bay leaves and red berries for color, plus fragrant oils and spices. She made this for her own personal use and to decorate a friend's gift shop, never dreaming the product would be sold. Her visiting friends and the gift-shop customers wanted to know where to buy the delightful concoction. Soon she was packaging small quantities in cellophane bags tied with colorful cords. Customers would buy the entire supply as soon as it got onto the shelf.

Patti Upton, Aromatique

Patti envisioned a new industry—decorative room fragrances—and launched Aromatique. The first just-for-fun product, called the Smell of Christmas, was followed by the Smell of Spring, and by other environmental fragrance items, which she sold directly to boutiques around the country. Within a few months sales reached $100,000. More retailers were added, but on a selective basis. The company's marketing strategy was to sell only to better stores willing to display their products in prime floor space, thereby assuring optimum sales per outlet.

Aromatique, still privately owned, has been phenomenally successful. The product line has been increased to eleven different room fragrance lines, and more than 5,000 upper-end retailers carry the firm's merchandise. An average of 200 employees work for the company year-round, with several hundred more added during peak seasons. Annual sales of the Heber Springs, Arkansas, firm are about $25 million.

ACTION PRODUCTS INTERNATIONAL

Judith Kaplan, Action Products International

Judith Kaplan turned a stamp-collecting hobby into a $4 million business.

Judy, a petite, four-foot-eleven-inch, avid museum- and planetarium-goer, was disappointed with what she found in their gift shops. Few of the items had much relevance to the exhibits, and in 1977 she began offering packets of commemorative postage stamps. Getting started wasn't particularly difficult since she knew stamps—collecting was a family hobby—and the lists of museums and planetariums were readily available.

The company, then known as Action Packets, was run from Judy's Queens, New York, basement. The first order—$100—came from a planetarium and was for a stamp grouping depicting recent rocket launches and astronomical discoveries. Within two years, sales reached $100,000.

The product line was expanded to include nonstamp, purchased items, doodads such as rubber snakes and zodiac key chains. In 1980, the rapidly growing firm moved to Ocala, Florida—into a 15,000-square-foot office and warehouse—and began publishing multipage catalogs, which were mailed to 800 museums, aquariums, zoos, and planetariums. Sales accelerated when corporate aerospace memorabilia were added for companies like Boeing and General Dynamics. In 1984, Judy went public with a stock offering to raise expansion capital. Action Products today employs about forty people and has annual sales in the United States and overseas of over $4 million. Judy is still CEO.

BROADMOOR BAKER

In 1986 Paul Suzman home-started a business that now provides a six-figure income, but only required ten to twelve hours a week of his time.

Paul, a Seattle real estate consultant, wasn't satisfied with the breads that were available at local stores. They lacked the hearty, grained texture of the breads he ate as a youth in his native South Africa. Tinkering at home with recipes on evenings and on weekends, he finally came up with a concoction that included whole-wheat flour, barley, rolled oats, cracked wheat, sesame, flax, sunflower, poppy and pumpkin seeds, molasses, and brown sugar. Friends and neighbors were used to taste-test the product and loved it. With their encouragement Paul decided to make the bread available to the general public.

But there was a problem. Paul was very successful at his real-estate business and didn't want to leave. So he came up with a solution that enabled him to work at both real estate and baking—he farmed out the baking, packaging, and distribution of the bread to Gais, a quality commercial baker. A contract was negotiated that gave him a royalty based on net wholesale volume.

Paul Suzman, Broadmoor Baker

Paul spends about ten to twelve hours a week on quality control of the bread produced, developing new recipes, and public relations. Other bakery items have been added and product sales are $1 million a year. The bread mixes are licensed to a wholesaler for national distribution outside the Pacific Northwest.

BONNE BELL

Jesse Bell believed in the American dream—and proved it worked. At the age of thirty-seven, ambitious and confident, he left his job as cosmetics salesman in Kansas City and moved to Cleveland where he started a "factory" in the basement of his rented house. He named the firm Bonne Bell. That was in 1927.

Using a hot plate, Jesse prepared and packaged makeup items for women and then sold the merchandise himself door-to-door. When a prospective customer objected to the somewhat primitive brown-paper-

Jesse Bell, Bonne Bell

bag packaging, Jesse had an answer. "Are you interested in a package or a product?" Most bought.

Sales grew and the company expanded into the wholesale market, hiring women to sell to beauty salons. In 1936, Bonne Bell purchased a facial cleanser formula developed by a chemist. The formula, named Ten-O-Six, won public acceptance and remains the firm's best seller.

Bonne Bell today markets a complete line of cosmetics and has worldwide sales in the $50 million range. It's still family-owned and run by Jess Bell, son of the founder, and his sister Bonne Bell Eckert.

MANHATTAN TOY COMPANY

With both grandfather and father Goldwyn Hollywood success stories, many believed son Francis (Fran) would eventually go into motion pictures. Instead, in 1982 at the age of twenty-eight, he left a good job at one of the Big Eight accounting firms and chose an entrepreneurial career in stuffed toys from a Manhattan apartment.

Fran named the firm Stuffed Oids and the first creation was an oid— a strangely shaped animal that resembled a prehistoric monster. The production work was contracted out and Fran handled the selling, personally calling on toy and gift stores in the New York metropolitan area. Oid bombed.

Changing the name of the firm to Manhattan Toy, Fran replaced the oid with a dinosaur line, which sold well in better toy and department stores. Independent sales representatives were hired to market the toys nationally, and outside money was brought in, which reduced Fran's equity in the business to 50 percent. With a national marketing network in place and capital available, Manhattan Toy started to grow to over $5 million by 1989. In 1991 Fran sold the remaining 50 percent share of the business to an outside group and went into other entrepreneurial endeavors.

MY OWN MEALS, INC.

My Own Meals operated out of Mary Anne Jackson's Illinois home only for a few months—but that was enough time for her to conceive and market test an idea that would achieve millions in sales within a few years.

In 1986, Mary Anne, a Beatrice Foods executive, was among the victims of a company restructured after a leveraged buyout. She liked corporate life, but being unemployed pushed her into an entrepreneurial career that, she admits, would not likely have occurred otherwise. She knew the food industry, so her search for a business focused on products that could be sold in supermarkets. As a working mother she remembered all those weekend hours spent cooking meals her kids could eat during the week. The idea Mary Anne came up with was nutritious, no-additives meals, vacuum-sealed in plastic pouches for two- to ten-year-olds. All a work-weary mother would have to do was drop the pouch into boiling water or put it into the microwave.

Mary Anne Jackson, My Own Meals, Inc.

Mary Anne thought the product would do well in the marketplace but she was trained in a big company where market research is a must. So she enlisted a diaper service to distribute 2,000 questionnaires, and the response was overwhelmingly positive. Working with a food-development company, she prepared sample meals and tested them at nursery schools and day-care centers. What the kids liked was put in the product line.

The Deerfield, Illinois, company was financed by several private stock offerings. My Own Meals is now carried by 1,000 supermarkets and KinderCare Day Care Centers. Revenues are about $900,000.

THE LEARNING ANNEX

The idea for an adult-education school came from a friend of twenty-six-year-old Bill Zanker. The friend, a crafts teacher, complained about the difficulty of marketing her pottery courses to the public. Adding self-help seminars (such as getting through job interviews) to craft workshops, Bill started the school in the basement of a New York City brownstone. It was 1980 and his investment was $4,000.

Business strategy of the Learning Annex was simple. Recruit professionals to conduct short-term, inexpensive classes in their own studios or rented classrooms and publish a compilation of the courses in a catalog, which would be distributed free in high-traffic locations. Instructors would share in the tuition revenues. All this added up to low administrative costs and a breakeven point that did not drain working capital. Initially Bill distributed the catalogs himself—sometimes dressed as a clown—and then ran back to the office to handle phone calls of the registrants.

Bill Zanker, The Learning Annex

It took only three years for the Learning Annex to reach $1 million in sales and a $76,000 profit. In 1984, the company went public and expanded to other cities.

VOLUMETRIC FUND

Gabriel Gibs, Volumetric Fund

Gabriel Gibs, a chemist by training, enjoyed dabbling in the stock market. There's nothing unique about that—many people invest as a hobby. But Gabe turned his hobby into a full-time activity—running a mutual fund out of his Pearl River, New York, home.

Gabe developed his knowledge of the stock market from personal investing and discovered a market-forecasting technique based on volume analysis during his MBA program at Pace University. In 1978, ten coworkers approached him about forming an investment group. They each put in $1,000 and the Volumetric Fund came into being. The fund was operated as a sideline until 1986 when Gabe left his job, incorporated the business, and went public with the fund. His garage was converted into an office.

The no-load Volumetric Fund has grown to more than 1,100 investors and assets of $17 million. The fund is now listed in the Mutual Fund section of newspapers. The staff still remains small, with Gabe serving as president and portfolio manager. Several assistants handle administrative chores.

◆ ◆ ◆

And there are other stories. Dorothy Noe, a North Carolina entrepreneur, built a $20-million firm from her garage. Her firm, Dorothy's Ruffled Originals, custom-makes curtains and other accessories to match the antique decor of a home. Barbara and George Spite named their basement-operated mail-order company after themselves, the Barbara George Collection. The firm did $30 million in merchandise sales that are selectively targeted.

Leanin' Tree Publishing was operated part-time for many years from the Colorado home of Ed and Pat Trumble. They started with four cowboy greeting cards. Their Western and wildlife subject cards are now sold in 15,000 retail stores. Moe Siegel picked plants during bicycle rides in the Rockies and home-mixed them to concoct herbal teas. His multimillion-dollar Boulder, Colorado, firm, Celestial Seasonings, is the industry leader. Most people will be surprised to learn that Nikes began in a home basement, where the first shipments of the imported running shoes were stored. Sales took off when the owners convinced marathoners to wear the shoes and the firm benefited from the advertisement.

Don't get the idea that turning a home business into a big business is a recent phenomenon. Pepperidge Farm bread began in 1937 with a husband-and-wife team. Margaret Rudkin baked the bread in her kitchen and her husband delivered the loaves on his way to work. Arnold Foods was started at about the same time by Paul Arnold with $600 after he was fired from a bakery. His wife made and packaged the quality bread and sold it locally. Mueller Noodles was started in 1867 as a sideline in a kitchen of a New Jersey home. In 1889, Sam Johnson custom-mixed his own paste-wax in a basement and gave it to customers who purchased his parquet floors. The firm he founded is now known as Johnson's Wax. Burpee Seeds was started in 1880 by Atlee Burpee as a mail-order operation out of his parents' home. Lane Bryant began as a home-based sewing operation in 1906. First it was lingerie, then gowns and maternity clothes—all specifically designed to flatter the wearer's figure.

The first Steinway piano was crafted in the 1840s in the kitchen of Heinrich Steinweg's home in Germany. Smith Brothers cough drops were initially cooked on a kitchen stove and packaged by the two brothers in plain paper envelopes. The now famous S.O.S pad began in 1917 as a giveaway by a salesman who sold aluminum cookware. Working in his San Francisco home, he dipped the stainless-steel pads in soap until they were saturated. Hershey's Chocolate was started in the back room of a Pennsylvania home. The first product was homemade caramels and later chocolate was added. This eventually led to the chocolate bar made with fresh milk. The concept for Avon began as a perfume giveaway by a home-based, door-to-door book salesman. He used it to get housewives to listen to his sales pitch.

Remember, a big business is often only a small business that grew and prospered.

2 GOING FROM KITCHEN TABLE TO EXECUTIVE SUITE

The Secrets of Growing a Business

The reasons for the phenomenal success of the firms profiled in Chapter 1 may appear to be a hodgepodge of unrelated factors. They are not. Weaving through the case histories are common threads—elements that reveal the secrets of business growth.

THE SECRETS OF GROWTH

1. *Offer products or services that can be marketed on a large scale.* Growth opportunities are not inherent in all ventures that can be home-operated. A secretarial service, for example, usually has too limited a market to attain million-dollar sales. To move into seven-figure revenues a business has to reach a large enough group of buyers. More often than not, this will require the enterprise to market nationally. Almost all of the megasuccessful went down this path. But there are exceptions. Consumable products with widespread appeal, such as bakery items, may find enough customers in metropolitan areas of major cities. Both Broadmoor Baker and The Little Pie Company reached seven-figure sales levels with only regional distribution of their products.

2. *Provide something different from what's already in the marketplace.* It's difficult for any business to sustain significant growth when its products

or services are hardly distinguishable from the competition. Entrepreneurs can create differences simply by finding better ways of serving selective segments of a market. This sometimes is accomplished just by adding a new twist to something old, or by marketing more creatively. For example, Lillian Vernon took essentially off-the-shelf merchandise and personalized the items. Discovery Toys packaged a variety of educational products and marketed directly to consumers using Tupperware-like home "parties." This selling method turned out to be much more effective, in informing the parents of the educational value of the games, books, and toys, than what could be conveyed from nonpersonal retail store displays. Paul Sebastian found a way of penetrating the highly competitive fragrance market by selling through men's clothing stores, a distribution channel ignored by others. Borland International rode in on the computer revolution. The firm sold good software cheaper than the competition and through mail order while most similar products were marketed through retail stores.

3. *Target specific markets that can be reached through affordable means.* All enterprises have practical limitations on the ways they can reach markets. Display advertising in major publications or establishing a national sales force, for example, are not usually viable options for small work-at-home sidelines. Many of the megasuccessful companies do well targeting narrow markets where business development costs are very moderate and profits achievable even at marginal response levels. Cases in point: Sierra On-Line got started by placing inexpensive ads for its video games in computer magazines. Thousands of dollars poured in with most of it flowing to the bottom line because unit manufacturing costs were low. That's what provided the business with the capital to expand. Action Products focused their selling efforts mostly toward souvenir retailers, a small but volume-buying market. Every catalog distributed produced hundreds, sometimes thousands of dollars in orders. Harbor Sweets concentrated its selling efforts initially at Atlantic Coast gift stores, a natural market for its nautical-theme chocolate designs.

4. *Generate volume revenues from each customer.* Million-dollar sales from home-started businesses generally are not built on one-shot selling or low-priced products or services. Developing customer demand is one of the more expensive components of a business operation, and a single sale of ten or twenty dollars will rarely cover the cost of producing that sale. A

must for a growth-oriented business is to either create products or services with repeat sales potential or have high unit-selling prices.

5. *Drive the business with new products or services.* Just about every product or service has a life cycle, and sales will almost always start to fall off eventually. Critical to the sustained growth of a business is the ability to pick up the slack with something new. ASK Computer Systems continuously offers additional software as well as add-ons and refinements to older programs. The Diet Center is always introducing improved nutrition products. Stanley H. Kaplan Educational Centers now offers self-improvement courses to its college admission and licensing preparation. Suzy's Zoo added paper goods to its greeting card product line. I Was Framed branched into promotional and premium markets.

6. *Continuously readjust to the marketplace.* Time will bring new opportunities as well as changes likely to affect what business is already doing. Shifting gears as demand moves up or down is critical to continued growth. When Yankee Candle started to lose sales to machine-made imports, more emphasis was put on handmade candle products. Lillian Vernon modified

---

DATA ON THE MEGASUCCESSFUL

Of the forty megasuccessful companies profiled in this book:

- ◆ Sex: Twenty-one of the entrepreneurs involved were male, fifteen were female, and four husband–wife teams.
- ◆ Age: Eighteen of the entrepreneurs were in their teens or twenties when they started their home business, sixteen were in their thirties, and six were in their forties.
- ◆ Products/services/sales: Twenty-four firms manufactured products, eight sold the products of others, and eight created services.
- ◆ Market: Thirty-nine of the forty companies developed products or services essentially for a consumer market. Only one (ASK Computer Systems) targeted only the business community.
- ◆ Distribution: Seventeen firms marketed through middlemen, eight used mail order, eight were involved in retailing, and seven distributed via direct selling.
- ◆ Idea creativity: Eighteen firms built their successes by improving on existing products or services, while ten companies actually created something that could be considered new. Seven businesses simply packaged products from various sources and marketed them more effectively. Five firms refined available products or services and channeled them to new markets.

its merchandise over the years to accommodate the increase in the number of working women in the population. Thirty percent of Georgette Klinger's skin-care business now comes from men.

7. *Grow at a controlled pace and keep failures manageable.* There's never any certainty in marketing. That "can't miss" idea sometimes does. New products or services may not take off right away and possibly not at all. Experienced entrepreneurs enter new markets in stages and never put themselves in a position where one failure jeopardizes everything that's been built over the years. Manhattan Toy bombed with a strangely shaped monster toy, but followed it up with a dinosaur line that captured the market. What works in New York City may not work as well elsewhere. That's what The Learning Annex found out in the 1980s when it expanded to other cities. But they quickly retrenched and were able to cut the losses.

8. *Hone management skills.* Small ventures can expand only if the entrepreneurs learn how to operate in a complex, multidimensional environment. Acquiring and upgrading business disciplines in finance, marketing, product development, and so forth is a continuing process and essential to survival in the roller-coaster world of big business. A number of the megasuccessful, at one time or another, had to go to the financial markets—banks, Wall Street investment capital firms—to raise expansion capital. The funds were provided because those former kitchen-table entrepreneurs had grown into professional corporate managers.

The Entrepreneurial Component

A home-started business that achieves sales of $1 million or more doesn't just grow by accident. Certainly following a set of guidelines helps keep the enterprise from wandering too far off the path to success. But something more is needed—a motivated entrepreneur with special qualities who will drive the business to heights that most ordinary people would consider beyond their wildest dreams.

Entrepreneurs who move up to the ranks of the elite see challenges and opportunities from changing circumstances—sometimes creating their own—while others see nothing. They work tirelessly, assume risks others would shy from, make personal sacrifices, and never get comfortable with the status quo. Doggedly determined to succeed, they develop a growth strategy and push the business ahead of them.

SUCCESS TIP

CONTINUOUS REVENUES PER CUSTOMER

Possibly the single most important factor in the success of the firms that went from home business to big business was the development of a solid customer base—consumer or retailer—for repeat orders with minimum selling cost. Lillian Vernon achieves this through the mailing of catalogs to previous buyers. Georgette Klinger's clientele return for regular skin-care treatments as well as purchasing products for home use. Food companies such as The Little Pie Company depend upon return visits from satisfied customers who have tasted their products.

Only high-priced, high-margin products or services, such as Stanley H. Kaplan Educational Centers, can afford to invest the selling time and effort to acquire a customer who is likely to make only one purchase.

ADVICE FROM THE MEGASUCCESSFUL

Profiled entrepreneurs were asked to provide advice to newcomers just starting out in the business world. Here are some of their comments:

◆ Respect the consumers. They can be fooled—once only (Paul Suzman, Broadmoor Baker).

◆ Do your homework. It's the only way to validate your hunches (Mary Anne Jackson, My Own Meals).

◆ To create, we must let our imaginations soar (Lane Nemeth, Discovery Toys).

◆ A lot of people think marketing is what you do after you develop your product. That's a mistake. It includes talking to the customer first (Scott Cook, Intuit).

◆ You should not dwell on your mistakes or setbacks—but instead learn from them and then move on (Lillian Vernon, Lillian Vernon Company).

◆ Success is achieved by focusing on the objective, but being flexible on the method. The objective was for the company to grow in terms of sales, profit, and net worth. Flexibility may mean changing the product mix, enlarging the customer base, and seeking new markets (Judith Kaplan, Action Products International).

◆ A company cannot remain stagnant. It must always be growing and, when necessary, changing (Jan Stanton, I Was Framed).

◆ There are those who dream that they could and some who do what they dream— that's what sets us apart (Leonard P. Cuozzo, Paul Sebastian, Inc.).

Here is an illustration of the stuff really successful entrepreneurs are made of. In 1981, a direct-marketing consultant was retained by Lillian Vernon to come up with a growth strategy for her company. He presented three alternatives: Expand the product line, mail catalogs more frequently, or mail larger catalogs to more people. Rather than choose one, Lillian adopted all three and took a business that was growing at 18 percent a year and made it grow at 40 percent. That's the courage it takes to turn a kitchen-table sideline into a $200-million operation.

Timidity is not a characteristic of entrepreneurs who make it to the top. Sandra Kurtzig of ASK Computer Systems personally marketed her own company the first few years. She designed a flier that looked like a wanted poster with her picture on it. It read, "Warning, dangerous woman on the loose. Do not resist this woman. She is armed with many ways to save you money." With that promotional onslaught, it was difficult for prospective customers not to see her.

Rebecca Matthias launched Mothers Work with $10,000 of her own money. Her first maternity-clothes catalog bombed. It was timed wrong, she later learned—the spring season starts in January and her ads appeared in March. By the time most people had received the catalog, they had already ordered from others. But she didn't quit, and eventually she went from mail order to franchised retailing. Entrepreneurs have to be resilient enough to bounce back.

Despite Rebecca's success—$100 million in sales—she provides a warning about the entrepreneurial lifestyle. "It's not for everyone. You have to seriously think about what you are getting into. There's no such thing as a partial commitment to a business. It must be a high priority, it requires 100 percent." But then she adds, "Setting and accomplishing goals against great odds is an incredible high. It's the greatest confidence builder there is."

The Essentials of Successfully Starting, Operating, and Expanding a Home Business

WHAT IT TAKES
TO SUCCEED

3

An Overview of Home Business

The next several chapters provide the information needed to get you going in a home business. They move you through the processes of selecting the right business as well as the mechanics of startup and management. All the material in these chapters is conveyed in a conversational format that anticipates the questions most likely to be asked by aspiring entrepreneurs and responds with practical here's-what-you-do advice.

♦ *I have little experience in the business world and am concerned about my ability to successfully run even a small, home-based venture.*

Too many people are so frightened off by the word "business" that they never attempt to start one. Many home businesses are simple to operate. For example, let's take the case of a craft hobbyist who started a home business to supplement nine-to-five job earnings. She buys small quantities of canvas and paints them with various designs that other needlecrafters will finish. Adding the right amount of yarn, she packages the product in plastic bags and sells the kits to local boutique and craft stores, as well as through mail order. In another case, a home-based entrepreneur receives catalogs from a well-known direct-sales cosmetics firm and distributes them to friends, neighbors, and acquaintances in places of business. When customers call in purchases,

NEEDLE POINT

Animals. Cats, dogs, pandas & more on handpainted canvases. Brochure $1 A Dragon's Tale Needlepoint Box 559/ST Cathedral Station NYC 10025

AVOIDING THE PITFALLS OF WORKING FROM HOME

While working at home saves commuting time and no boss looks over your shoulder, there are also some negatives. One problem is intrusions from family and friends. Neighbors think that if you're at home you can't be working and will phone or barge in at any time for a social chat. Another problem is that it gets lonely, especially if you've been used to working with others. Then there is the problem of the business consuming your life—there's always something to do. Here are some suggestions on dealing with these problems.

◆ Make your work hours clear to friends and neighbors and be firm about enforcement.
◆ Battle isolation by regularly meeting others for lunch.
◆ Discipline yourself to mentally leave the work behind at the end of the day.

she buys the merchandise, repacks it into individual orders, and makes the delivery. These home-run businesses don't take more than average ability and take only modest amounts of capital. There are many similar work-at-home opportunities for anyone able to come up with a sound, marketable idea and who is sufficiently motivated to make the effort to turn the idea into a profitable business.

◆ *How would I go about choosing a business?*

Ideas for a business can come from a variety of sources. Often they come from something you know best—your present occupation, hobby, or personal interest. Tens of thousands of people have simply turned leisure time activities into money-making enterprises. Changes in technology sometimes generate new opportunities. Some of the most successful home businesses today are computer-related. Frequently new business ideas come from the identification of a need from a personal experience—a product or service that is not available locally, or in some instances, not at all. For example, you're having a small party and prefer to have the food catered, but can't find anyone willing to do it. So you cater it yourself and then others ask you to do it for them.

Many new businesses sort of stumble into existence in just this way. Changes in the way people live may also trigger new venture startups. The demand for child day-care centers was brought about by the growth of two-income and single-parent families. Employment advertising can sometimes provide hints to business needs. Ads for certain types of jobs—telephone-marketing people, secretaries, bookkeepers, and so on—are strong indicators that demand may exceed supply and a home venture might very well survive on overflow business alone. Just remember one essential: The business you choose should fulfill a need if you expect to generate any long-term market demand and possibly achieve seven-figure sales in the future.

◆ *There are some needs I can identify right now.*

That's fine, but that's only half the equation. The second half is to match those needs with your own interest and capabilities. To have any chance of succeeding you obviously must possess the personal desire, technical talents, and investment capital to produce and market the product or service you've selected. The business choice also has to be practical for your time schedule, home-space availability, and location. And don't forget legal considerations. The law sometimes restricts the types of businesses that can be operated from the home.

◆ *Do all home businesses have million-dollar sales potential?*

Some much more so than others. Businesses that can develop repeat sales or can be expanded geographically to reach national markets obviously have a much better chance of making it to the million-dollar figure. The success of mail-order ventures is a good example. Localized personal service enterprises, while capable of producing comfortable incomes for their owners, are likely to remain small unless they can be packaged into licensing arrangements or franchised.

◆ *Are there business advantages in operating from home?*

For the right businesses, yes. The reduced overhead means a lower operating break-even point. Where a non–home-based firm may struggle, a home enterprise can not only survive, but prosper. And being small can also be an advantage. Large companies tend to be impersonal and inflexible. More often than not localized segments of a market are better served by one-person, owner-managed enterprises.

◆ *What personal traits go with successful entrepreneurship?*

Individuals who do well frequently possess similar characteristics. They're self-starters, well-organized, and capable of making decisions. Doers, not thinkers, they don't discourage easily. They bristle with confidence, certain that things can somehow be worked out. And, most important, they are able to commit themselves to strict work discipline. A home business, by its nature, competes with kids, television, social activities, and other distractions.

◆ *What if I have only limited knowledge of the business I select?*

Many startup entrepreneurs have had the same problem, but through education and job experience they were able to develop sufficient skills to go into the business of their preference. Take the case of a young woman with two children who thought she could make a go of a home venture that provided a variety of business services, such as word processing and simple bookkeeping. She prepared herself by taking typing and business courses in night school and then worked part-time at office temporary jobs. It took a year, but it was worth the effort. Her home sideline earns her $8,000 a year. There are always a wide variety of educational courses available in local schools that can serve as the seed for starting a home business. Some worthwhile courses are available through mail correspondence.

◆ *Suppose I choose a business that requires more money than I have. Can I borrow what I need?*

While most home-based entrepreneurs use personal savings or obtain loans from friends to start new ventures, you can, in most instances, also borrow small amounts of money from local banks for periods of up to three years. An unsecured loan requires only your signature, but more than likely a secured note will be offered to you. This has lower interest payments than an unsecured note, but will require you to pledge some assets, such as stock, or to have someone guarantee the loan. Another frequently overlooked source of startup funds is borrowing from life insurance. Loans are almost always obtainable against policies with savings features. Some entrepreneurs have obtained a number of credit cards that they used to provide a substantial cash bankroll for the business startup. Terren Dunlap cofounded Go-Video, an electronics firm, with $60,000 drawn against personal cards.

◆ *I see many advertisements in newspapers and magazines for easy-money-at-home business opportunities. Can't I just mail those firms a check and avoid all the hassles of startup?*

You'll save the price of this book many times over if it helps you avoid the many work-at-home gyp schemes. Typical are those that require up-front money for instruction, materials, and equipment, implying you are being offered piecework employment at home, while in reality you're only being asked to buy something. Envelope stuffing, newspaper-clipping services, and worm farming in your basement are some of the most popular scams. But there are many variations of the

10. Publishing Your Art As Cards & Posters, by Harold Davis. This is a practical, definitive manual for artists working with oils, water colors, pastels, graphics, computer art and photography. It is complete guide to creating, designing and marketing cards and posters. It provides a road map for both the self publishers and those who choose to have their work published by others. A glossary of business and technical terms provides an instant introduction to production and business terms. An index permits quick access to topics of interest. Multiple resource sections provide valuable names, addresses and phone numbers of printer, card and poster publisher/distributors. *ISBN 0-913069-22-1, $14.95, 96 pp., Distributors: Baker & Taylor, Amphoto, and Quality Books—The Consultant Press, 163 Amsterdam Ave., #201, New York, NY 10023*

Startup help for new entrepreneurs can come from a variety of sources—books, workshops, seminars, specialized schools, home-study courses, and so forth. Some temporary-job agencies even provide training before sending applicants out on assignment.

same basic theme, and the promotions are usually supported by I-got-rich-in-one-month-type testimonials.

One classic "opportunity" that really wasn't turned out to be very costly to a retired couple. They mortgaged their house to pay a promoter $24,000 for equipment and supplies. They contracted to make signs—"Open," "Closed," "Beware of the dog," and the like. The company that sold them the equipment was supposed to buy back the finished products at fair prices. An ideal work-at-home business, right? Wrong. The company didn't buy anything, leaving the couple with a new mortgage and no income. By the way, the equipment and supplies were worth about $4,000.

There are some legitimate work-at-home business opportunities, but beware of those fraudulent ones that make unrealistic promises.

◆ *I guess there isn't any easy way to get started, but how about buying an existing business?*

Buying an existing business may have some advantages, especially if the owner is retiring, moving, or selling for health reasons. Just make certain the business's success is not tied to the personal qualities or acquaintances of the seller, and that future profits will not be hurt by visible changes in product or service demand. A fair price of an existing business is roughly four or five times the average earnings of several years. A payout of 20 percent of the purchase price for a five-year period is usually considered quite reasonable.

◆ *What about a franchise?*

For entrepreneurs who prefer the purchase of "turnkey"-type packages, there are a number of firms offering franchises or other business opportunities. Franchises usually involve a higher initial investment and the payment of royalties based on gross receipts. In nonfranchise opportunities the sponsoring companies almost always earn their money through the services they provide on a continuing basis or the selling of supplies. In addition, there may be some initial investment for instructional material and equipment. Training in a nonfranchise arrangement is likely to be less comprehensive and usually consists of training manuals and telephone consultation.

DO YOU HAVE WHAT IT TAKES TO BE AN ENTREPRENEUR?

Not everyone is cut out to be an entrepreneur. The following self-analysis test will help determine whether you have the necessary personal traits to succeed on your own. If you can respond positively to at least seven of the ten questions, entrepreneurship is a worthwhile pursuit for you.

- ◆ Achievement: Are you strongly motivated to succeed in anything you do?
- ◆ Confidence: Do you make up your mind quickly after reviewing the options and believe you can take a business from zero to a profitable enterprise?
- ◆ Risk taking: Are you willing to take reasonable risks and handle the pressure that results from a degree of insecurity?
- ◆ Responsibility: Do you welcome the responsibility that goes with your own business?
- ◆ Self-starter: Can you move on your own without someone pushing you?
- ◆ Discipline: Are you able to stick to a schedule?
- ◆ Orientation: Do you believe in giving priority to getting the job done?
- ◆ Communication: Do you recognize that much of your success will depend upon how well you deal with people?
- ◆ Creativity: Are you someone who is always coming up with new ideas?
- ◆ Leadership: Do you prefer to give orders rather than follow the lead of others?

◆ *I know there is nothing certain about business, but is there anything else I can do to make sure my selection is the right one?*

Do market research. This involves the gathering of information to determine in advance who might buy the product or service and what they might be willing to pay for it. Good research will also collect data on the competition. Many new businesses avoid some risk by copying the best features of a competitor's product or service—it's safer than trying to reinvent the wheel. In some instances markets for products can actually be tested by placing sample quantities of the merchandise in retail stores. No significant commitments of time or money have to be made until the tests prove out. Major companies frequently do this type of consumer market testing before nationally marketing new products. A word of warning: A positive reaction to market research doesn't assure success. People sometimes say one thing and then act differently. But doing some research is still better than acting on a gut feeling.

◆ *Let's assume I've done the market research and there is a demand for my product or service. Now what?*

All business startups should follow a logical path, and home operations are no exception. The preparation of a detailed business plan is essential. It is a sort of road map for establishing the business and consists of putting down on paper all the steps that have to be taken to "go live." The plan will bring to the surface some of the problems you are likely to encounter and translates everything into bottom-line dollars. Many ventures, home-based or otherwise, start out undercapitalized and find their funds exhausted before they've had a chance to turn the corner. Planning helps keep receipts and expenditures in proper balance.

◆ *Won't I need a lawyer and accountant to get started?*

Other than cost, it never does any harm to consult professionals. But many small businesses can be started without professional help if the entrepreneur doesn't mind doing the work. By consulting with various government agencies and perusing business books found in libraries, most professional fees can be kept to a minimum. However, if you intend to go into a business in which personal liability may be involved, you should definitely seek professional assistance.

◆ *Is that it?*

Pretty much so. Start the business by taking the steps called for in the plan. Give the business a name, legally establish it, prepare the workspace, acquire insurance, open a business checking account, get a business phone or answering service, order the equipment and supplies, get listed in the Yellow Pages, estimate prices, start manufacturing the product or prepare the service, and so on. In brief, phase one of the startup gets you ready to serve customers.

Phase two is to let potential customers know you're open for business. This is done through advertising and promotion. Get business cards and stationery, prepare and distribute promotional literature, run ads in newspapers and magazines, solicit by phone. And don't forget to take advantage of free publicity by issuing news releases to the appropriate media.

Producing sales is phase three. This includes convincing customers to buy, delivering the product or service, and getting paid for it.

◆ *What about managing the business?*

Of course you're going to have to keep accurate records of income and expenditures, both for tax purposes and to know whether the business is profitable. Inexpensive bookkeeping systems are available from stationery supply stores for posting simple transactions, or you can use an accountant to set up the books.

Don't expect to get rich overnight. Often it takes from six to twelve months before any business will produce a sufficient profit to even come close to compensating you for your time and investment. The first year should be thought of as a learning experience and some adjustments to your original plan will almost assuredly be needed. But stay flexible and react quickly to market feedback. No two businesses are alike and the right combination of elements that will make your venture successful has to evolve over time. That will only bring you to the first plateau. But there's no reason you have to stop there.

THE MOST POPULAR HOME BUSINESS OPPORTUNITIES

Here is a comprehensive list of income-generating product and service opportunities that have successful work-at-home track records. Many are grouped by activities that are either similar in skill requirements or logically fit together and can be combined into a single business package.

Basic homemaker skills
> Childcare
>
> Clothing sewing/alterations
>
> Laundry services
>
> House sitting (pet care, plant watering)
>
> Pet boarding

Auto detailing (car cleaning)

Direct selling product distributor

Special Events

Event planning/coordinating

Catering

Cake baking and decorating

Calligraphy

Children's party services

Printed invitations supplier

Bridal gown, headpieces supplier

Floral centerpieces supplier

Party item rentals

"Not new" gown supplier

Customized party favors supplier

Bridal party makeup

Party-help personnel referral

Crafts and hobbies

Handicraft products

Craft/hobby instruction/patterns

Craft/hobby workshops

Craft/hobby kits

Seasonal holiday crafts

Seasonal personalized children's greetings

Holiday boutique sales

Food

Catering

Food specialties

Cake/pie baking

Cooking instruction

Recipe publishing

Gift baskets

Repair services

    Auto maintenance/repair

    Chair caning

    Furniture repair/refinishing

    Electronic equipment repair

    General fix-it

    Small engine repair/maintenance

    Upholstery services

    Taxidermy

    Tennis racquet restringing

Mail order

    Products—general

    Products—personalized/customized

    Specialized catalog merchandising

    Plans/instruction

    Kit assemblies

    Newsletters

Pets

    Pet boarding

    Pet grooming

    Pet shampooing

    Dog training

Group instruction

    Weight-loss clinic operator

    Stop-smoking clinic operator

    Arts and crafts workshops

    Cooking lessons

    Exam preparation

    Language courses

    Leisure-time activity instruction

    Personal growth/improvement seminars

Special subject education

Computer training

Personal assistance

Income tax preparation

Medical forms processing

Tutoring

Career counseling

Investment/financial advisor

Personal help counseling (marriage counseling, for example)

Musical instrument instruction

Job résumés and search

Personal analysis (astrology, for example)

Personal services

Hair stylist

Manicurist

Pedicurist

Electrolysis

Makeup/fashion consultant

Manufacturing

Proprietary products

Assemblies/kits packaging

Sewn products

Information/matching/referral services

Domestic/temporary help services

College guidance and financial aid services

Entertainment talent booking

Ticket brokering

Miscellaneous matching (apartment finding, roommate matching, dating, class reunion, tourist information, summer camp information)

General business services

   Bookkeeping/payroll

   Bill collection

   Fund-raising

   Mailing services

   Mail receiving and forwarding

   Computer data entry

   Secretarial/typing/word processing

   General clerical

   Telemarketing

   Telephone answering

   Transcription

Creative arts

   Artist (painter or sculptor, for example)

   Craft artisan

   Art/antique dealer/gallery

   Art/antique appraiser

   Art/antique restorer

   Art instruction

   Commercial art/designing/illustrating

   Creative writing

Photography

   Commercial photography

   Portrait photography

   Photographic processing

   Photo restorer/touch-up

Specialized business services

   Advertising

   Public relations

   Graphic arts

Computer programming

Language translating

Technical writing

Business writing

Market research

Specialized employment services

Cooperative advertising service

Publishing activities (copyediting, book reviewing, proofreading)

Desktop publishing

Other

Bed-and-breakfast establishing

Home retailing

PICKING A WINNER

Guidelines for Business Selection

4

BUSINESS IDEAS

♦ *I'm ready to move ahead on a home business. Where do I begin?*

The first step in becoming successfully self-employed is finding a business that combines your entrepreneurial strengths with a marketable product or service. Getting to that point involves navigating through a maze of business choices with varying degrees of business suitability, profit potential, and growth possibilities.

♦ *What work-from-home options are available?*

About one hundred specific opportunities seem to do well in home-based operations, and they fall into three general categories. Product-oriented enterprises involve manufacturing similar or one-of-a-kind items. Service-oriented activities are just that, a service—personal or business—provided for a fee. Finally, there are sales-oriented businesses that deal with the resale of purchased, not created products. Product distributorships, such as Mary Kay and Discovery Toys, are examples of businesses in the sales category. While there are no absolutes, product businesses tend to be somewhat more complex to run, need a larger space, and require higher amounts of startup capital than service or sales ventures.

◆ *How would I go about coming up with ideas for a business?*

It's a two-step process. Begin by narrowing the field to activities you enjoy and feel comfortable with. What types of work do your talents and interests naturally move you to do? Persuading, handling children, tinkering with machines, cooking, teaching, working alone on hand-crafted items, something professional—these are typical choices. A business that's stimulating and challenging can help dispel self-doubt. The promise of money is not enough. The venture itself must inspire and drive you.

Next, brainstorm business ideas, limiting them, obviously, to those that will mesh well with your interests and lifestyle. Start with ideas related to things you already have some familiarity with—work experiences and hobbies. But don't limit your creative thinking to that. What about products and services you sought and found unavailable or not completely to your satisfaction? Consider the latest trends in technology, legislation, and social change. Do they offer any work-at-home opportunities? How about variations on items already on the market? Many "new" products and services are really only modifications of things that have been around for years. Were there any remarks over-

FADS

Fad items can sometimes make home-based entrepreneurs wealthy. The Pet Rock did just that in 1975 for Californian Gary Dahl. The idea for the novelty item came out of casual conversation with buddies during a social hour. Then it was good for a laugh—and later, for a million dollars.

The Pet Rock—a round stone plus miniature pet-training booklet packaged in a box with a carrying handle—wholesaled for two dollars and retailed for four dollars. No money was spent on advertising but $4 million of the product was sold in three months.

What made the Pet Rock so popular? At least one partial answer was that the idea of a Pet Rock was so outrageous, so ridiculous that it became media news. The publicity, worth millions of dollars, created the craze. But also the timing was just right—after Vietnam and Watergate—and, as Gary Dahl says, "The country needed a laugh."

heard in conversation that might be worth further investigation? What about businesses successful elsewhere—would they work in your areas? No formula exists for creativity, but many good ideas are conceived through logical, pragmatic thought.

♦ *Can't I just go with an established type of business?*

Many entrepreneurs do just that—start "old" concept businesses in crafts, clerical services, child day-care, and so on—and do quite well. But the marketplace for look-alike ventures is almost always competitive and this keeps the lid on profits and, indirectly, on growth. The key to real business success is creating or finding a market niche.

♦ *What's a market niche?*

It's a segment of the market—a group of buyers—willing to purchase products or services distinctively different from what's already available. The marketplace isn't a monolithic mass, but is more similar to a radio band on which many stations operate side by side and appeal to different audiences. Each station has created its own market niche by programming—news, rock, classical. A business fortunate enough to have a market niche can distance itself from the competition and price higher. Better profit margins can provide the capital needed to fuel growth.

♦ *Do you have any suggestions on how I can create or find a market niche?*

Think about product or service differences—in design, price, quality, service, or buying convenience. For example, one entrepreneur created a market niche for her Christmas ornaments by designing them depicting black rather than white people. Bloomingdale's bought the product. Another entrepreneur duplicated designer fragrance scents and sold them for one-fifth the price. Some products can be personalized. Add monogramming and charge more. Some services lend themselves to customization. Computer programmers frequently tailor standard software to specific companies.

Customizing doesn't have to be particularly sophisticated. One entrepreneur made and imprinted little vests with "I Love . . ." (filling in the name of the customer's town or school) and put them on purchased

SAME INDUSTRY, DIFFERENT NICHES

Of the forty "kitchen table to executive suite" entrepreneurial companies profiled in this book, eight rode to success on the development of computer technology, each carving out a different niche in the marketplace. Borland cut its teeth supplying tools for computer programmers. ASK focused on small manufacturers who wanted to trace inventory of finished work and manufacturing materials. Sierra On-Line created entertainment software, while T/Maker specialized in graphics and desktop publishing programs. Intuit targeted the consumer and small-business market with an easy-to-use check-writing system.

In the nonsoftware area Computer Express built a retail business on the electronic-shopping concept. Dell chose the hardware route, but marketed direct to consumers via mail order, selling quality computers at prices that were hard to beat.

teddy bears. They were then sold at gift retailers, college stores, and airports. Sometimes all that's needed to create a niche is to serve a market better than existing suppliers. Making something easy to use may create a market niche. The components for craft items may be purchased separately, but some customers will pay extra to obtain them in kit form. A market niche can arise from offering special services. Providing pickup and delivery or evening and weekend hours could entice enough buyers who need or want those conveniences away from the competition.

♦ *After I've come up with a number of ideas for my home business, then what?*

Compare them by answering the following questions. Can the idea be turned into a money-making business? Is the market large enough to provide the income level you're seeking? Would the business have growth potential?

♦ *Suppose all I'm seeking is some extra money. Why should I care about growth?*

Most first-time entrepreneurs start out with limited goals, willing to settle for "a few bucks on the side." But after tasting success and gaining confidence, there's a desire to take another step up the ladder, then another.

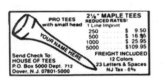

Varying a home-business product or service so it is somewhat different from the competition helps find a market niche. The variations can take many forms: unique or special services, customization, quality, price, or simply more convenient appointment times.

♦ *I've answered the questions, now can I start the business?*

Not just yet. Your business options may be further restricted when judged in relation to your circumstances. These items have to be considered before making the final decision on a home business:

1. *Skill and talent.* You must possess or know where to acquire the technical, marketing, and administrative capability to produce the product or provide the service.
2. *Time availability.* When do you intend to work at the business—days, evenings, weekends? Family commitments, such as taking care of children, or individual preferences, such as not wanting to

---

SCHEDULING BIG LEAGUE BASEBALL: A HOME BUSINESS

Scheduling over 2,000 regular-season games of the national pastime around restrictions such as religious holidays and players' association regulations that limit day games after night games that would require an airplane flight of more than ninety minutes is too complicated a task for computer programming. What may come as a surprise is that the schedule is prepared by a Staten Island, New York, company—Stephenson Systems—consisting of a husband-and-wife team working at home. Henry and Holly Stephenson are under contract to Major League Baseball for "something less than $1 million a year." It takes about eight months to schedule the thirty teams.

work weekends, can very much limit the number of hours and time schedules for a home business.

3. *Money for investment.* Some businesses can be started and operated on a shoestring, while others may require substantial investments in equipment and inventory.

4. *Space availability.* While many enterprises can be run from an apartment, others require the large square footage of a basement, garage, or attic of a private home.

5. *Community where you live.* Big city, suburb, rural village, or farm—each can support successfully only certain types of home-business activities.

6. *Location of home business.* Some ventures require visibility and accessibility (being on a main road, for example), while for others location is secondary.

7. *Ability to conform to legal requirements.* Authorization in the form of licensing by a government agency—federal, state, or municipal—may be needed. The requirements must be met and the license obtained before startup. Usually operations involving public health and safety fall into the licensing category.

8. *Local zoning.* Some types of home business can't be legally operated in residential areas because of local zoning ordinances.

ZONING RESTRICTIONS

◆ *How do I find out whether my home is zoned for a business operation?*

Check with the city or town clerk to determine which home activities are legally allowed. Professional businesses—teaching, counseling, bookkeeping—are usually permitted, as are incidental occupations customary to the home, such as dressmaking.

◆ *Suppose my special type of business isn't specifically mentioned in the zoning regulations?*

You can apply to the local zoning board for a variance. This involves completing some forms detailing the activities you intend to carry out. Property owners within several hundred feet of your home will be notified. If no one objects and the business isn't likely to change the residential character of the neighborhood, chances are good that approval will be given.

♦ *And if someone does object?*

If you can show that similar operations in the neighborhood have been approved in the past and that the income is your only means of livelihood, then you may be able to convince the zoning board to give you the variance.

♦ *What happens if I can't get zoning clearance?*

Some home ventures are operated in technical violation of local zoning boards. While this can't be recommended, authorities in the municipalities are known to ignore such situations if traffic and parking are not disruptive to the neighborhood and the neighbors make no official complaint. A word of caution, though: If you do decide to operate in an area that restricts your type of business you will not be able to obtain other permits of licenses. Also, avoid local publicity. Even if no one objects, once the authorities become aware of a nonconforming business, they're legally obligated to close it down.

Zoning Code Closes Lemonade Business

FORT WORTH, May 31 (AP) — The bureaucracy has forced a teenager and his brother to close a lucrative business that had become a neighborhood institution.

The brothers, 14-year-old Chip and 7-year-old J.J. Merrick, had to close their lemonade stand because it violated a city zoning ordinance.

The business had slaked the thirst of Fort Worth residents for three years, but it is gone now because of an anonymous caller.

The bad news was delivered last week by C. C. Smallwood, a city code enforcement official. The area is zoned for residences, but the lemonade stand is a business and it costs $650 to apply for a zoning change.

"On my own I wouldn't have done it," Mr. Smallwood said. But he said that when a complaint is filed officials have to take action. He said the complainant refused to give a name.

PERMITS AND LICENSES

♦ *What sorts of businesses require permits or licenses?*

Laws will vary by locality but almost always there are occupational regulations or building regulations covering some aspects of public health and safety. Premises used for food preparation, lodging, and the employing of others require periodic inspection for compliance with fire and health standards. Occupations such as child day-care, marriage counseling, cosmetology, and hairdressing are usually licensed to protect the public from unqualified providers of such services. You will have to take an examination or show proof of the proper educational background and experience before a license will be issued. Other trades that may require licenses include employment services, dating services, and antique sales. Also, some states have

GETTING AROUND ZONING RESTRICTIONS

Zoning restrictions sometimes present the biggest hurdles to home business startup. Here are four ways to work around them.

1. Provide customer pickup and delivery services.
2. Use retailers as drop points.
3. Select a home business that can be conducted primarily by mail, telephone, or telecomputer communication.
4. Operate on an appointment-only basis.

Case in point: One entrepreneur sells and mounts auto tires from his two-car garage, not a business that is easily run from home. Customers call with the tire size, a price is quoted, and an appointment is arranged. The entrepreneur then picks up the tires at a wholesaler and has them on hand when the customer arrives.

labor laws that require all home workers to have special permits for any sort of commercial activity.

◆ *Does that mean some products can't legally be produced in the home?*

Federal regulations ban home manufacturing of women's apparel. However, these policies are going through some changes so it's best to check with the U.S. Department of Labor to find out what restrictions, if any, still apply. Some states also have limitations on home-produced products, so it's wise to get applicable regulations from your own state's labor agency.

◆ *Are all home businesses operated legally?*

Some do not conform with all legal requirements. Often this is done to keep the activity underground and away from IRS scrutiny. As a result it's likely hundreds of millions of dollars in home-business income is never reported or taxed.

But if you intend to open a business checking account or be listed in the Yellow Pages, going legal is a must, and it makes good sense if any sort of liability is involved. If you plan to be in the business over the long term, it's in your best interest to operate within the law and take advantage of the legitimate benefits available, such as business expense–related tax deductions and retirement plans for the self-employed.

PATENTS, TRADEMARKS, COPYRIGHTS

◆ *Suppose I come up with something unique. How can I prevent someone from stealing it?*

There are three forms of legal protection. A patent is for inventions, trademark registration covers product names and logos, and copyrights protect the written expression of an idea.

◆ *Is protection an expensive process?*

For a copyright, no. It can be obtained for only twenty dollars through the copyright office in Washington.

TAKING ON GOLIATH—AND WINNING

When you come up with something successful, it often is only a matter of time before someone tries to copy it. In the 1980s, that's what happened to Colorado-based Blue Mountain Arts, a home-started greeting-card firm that developed into a multimillion-dollar company. Their biggest seller was a line of nonoccasion cards that were reflective free-verse poetry with delicate paintings. In 1986 Hallmark tried to buy the firm, but the owners Stephen and Susan Schutz refused to sell. Hallmark, not willing to give up a share of a growing market, essentially copied the cards and then used its marketing clout to displace Blue Mountain Arts products in the stores. Blue Mountain sued for $50 million, citing a concept known as "trade dress," which protects copyrighted creative works against "confusingly similar" infringements. The case was settled out of court and Hallmark agreed to stop copying the cards.

Trademark registration costs $245 and approval is usually granted within a year. Since the expense is minimal, it makes sense for small business entrepreneurs to obtain one or both forms of protection.

Patent protection is much more involved and costly. For a small entity the application alone costs $395 and then there is $660 that has to be paid when the patent is granted. The process takes about two years. The problem is that patents are easy to circumvent and have value only if the application is properly prepared. Unfortunately this usually requires an experienced patent attorney who knows how to come up with the right drawings and language. Patent attorneys charge $4,000 to $5,000 for their services.

♦ *What about companies that seek out inventions to market? Don't they obtain patents as part of their service?*

No. What they usually do is register the inventions under a disclosure document program, which costs six dollars and offers no real protection. As a general rule, these invention-marketing services should be avoided, since it seems inventors rarely recoup the upfront fees charged—about $800 and sometimes much more. Before signing anything see whom the firms have helped in the past and call them. Also check to see if any complaints have been lodged with the Better Business Bureau.

5 TURNING PRODUCTS AND SERVICES INTO DOLLARS

The Magic of Marketing

MARKETING—GENERAL TIPS

♦ *Shouldn't I also give some consideration to how the products and services will be sold?*

Too many neophyte entrepreneurs get carried away with the euphoria of their idea and neglect to effectively deal with the most important aspect of any business—convincing people to buy what's being offered. A marketing plan is essential.

♦ *Marketing—isn't that just another term for selling?*

This limited view is a widely held misconception. While marketing does incorporate the selling effort, for many businesses much more is involved in moving a product or service to user. Marketing is a composite of five interrelated, sales-focused activities: (1) market research, (2) distribution channels, (3) pricing, (4) advertising/promotion/publicity, and (5) selling. If the first four elements of the marketing process are on target, the final element, the actual sale, comes about with relative ease.

♦ *How important is marketing for a small, part-time venture?*

While the complexity of marketing varies by type of business, all situations require answers to six basic questions:

1. What's the right product or service?
2. Who will buy it?
3. How much should be charged?
4. What's the best way to reach the buying market?
5. How can people be convinced to buy?
6. What will trigger a sale?

MARKET RESEARCH

♦ *What kind of market research is suitable for a small home-based business?*

There are a number of things you can do to make sure the business heads down the right path. If you've chosen a product or service that's advertised in newspapers or magazines, check issues a year or two old to see if the firms are still operating. Repeat ads are good evidence that sales are being made. Next, shop the marketplace and get some feel about business conditions. Do the businesses appear profitable? Are customers waiting in line and paying high prices? A strong demand means there's probably room for another supplier. If the vibrations are negative, rethink the whole business idea. Another excellent information source is suppliers of materials. They know what's selling and what's not and generally have a good feel for market trends. Also survey prospective customers in face-to-face conversations, telephone interviews, or mail surveys. Don't be shy, ask them directly—would they buy your product or service, how frequently, and what would they pay? And especially listen for any indication of unique features that, if offered, will provide an advantage over the competition. If possible, do a market test.

QUESTIONS MARKET RESEARCH SHOULD ANSWER

◆ Demand: Is there a sufficient demand for the product or service to make the business profitable? Is this demand permanent, temporary, seasonal, or likely to be affected by changes in the future?

◆ Customers: What is the profile of potential customers (sex, age, income, education, and so forth), and where do they reside? Are they easily identifiable? Can they be reached economically through advertising and promotion?

◆ Product/service and price: What product or service features are important to customers? What are they willing to pay for them?

◆ Competition: Who is the competition? How much do they sell? Are they profitable? What features in product or service do they offer? How much do they charge? What channels of distribution do they use? What methods do they use to advertise and promote the product or service?

◆ *How do I do a market test?*

For retail products, place some items into one or two stores, on a consignment basis, if necessary, and monitor results. If the store owner calls and wants more merchandise, that's a good signal you're a winner. But if the items are still sitting on the shelf two months later, that's bad news. Try to find out why, correct the problem, if possible, and retest. If it still doesn't fly, drop the idea. Demand for mail-order products can be gauged by running test ads in selected media and measuring response.

◆ *Should I talk to others about my idea?*

Yes, but don't take their response as the final word. The opinion of friends and acquaintances, whether enthusiastic or negative, is only of value if their reasons add some dimension to your thinking.

◆ *If the market research is positive, can I then pull out all the stops and move ahead with the business?*

Market research will help to improve the success odds, but is by no means foolproof. Proceed with caution and always watch for early signs that something is working—or isn't working and needs changing.

DISTRIBUTION CHANNEL

◆ *What is a distribution channel?*

It's the way products or services reach users. Direct distribution is most commonly used in small, home-based businesses and involves just two parties—seller and buyer. Indirect distribution channels use various types of middlemen who sell the products or services to users through their own marketing outlets.

Direct distribution has two major advantages. First, it's far less complicated than indirect distribution. Just about anyone can start a direct-distribution business, frequently with little money and limited or no business experience. Second, since only seller and buyer are involved, the entrepreneur retains the full selling price.

◆ *When should I use indirect distribution?*

If it's not practical to use your home for selling for zoning reasons or if it is too out of the way for customers to get to, selling through middlemen may be the only alternative. Some entrepreneurs enjoy creating products but don't like the other or the time involved in selling. Spending weekends at craft fairs is not for everyone. And, of course, one person can achieve only limited sales volume. Going wholesale, as they say, provides an instant selling organization and the ability to quickly multiply sales.

◆ *How would I go wholesale?*

One way is to sell through retailers, especially those that are local and owner-operated. Items can be sold on a cash, credit, or consignment basis. ("Consignment" means that merchandise isn't paid for until sold; craft items and works of art are frequently retailed this way.)

Another way of going wholesale is to sell through wholesalers, distributors, or jobbers. These groups function alike but each industry refers to them by different names. They move a variety of merchandise through their own marketing network. Or you can market through agents, brokers, and representatives—reps, for short—who serve each

THE COST OF USING VARIOUS CHANNELS OF DISTRIBUTION

When an entrepreneur starts using outsiders to help market the product or service, sales volume usually increases. But this also means part of the selling price will be retained by those involved in the distribution pipeline.

DISTRIBUTION CHANNEL	WHAT IT COSTS AS A PERCENTAGE OF THE FINAL SELLING PRICE
Direct to buyer (no middlemen)	
Face-to-face selling	0%
Telemarketing	0%
Mail order	0%
Direct mail	0%
Direct to buyer (working with outside selling organizations)	
Agents, brokers, representatives	10%–20%
Indirect (selling to retailers)	
Outright sale	50%–60%
Consignment sale	25%–40%
Rack merchandising	30%–40%
Indirect (wholesaling)	
Wholesalers, distributors, jobbers	20%–30%
Indirect (selling to mail-order houses)	
Catalog houses	60%–70%

industry. Unlike the wholesaler group, they don't actually buy the products or even handle the merchandise but simply serve as an independent sales network trying to persuade retailers to add the products they carry to inventory shelves. Commissions are paid to them only for what is sold.

♦ *Where would I find wholesalers or agents to handle my products?*

Finding them usually isn't too difficult, but convincing them to take on your product is. Virtually every industry has a trade association and publications that carry ads soliciting products to sell. Contact the marketing organizations and send them samples and sales literature. If you live near a city with a trade mart it pays to make a visit and note the names of the forms that carry products similar to yours. Also, attending trade shows is a must for serious entrepreneurs. Many wholesalers and agents are represented at the show and attending will enable you to find out who they are and give you an opportunity to discuss your merchandise.

♦ *Is there anything different about distribution through wholesalers and agents?*

Most definitely, yes. While neighborhood store owners might work along with neophyte entrepreneurs, most of those engaged in business for a living expect suppliers to be familiar with trade practices and those who don't take the time to learn are likely to be ignored.

If you do venture into selling through wholesaler and agent groups, have available descriptive promotional literature, usually a full-color catalog sheet with product specifications on the other side, plus ordering information and published price lists. Entrepreneurs are also expected to know trade pricing and advertising allowance policies. Small retailers, for example, receive a 50 percent discount from list prices while chain and department stores get "50 and 10." Agents frequently require samples along with promotional material and they should be charged enough to at least cover basic costs.

♦ *I think I get the picture.*

There are good reasons for these practices, which are intended to weed out little entrepreneurs who get in over their head and can't provide timely delivery of merchandise. When dealing with this middleman market, it is essential you project a professional business image. Even if you do everything right chances are you'll have to contact a number of firms before convincing some to represent you.

FINDING THE RIGHT DISTRIBUTOR OR REP

If you produce products that can be sold through chain and department stores, the best marketing results will come from dealing with salespeople who already have their foot in the door, that is, people who already sell those accounts. How to locate them? Call the buyers of your type of product at each of the chain or discount store's headquarters and simply ask who they buy from. Then call the distributor or rep and mention that you were referred by the buyer from JCPenney or Kmart. You can be certain they'll pay attention.

TYPICAL DATA SHEET FORMAT FOR WHOLESALING MERCHANDISE TO RETAILERS

Regency Kits
P. O. Box 3000
Roselle, NJ 07203
(908) 555-7777

Retailers Information Sheet

Effective:	January 1, _____.
Products:	Needlecraft Kits—Patchwork Pillow.
Quantity:	Minimum order of any six (6) kits on one (1) purchase order received retailer pricing.
Returned Merchandise:	Damaged merchandise must be returned within ten (10) days after receipt of order.
Quotations:	Customer orders or special quantities are available on request.
Delivery:	F.O.B. Roselle, New Jersey. Two- to four-week delivery.

If you decide to expand your home business beyond neighborhood retailers, it's essential that trade practices—such as providing product data sheets—be followed.

◆ *Does it ever make sense to hire my own salespeople?*

Some home entrepreneurs do hire part-timers—friends, housewives, students, retirees—to sell locally on a commission. But it rarely pays for a single product. The major advantage of using established marketing wholesale or agent organizations is that they already have trade contacts and can get to see buyers who might refuse to meet with you.

◆ *How would I select a channel of distribution?*

It is best to follow the current practices in the industry. If certain chain and department store buyers traditionally purchase through wholesalers and agents, it's highly unlikely that you'll be able to sell to them directly. Sure, it sometimes happens—an entrepreneur who sold antique Chinese jewelry approached Neiman-Marcus and was given an order. But this is the exception rather than the rule. To save you from wasting effort, initially stay with what works in the trade and then try other methods.

SELLING

♦ *How are products and services sold?*

In many ways. The technique most common among home-based entrepreneurs is face-to-face personal persuasion. This can be done at home, at the customer's home or place of business, or at retail sites such as craft fairs. Face-to-face selling doesn't have to be done on a one-to-one basis: Group selling at house parties has long been used in direct-selling product distributorships (Tupperware, for example). The selling doesn't even have to be face-to-face: Some products and services can effectively be sold using the telephone.

♦ *Such as?*

Anything that can easily be visualized—name-brand merchandise and magazine subscriptions, for example. Many product distributor representatives for such firms as Mary Kay solicit orders over the phone and deliver the items at a later date. That makes phone selling an especially practical home business in restricted zoning areas.

♦ *Where does mail order fit in?*

Mail order is a multibillion-dollar direct sale to consumer business. Sales originate from media advertising or direct mail—letters or catalogs. Sometimes printed promotional material is grouped with sales literature of other advertising in cooperative mailings. Home entrepreneurs with the right products may be able to market through mail-order catalog firms that display the items in their catalogs.

♦ *Which selling method is best?*

For some types of business, the choices will be limited to a single selling method. For others, however, several options may be available,

> ### RETAIL RACK MERCHANDISING
>
> Rack merchandising is a form of retail consignment selling. The seller doesn't just deliver the merchandise to the retailer but is also responsible for displaying (or racking) the items, keeping track of the inventory, and replenishing sold items periodically. Rack merchandising is most effective for items retailing for three dollars or less and attractively packaged. The seller may also have to supply the display racks.

SELLING TO MAIL-ORDER CATALOG HOUSES

Another wholesale-type distribution channel for home-produced products is mail order catalog houses. Such firms as Lillian Vernon, Harriet Carter, Hanover Direct, and Miles Kimball offer marketing outlets to the consumer. Selling to this market involves mailing them a package of promotional material consisting of descriptive literature, glossy photographs or illustrations of the product, proposed advertising copy, and prices. If interested, they will ask you to complete a merchandise data sheet and return it with a product sample. A purchase order will be issued for a small quantity if they feel the product has a good chance of selling through their catalog and they are confident you will be able to deliver the merchandise. Mail-order firms take a percentage of the catalog price, which can be up to 75 percent for low-priced products.

and you don't necessarily have to settle on one. Many businesses, for example, use both retailing and mail order to move merchandise. The answer to your question is that the best selling methods are those that produce a profitable sale; that is, a sale in which the cost of selling the product is less than the cost of producing it.

CREATING THE DEMAND AND GETTING THE ORDER

Advertising, Promotion, and Sales

6

♦ *What is the difference between advertising and promotion?*

Both are intended to influence the buying decision. Advertising does this by creating an awareness of a product or service using the media, while promotion focuses on stimulating a purchase. In some advertising, the distinction between the two is fairly clear-cut. Television and magazine advertising for detergent soap informs the audience of the product's advantages, while the cents-off coupon attempts to motivate a choice of that product in a supermarket. That part is promotion. In small-business operations advertising and promotion may blend and the differences are less obvious.

There are three basic steps to any advertising program. It certainly makes no sense to waste time and money on those who are not likely to make a purchase, so step one is to make sure the advertising is directed to audiences with the greatest potential to become customers.

♦ *How can I tell who the customers might be?*

The best prospects are those who already use the product or service. They are considered educated or informed buyers—they are familiar with the advantages of the particular product or service and need only be sold on buying from you instead of your competition. Then there are groups who buy related items. For example, someone who shops for needlecraft supplies tends to also be a customer for needlecraft kits and workshop courses. Individuals with related interests in products or services are frequently good prospects. For example, parents with children in college respond to "survival" food package mail-order solicitations.

Look-alikes—that is, those groups that have characteristics similar to those of existing customers—are a target market. For example, since small tradespeople often use outside bookkeeping and tax services, it can reasonably be assumed that tradespeople who are not now customers will provide a better than average response to advertising for such services. Finally, there are groups that logic tells us should be buyers. Women wear jewelry, homeowners use mower repair services, teenagers prefer trendy clothing, and so forth.

◆ *After I identify potential buyers, what then?*

The best advertising in the world will not produce results if it runs in the media that do not reach the desired buying groups. Step two of an advertising program is to match the right media with the buying groups you've already identified. This requires an understanding of the type of

---

CUSTOMER PROFILE DATA NEEDED FOR MEDIA SELECTION

1. Special interests (craft, business, etc.)
2. Geographical area customers are likely to come from (neighborhood, city, metro region, national, etc.)
3. Sex
4. Age group (teen, college, senior citizen, etc.)
5. Marital status (working single, married with family, married with no children, etc.)
6. Income group (affluent, middle-income, etc.)
7. Education level (completed eighth grade, college graduate, etc.)
8. Occupation (blue-collar worker, professional, etc.)
9. Resident type (owner occupied home, high-rise apartment, urban row housing, etc.)
10. Community (large city, suburban, rural town, etc.)
11. Religion, race, ethnic background, if applicable

audience each medium is capable of delivering. The problem is that the media classify audiences by demographics, not by buyer type. In order to make a match, the buying groups must first be converted into compilations of demographic characteristics known as customer profiles.

◆ *Makes sense. What's step three?*

Step three is creating advertising and promotional material that will convince prospective customers to purchase your product or service, not your competitors'.

◆ *I know there are many advertising and promotion techniques, but which ones are really practical for small home-business operations?*

Surprisingly, there are quite a few. Let's begin with the ones that are relatively inexpensive.

Business cards can simply show the name, address, and telephone number of your business, or like the fold-over card shown above, cards can include detailed information on business products or services. ◌

1. Display a sign in front of your home, if it is legal to do so. Better yet, display the products themselves on the lawn, as they will attract more attention than a sign.
2. Distribute fliers on the street or door-to-door, or place them under wiper blades on autos parked in the street and in shopping-center parking lots. If possible, have fliers inserted in newspapers by local carriers.
3. Display posters in high-traffic areas, such as on supermarket bulletin boards, in laundries, in bus shelters, on company bulletin boards, or on telephone poles. Use eye-catching graphics with tear-off reminders.
4. Post signs in retail store windows and make available promotional literature or business cards on store counters. Retailers may let you do this in exchange for products or services.
5. Drop off business cards at prospective customers' homes or places of business—this is a simple but very effective way of letting people know you exist.
6. Advertise in community service, social, and religious organization newsletters and bulletins.
7. Participate in fund-raising events with charitable organizations, splitting proceeds with them.

Posters are a low-cost promotional technique. This poster was displayed on a bus shelter and has tear-offs for carry-away reminders.

8. Exhibit at libraries, colleges, and motion-picture theaters. This is good exposure for arts and crafts products. Or take a booth at county fairs.

9. Affix a magnetic sign on the family auto and supply friends with bumper stickers.

10. Include promotional literature in mailouts of others. Pay for it or barter products or services.

11. Ask others to spread the word and give them an incentive in the form of discounts on future purchases.

12. Have someone walk around with a sandwich-board display. This can be combined with flier handouts. Many a business got started just this way.

13. Be included in the Welcome Wagon package if new people in the area are potential customers.

♦ *What's available in the more formal types of advertising?*

Direct Mail—postcards, printed fliers, personalized letters, brochures, and catalogs—is usually appropriate and modest in cost. For a small annual fee, the Postal Service allows quantities of two hundred or more

SURPRISE GREETINGS

SEND A PERSONALIZED LETTER FROM SANTA CLAUS OR THE "BIRTHDAY CLOWN" TO A SPECIAL SOMEONE...SEND $2.00 FOR EACH LETTER TO: SURPRISE GREETINGS
                                  P.O. BOX 7111
                                  ROSELLE, N.J. 07203

DETACH AND MAIL _____

PERSON'S NAME: _____

ADDRESS: _____

DATE OF BIRTH:_____(if ordering birthday letter)

Fliers: inexpensive promotion technique. Fliers are affordable methods for home entrepreneurs to advertise products and services. They can be distributed door-to-door, left on car windshields, inserted in home-delivered newspapers, placed on countertops in retail stores, tacked on supermarket bulletin boards, included in other business mailings, and handed out on the street. Costs can be kept to a minimum by creating mini-fliers such as the one above.

Standard countertop brochure holders can be purchased for a few dollars.

pieces to go under a special bulk rate, thereby cutting the first-class postage costs approximately in half. Mailing lists permit businesses to target their message to specific groups with a minimum of waste.

◆ *How would I acquire the mailing lists?*

Many home entrepreneurs develop their own from directories—telephone, industrial, trade, local chamber of commerce, and so forth. Addresses on peel-and-stick labels are available from firms specializing in mailing lists for just about any category you can think of—geographical, demographic, type of business, type of professions, income, job title, and so on. Some local printers provide addressing services to residents of households, so a zip-code area can be economically saturated with a mailing program.

There are also packaged or cooperative distribution programs that combine into one mailing a number of advertisers interested in a specific market. Fliers, coupons, or brochures can be included. A variation of cooperative mailings are direct-response postcards. Here the inserts are return postcards with promotional information printed on the other side. The convenience of response frequently produces better results than conventional direct mail.

◆ *Are newspapers also a good choice?*

Less sharply focused but still effective in getting the message out are newspapers. Choices include community weeklies and advertising

Cooperative mailing. Almost all areas have cooperative advertising services that group a number of promotion pieces from different businesses in the same mailing. The cost is four to five cents per household and the minimum coverage is usually about 10,000.

shopping guides like the "Penny Savers," which are distributed free to area residents. Readership patterns very widely so you'll have to test each to see which works best.

Always run ads in the sections that are most likely to be read by the maximum number of prospective customers. For example, a bookkeeping service will probably get the best response from an ad in the business services directory or in the business section. An ad for a recipe booklet or cooking class will do better if it runs in the food section.

Don't overlook the specialty newspapers—business, religious, ethnic, occupational, union, senior citizens, and the like. If their readership comes close to matching desired customer profiles, they can get results at affordable costs.

♦ *Isn't newspaper advertising expensive?*

Costs vary with ad size, the circulation of the newspaper, and the frequency of the insertions. Volume discounts are usually available. To make it economical for local business to advertise, many large-city dailies offer zoned editions at a lower rate. They circulate in smaller areas but can be a good choice if the audience you are trying to reach is limited geographically.

♦ *Are magazines a realistic media choice?*

Magazines, selectively used, can be an excellent advertising vehicle for home businesses. Mail-order products are frequently sold through the shopping-guide sections of nationally distributed publications. Limited-circulation magazines—special interest and regional—are within the pocketbook of small business entrepreneurs. Freely distributed, and known as controlled-circulation magazines, these can target select groups—executive, professional, and industry—at moderate cost. Classified ads, even in magazines with circulation in the millions, are affordable.

While magazines generally have a higher advertising unit cost, their selectivity frequently means better results from smaller audiences. Consequently, their cost per order may compare favorably with other media.

Ramsey
Bergen Co.

HOME & STORE NEWS
(Tabloid)
Box 329, 6A E. Main St., Ramsey, NJ 07446.
Phone 201-327-1212, FAX, 201-327-3684.

CAC

Media Code 2 141 2600 0.00   Mid 022693-000
Published weekly—Wednesday.

1. **PERSONNEL**
Publisher & Gen. Mgr.—Thomas E. Dater.
Advertising Director—Harold Korsen.
3. **COMMISSION AND CASH DISCOUNT**
15% to recognized agencies if paid within 30 days.
No cash discount.
4. **GENERAL RATE POLICY**
30-day notice given of any rate revision.
Alcoholic beverage advertising accepted.
ADVERTISING RATES
Effective January 1, 1989.
Received March 17, 1989.
5. **BLACK/WHITE RATES**
Flat, per line .... .5322
13. **CLASSIFIED**
1.80 per line; 1 time; min. 3 lines; 5 words per line.
Classified Display: .5714 per line; min. 14 lines.
Closing time: Noon, Friday.
14. **ROP DEPTH REQUIREMENTS**
As many inches deep as columns wide.
15. **CLOSING TIMES**
5:00 p.m. Thursday before publication.
16. **MECHANICAL MEASUREMENTS**
PRINTING PROCESS: Offset.
7/8-6/4—7 cols/ea 8 picas-6 pts/4 pts betw col.
Lines to: col. 224; page 1568; dbl truck 3136.
17. **POSITION CHARGES**
Specified position, extra 25% when available, at publisher's option.
18. **SPECIAL CLASSIFICATION/RATES**
Political, per inch 7.45; cash with order.
20. **CIRCULATION**
Established 1961. Per copy .25.
C.A.C.—12-31-88
                                       Non-Paid Paid Total
Wednesday .... 28,495 ... 28,495

Media information source. Advertising data for all media are listed in the *Standard Rate* and *Data Service* series of manuals found in many libraries.

PER-INQUIRY/PER-ORDER ADVERTISING

Few in the media will talk about it or will even admit to doing it, but many radio, television, and cable TV stations, as well as magazines and newspapers, accept advertising with little or no up-front cost. Shared-revenue payment arrange-ments are tied to response—that is, they get paid on each inquiry or order received. This form of advertising is an attempt by the media to sal-vage some monies from unsold time and space and to convert users to regular advertising. This sometimes happens when the response is good.

In per-inquiry advertis-ing, in which the advertising is intended only to develop leads for follow-up and money may not be remitted, each response is paid for at an agreed-upon commission rate. Since fulfilling requests can be costly and there's no assurance of a sale, some businesses charge for each inquiry to partially offset some of the expenses.

Where products are sold from ads the media company and advertiser split the pro-ceeds. This can range from 25 percent to 50 percent going to the media with the lower percentage almost always for higher-priced merchandise.

(Continues)

◆ *Is radio and television advertising ever worth considering for a home business?*

Very infrequently. Radio falls somewhere in between newspapers and magazines when it comes to audience selectivity. Station formats—rock, classical, news, and so forth—pretty much determine audience demographics.

Focus can sometimes be sharpened by advertising on or around programs covering special topics, such as those related to business, news, or gardening. Radio in a localized market may be effective for announcement-type advertising, as for a home holiday craft sale.

Television advertising may only be practical in small cities where the cost is low. Text-type advertising on cable TV is inexpensive but results can very widely.

◆ *What about Yellow Page advertising?*

Directories offer instant reference for buyers who know the product or service they are seeking and should be included in most advertising budgets. The telephone Yellow Pages, the most popular directory list-ing, is available by geographical region, which is affordable even for small, neighborhood-type businesses. Directories published by indus-trial, trade, and professional associations are also worth considering because of their audience selectivity. In many instances listings are free if the products or services are relevant.

◆ *All areas have community publications. Are they worthwhile?*

Local specialty publications, such as community service, ethnic, and religious organization newspapers distributed to memberships, some-times accept advertising. They're worth a try if the readership might be customers.

◆ *That's quite a variety of choices. How do I select the right ones?*

Match the media with your target market. The target market is the class of people to which your product or service is most likely to appeal. These prospective customers may be in specific locations, have special interests, or be in a certain sex, age, income, or educational group. Each form of advertising and promotion is especially effective in reaching only certain types of audiences. For example, a display poster is seen by area people, a trade journal ad is read by those interested in the specific subject, and newspaper advertising gets to a large mixed audience. As a home-based entrepreneur, like any other business person, you're responsible for selecting the forms of advertising and promotion that best expose the business to the optimum audience of potential buyers.

♦ *The selection process seems difficult.*

It is. There is a wide range of choices and much uncertainty about which ones will produce the best results. Media categories themselves are not directly comparable. The printed word, for example, is considered to have better advertising impact than spoken communication. Even written communications have various degrees of impact. Direct mail produces a response pattern different from, say, display advertising.

There also can be differences in effectiveness within media categories. Special-interest magazines justify higher advertising costs than general circulation publications because they have less waste circulation. Paid-for media tend to be better read than those that are freely distributed. As a result, identical audience numbers don't necessarily translate into identical order response. Some magazines have more pass-along readership than newspapers and other publications. That makes their circulation numbers more valuable.

♦ *Is there a way I can narrow down the options?*

Yes. First, quickly discard the advertising and promotion methods that obviously don't make sense for your product or service. For example, if your home business is geared to a neighborhood trade, don't bother considering nationally distributed newspaper Sunday supplements. Next, check out the advertising and promotion techniques being used by companies with similar products or services. They are likely to be effective if the same methods and media have been in use for a period of time. Third, take advantage of all established advertising marketplaces for your product or service. Odds are they will give you the best response. Fourth, promote directly where it should do the most good.

Since processing entails some work on the part of the media company (it's customary that replies first go to them), they will handle only products that in their judgment have volume appeal to their type of audience, and the offer contains a money-back guarantee. They quickly drop products when the response is poor or when they receive an abnormal number of customer complaints.

Media accepting per-inquiry and per-order advertising rarely promote that fact, so you must send a letter to the company outlining the proposal. Acceptance of per-inquiry and per-order advertising will more likely come from independent rather than network stations in large cities and stations in smaller cities. Magazines prefer to offer discount advertising rates for unsold pages in zoned editions but some of the smaller and specialized ones are known to accept ads on a revenue-sharing basis. Card-deck direct-marketing firms on occasion will include per-inquiry and per-order advertising in their coop mailings if they think the response could be profitable. The responsibility for preparing the advertising—camera-ready and mechanicals for print media, announcer scripts for radio, visual presentations for television—is the advertiser's.

(Continues)

While a small business may be able to work out revenue-sharing arrangements with specialized magazines and small, independent radio, television, and cable TV firms, it's better to use the services of direct-response advertising agencies when approaching the major cable media. In a typical situation the agency receives a commission of 10 percent while the medium's share is about 25 percent. More than likely the cable networks will require advance deposits of $2,500 to $10,000 from which commissions are deducted.

If your business is child tutoring, hand out fliers to kids getting on or off school buses and mail information to teachers. Leaving business cards at antique stores could produce tangible results for those restoring and refinishing furniture. Finally, analyze the various advertising media alternatives and promotional techniques and compare the cost per thousand of each in reaching your target market.

◆ *Cost per thousand? What's that?*

The various forms of advertising and promotion differ in the size of the audience each can deliver and in cost. The only way a comparison can be made is by determining the cost per thousand viewers or readers. As an illustration, a $500 ad in a publication with 50,000 circulation translates into a $10 cost per thousand. The lower the cost, the more advantageous it is for the advertiser.

But knowing comparative cost may still not be enough to allow you to make an intelligent media selection. Different techniques can vary in pull, so it is essential to find out the source of the response. This is accomplished simply by asking customers, "How did you know about us?" In mail order, it's done by coding. I'm sure you've frequently seen a department number or letter listed in the address of mail-order advertising. This key, as it's called, permits identification of where the response is coming from.

◆ *Does a home business mean personal selling on my part?*

Unless all your selling will be done by mail, personal contact with prospective buyers, either consumers or middlemen, is inevitable. In most instances it will be face-to-face and the persuasive abilities needed will vary with the type of business. For example, a craft item that can be seen and touched pretty much sells itself. But if it's a service business, such as catering, your pitch will have to be very convincing to have someone turn over to you an important social event.

◆ *Can selling be taught?*

To a degree, yes. The selling process itself is a combination of intertwined steps, which can readily be identified. The problem is that effective selling involves two-way communication. Good salespeople have to be able to feel their way through the presentation, reading the prospect's verbal and nonverbal reactions and making adjustments as necessary. They also have to know when to expand or telescope steps in the process to bring the exercise to a natural close. That's why sales messages can't simply be memorized.

♦ *What is the first thing I have to do in my personal sell?*

Prepare for it by putting yourself in the customers' shoes and attempting to understand their needs and desires. Then develop a responsive verbal presentation that conveys your knowledge of the product or service and answers anticipated objections. Whenever possible your verbal presentation should be supported by documentation.

♦ *What sort of documentation?*

Let's begin with a fresh-looking business card. A soiled one is a turnoff. Documentation can take various forms. Promotional material, price lists, lists of satisfied customers, and facts and figures are some examples. A crafts artisan might show published articles and awards. Color pictures would help a cake baker and decorator make sales. Snapshots of table settings and prepared food would help a party caterer.

♦ *Would a prospective buyer be more difficult to deal with because the business is being operated from a home?*

Obviously a customer who drops in with some secretarial work will not likely be impressed to see a word processor sitting on a kitchen table next to jars of peanut butter and jelly. Appearances count in selling, and this goes for both the physical part of your home designated for the business and your own dress and attitude. Look professional, communicate friendliness, and use good manners. These things are frequently as important in selling as the product or service being offered, and sometimes more so.

♦ *What goes into the actual selling process?*

Good selling includes several fundamental steps. A salesperson has to learn how to qualify a prospect, first as a buyer, not a shopper, and

SUCCESS TIP

STRETCHING ADVERTISING DOLLARS

1. Sign an advertising contract to receive volume discounts from newspapers and magazines. Many will not ask the advertiser to pay the difference if contract levels are not met. (This is known as short rating.)
2. Take advantage of standby and remnant rates if you can. Newspapers and magazines almost always have some unfilled space at press time, while radio and television stations have unsold air time. Frequently these are sold at up to a 50-percent discount to advertisers who don't mind running on an as-available basis.
3. Don't just accept prices listed on the advertising rate card. Bargain for a better deal. Media people sometimes will throw in extra time spots or ad space just to close a sale.

(Continues)

second, as the type of buyer he or she is. Questions have to be asked that quickly size up the prospect and help tell an entrepreneur the selling strategy that will be most effective.

◆ *Selling strategy—what's that?*

The strategy has to focus on a prospect's needs. Basic instincts don't change. People buy for at least one of six reasons: monetary gain, health and safety, convenience, avoidance of worry, recognition, and self-improvement. Once the human motivation is identified, the sales presentation can be modified to show how the customer's needs can be filled by the product or service being offered.

◆ *Can you clarify this?*

A home entrepreneur with a bookkeeping service could try to persuade a prospect on monetary gain by highlighting that the service will allow more time to spend on sales, "where the real money is." A health-aid product distributor might emphasize "longer life" to senior citizens and "looking younger" to other prospects. A craft item would be pitched one way if the prospect were buying it as a gift and another way if the would-be purchaser wanted it for him- or herself. One sell might be on the basis of good value—"costing little more than a mass-produced gift." The other sell might deal with recognition—the desire to be admired—by talking about the uniqueness of the craft item and suggesting that by possessing it the buyer would be the envy of his or her friends. Emphasizing the points that motivate people to buy is probably the most important factor in successful selling.

◆ *When do I close the sale?*

Only when you're sure the prospect understands all that has been said. Expressions and body language can help you read the mind of the prospect, as can the questions you asked. Chances are someone who examines the merchandise or asks about delivery is ripe for a close. Sometimes you have to take the initiative. "Have I made everything clear?" and "Is there any other information I can give you?" are questions that will tell you whether anything is bothering the prospect.

ADVERTISING AND PROMOTION METHODS FOR REACHING VARIOUS MARKET GROUPS

MARKET GROUP TO BE REACHED	MOST EFFECTIVE ADVERTISING MARKET AND PROMOTION METHOD
A. General public in local area.	1. Advertising in community publications. 2. Display sign on home. 3. Flier distribution. 4. Direct mail. 5. Posters in high-traffic areas.
B. Special groups in regional or metropolitan area.	1. Direct mail. 2. Advertising in special interest regional publications.
C. General public in city or large regional or metropolitan area.	1. Newspaper advertising. 2. Advertising in zoned editions of regional magazines. 3. Local radio and cable TV advertising.
D. Special interest groups located nationally.	1. Advertising in specialized magazines and trade journals. 2. Direct mail.
E. General public nationwide.	1. Advertising in national magazines, newspapers, Sunday supplements. 2. Television advertising.

4. Request better ad positions or time slots. If you demand a preference you'll have to pay extra, but it doesn't do any harm to ask for an up-front location or air time around popular programs.
5. Strike a per-inquiry/per-order deal that allows you to run ads with no up-front cost. Shift to paid advertising if the advertiser's share of the revenues exceeds the ad cost.

♦ *Is there a proven closing technique?*

There sure is. Assure the buyer that the value is there and what's represented will be delivered. Give a choice, not a chance. "Is it charge or cash?" "Do you want this one or that one?" Apply pressure but don't force the sale. Let the customers feel they are making the decision.

♦ *What do I do if there are still objections?*

Stalling is not uncommon when a prospect is uncertain about a purchase. Deal with this by putting him or her on the spot. "What's

SOME PHRASES THAT HELP MAKE THE SALE

- ◆ Don't just take our words for it, try it yourself.
- ◆ Just check around—we stand behind our claims.
- ◆ With our warranty, there is no risk.
- ◆ You'll wonder how you got along without it this long.
- ◆ You owe it to your family.
- ◆ Can you think of a good reason for not buying at this time?
- ◆ I'm sure you'll agree—you can't lose.
- ◆ Try it—see for yourself.
- ◆ It sounds too good to be true, but the facts speak for themselves.
- ◆ The supply is limited, so it really doesn't make sense to wait.
- ◆ We're expecting a price increase, so waiting could cost you money

MAKING COMPARISONS OF ADVERTISING RATES FROM VARIOUS MEDIA

Deriving a cost per thousand (CPM) of audience units is a convenient way of making media advertising cost comparisons. The basic formula is:

$$\text{Cost/thousand} = \frac{\text{Advertising rate} \times 1,000}{\text{Total audience}}$$

Here is how it might be applied to magazines:

MAGAZINE	ADVERTISING RATE (PAGE COST)	TOTAL AUDIENCE (CIRCULATION)	CPM/AUDIENCE UNIT
1	$5,600	200,000	$28.00
2	$4,000	150,000	$26.66

bothering you? What haven't I made clear?" If cost is the problem, you'll have to repeat your description of the features that make your offer a good value. If competition is causing the indecision, highlight the competition's deficiencies. Sometimes adding an extra incentive, such as a discount or gift, helps to make the sale.

◆ *I guess that wraps up selling.*

Just one more item. It doesn't do any harm to encourage additional purchases. A special discount, such as 20 percent off on a second purchase, adds revenue and profit with very little extra effort.

One must learn to sell, so don't be discouraged at the outset. Your ability to make sales will increase with time. The important part of selling in the early stages is that you reappraise your performance and try to understand what factors caused the successes and the failures—and take these factors into account in the next selling situation.

FREE ADVERTISING IS YOURS ALMOST FOR THE ASKING

7

Publicity

♦ *As a home entrepreneur, my advertising budget is likely to be somewhat limited. What about exposure at no cost through publicity?*

Publicity can be a very effective marketing tool for new firms and should be actively sought. But the impact is short-lived and doesn't have the continuity of exposure needed to maintain continuous public awareness of the products or services offered. Only advertising can do that.

♦ *What receives publicity?*

Happenings, such as holiday craft sales, anything related to current events and the latest trends, human interest items—individual accomplishments, for example—new products and services, and the unusual. The media have to deem it newsworthy and likely to be of interest to an audience.

♦ *How do I go about getting this publicity?*

The most frequently used method is preparing a press release—usually 150 to 450 words of information about the business that won't be

77

viewed by the media as advertising. Address the release to the appropriate person—the editor or newscaster who deals with the subject. Some media publish regular columns featuring new products and there is no charge for the editorial mention.

◆ *Sounds simple enough.*

The process is, but getting media space or time isn't easy. There's plenty of competition for free advertising space and time. But there are some things you can do to improve the chances that your release will be accepted over others'. First, try to find an angle, such as tying the story to a special event or holiday. Editors also prefer new products

A TYPICAL PRESS RELEASE

For More Information Contact: September 1, ____
Doris Smith
33 Rock Road
Center City, MO 11735
(816) 555-6751   For Immediate Release

JOB FINDING TECHNIQUES LECTURE

A "How to Find a Good Job" lecture will be given by Doris Smith at the Center City Public Library, Main Street, Wednesday, September 21, at 7:30 P.M.

Ms. Smith operates the Acme Job Search Service. She will be discussing how to prepare a résumé, ways to find jobs that are not advertised, and changing careers. For more information call (816) 555-6751.

A professional career counselor, Ms. Smith is an adjunct instructor at the community college. A graduate of Bollard College, she has worked in personnel management for twelve years.

◆ ◆ ◆

All press releases must be prepared in a standard format. This is typed, double-spaced on 8½ by 11-inch bond paper with one-inch margins on all sides. The originator's name, company name, address, and telephone number should be typed single-spaced in the upper left-hand corner. The date of the release appears in the upper right-hand corner along with "For Immediate Release" or a future date for release. A headline is optional—it can be written by the press release originator or left to the editor. The publicity story should be factual and written in narrative form with no more than 450 words. The most important information should come first, followed by information less critical to the story.

and services over old-hat material, so emphasize a new or unique twist.

Second, include a photograph or illustration. Depending on space availability, it may or may not be used, but either way it will be a plus for your story. Finally, make the release easy for the editor to use. The opening paragraph should contain key information and answer five questions—who, what, when, where, and why. Follow this paragraph with more detail in decreasing order of importance so an overworked editor can simply cut the story to fit the space available. Material that requires extensive rewriting will most likely be discarded.

♦ *Press releases seem to be good for brief announcement-type news. Isn't there a way I can get more extensive coverage?*

Editorial mentions are product news, frequently accompanied by a photograph, published by magazines or trade papers. This type of publicity usually runs in the new products or mail-order shopping sections and must be written to resemble the editorial style of the publication to which it is going to be submitted. So it's best to peruse the publications before preparing the material.

Understaffed newspapers and magazines also seek out feature stories, which are another form of publicity. However, these require a professional editorial touch. Home entrepreneurs without writing skills should probably use the services of a freelance writer.

♦ *Will the media ever cover a story themselves?*

If the business is doing something of high reader, listener, or viewer interest the media might do feature stories with their own reporters. Send a proposal letter providing the story idea and slant to the media editors. You can use the same type of proposal letter to get yourself on radio and television talk shows, another publicity source.

♦ *What other types of publicity are worth considering?*

Where the business involves conveying information—teaching, counseling, and the like—personal appearances, as a speaker or by holding seminars, will provide excellent promotional exposure. But other types of businesses may lend themselves to some form of personal

Art Exhibit at Waldwick Library

WALDWICK - Portraits, florals, landscapes and wildlife oils by Dorothy Shuit of Allendale are on display at the Waldwick Public Library during the month of December.

Shuit founded the Community Arts Association in 1965 and now serves as Historian and honorary member. At the present time the membership totals over 200. Shuit has an art teaching background which extended over 30 years.

A timely exhibit of old-fashioned toys, collected by the Koob family of Carlstadt, may be seen in the library's main room display case.

Home entrepreneurs should not overlook any opportunities to obtain publicity by displaying creative works in public places.

WHAT'S NEW!

SUN-POWERED RADIO • CHILD'S CART SEAT • DOUBLE SHOVEL • MORE

▶ "Seat belt" cushion attaches to shopping cart, holds a small child securely in place for a more comfortable ride. $8
My Pal
Pansy Ellen Products 7075-A
Amwiller Industrial Drive
Atlanta, Ga. 30360

In the biker's seat? Inflatable cushion cover fits snugly on all bike seats, reduces the impact of bumpy road, long rides. $11.
Sports Comfort
Training
Equipment,
10 King St.,
Lynn,
Mass.
01902

▶ Dual-purpose shovel provides traction for spinning tires. $16. EZ-Tread, Hardware & Industrial Tool Co. Inc. 7601 River Road, Cinnaminson, N.J. 08077

▶ Solar-powered AM/FM radio has headphones, jogging strap, clips. Great for outdoor sports. $40. Sunstepper Mura, 5 Research Drive, Shelton, Conn. 06484

▲ Door wedge/burglar alarm slides under any in-opening door, triggers a shrill alarm when pressure is applied. $5 Wedge Alarm, Hanover House Bldg. #3, Hanover, Pa. 17333

▼ Light-up key covers have push-button, battery-operated light for finding keyhole. Set of 6, $10. Lillian Vernon, 510 S. Fulton Ave., Mount Vernon, N.Y. 10550

▲ Pretty, durable place mats for children have whimsical designs they'll love; clever, cutout shapes add interest, color to any table. Choose from bears and honey, rabbits galore, more. Each $3. Crown Corning, 1014 Sprague Ave., Los Angeles, Calif. 90040

BY ANN ELKINS

Anything new or different especially interests the media. Some publish regular columns featuring new products and there is no charge for the editorial mention.

Promotion stunts frequently are effective in attracting media attention. In 1982, Bill Zanker, president of the then two-year-old Learning Annex, announced that he was going to throw $10,000 from the eighty-sixth floor of the Empire State Building in New York City. On the day of the event reporters and cameramen congregated in the street to cover the story, as did the police to keep order. Just by coincidence two bank robbers chose that day and time to make a "withdrawal" from a branch of Bankers Trust located in the same building. They fired a warning shot into the ceiling, took some cash, and fled. Chased by bank guards, they ran right into the media people and were arrested. When Bill exited the taxi a few minutes later with the bags of money, it was a mob scene. He was told that throwing money off a building was illegal. Bill left with a police escort, pursued by hundreds of event attendees who grabbed at the money.

While the stunt didn't come off as planned, it received far more media coverage the following day than was expected, including a page-one story in *The New York Times*.

HOLIDAY AND SPECIAL EVENTS CALENDAR

Holidays and special calendar events offer home entrepreneurs exceptional selling and promotional opportunities. Sales are usually best the weeks preceding St. Valentine's Day, Easter, Mother's Day, Halloween, Thanksgiving, and Christmas. The media also use calendar events as lead-ins to local news stories. For example, they might use a press release or do their own feature story about a product distributor during National Salespersons Week, or a home secretarial service during Secretaries Week. Listed below are holidays and some special events that might be related to a home-business activity. A complete list of special events can be found in *Chase's Annual Events,* published annually by Contemporary Books.

- ◆ January: New Year's Day; Dr. Martin Luther King, Jr., Day (January 15); International Printing Week; Thrift Week; National Boat Show.
- ◆ February: Lincoln's Birthday (February 12); St. Valentine's Day (February 14); Washington's Birthday (February 22); American History Month; National Crime Prevention Week; Future Farmers of America Week; Boy Scout Week.
- ◆ March: St. Patrick's Day (March 17); National Salespersons Week; Red Cross Month; National Agriculture Day; Girl Scout Week; Easter (in some years).
- ◆ April: Easter; Passover; American Lawn and Garden Month; National Automobile Month; National Home Improvement Month; National Library Week; National Coin Week; Bike Safety Week; Secretaries Week.
- ◆ May: Mother's Day; Memorial Day (May 31); International Air Travel Month; National Radio Month; Senior Citizens Month; National Music Week; Let's Go Fishing Week.
- ◆ June: Father's Day; Dairy Month; Let's Play Golf Week; Flag Day (June 14).
- ◆ July: Independence Day; National Barbecue Month; National Farm Safety Week.
- ◆ August: Sandwich Month; National Clown Week.
- ◆ September: Labor Day; National Knit and Sweater Week; National Hunting and Fishing Day; Jewish New Year (September–October).
- ◆ October: Columbus Day (October 12); United Nations Day (October 25); Halloween (October 31); American Home Gardening Month; National 4-H Week; International Letter Writing Week; Jewish New Year (September–October).
- ◆ November: Thanksgiving; National Model Railroad Month; Cat Week International; Youth Appreciation Week; American Education Week; National Children's Book Week; General Election Day; Veterans Day (November 11).
- ◆ December: Christmas; Hanukah; New Year's Eve; Bible Week; International Arbor Day.

publicity. A caterer, for example, might talk to women's groups on how to throw a successful party.

Such products as works of art and crafts can be publicized through exhibits at libraries, municipal buildings, theaters, malls, schools, and events attended by large numbers of people. Trade shows are also places where publicity can be had through the distribution of press kits (packages of information) to the media.

♦ *What do I include in the press kit?*

The press release, a photograph that looks professional—Polaroids are not usually acceptable—and a fact sheet that provides background material, statistical information, and biographical data. Members of the media are more likely to give your company more space or time if they have material to work with.

Under no circumstances should you plan business advertising around publicity. The media will give you coverage only when it's convenient to them, which may not fit your business promotional effort. Publicity works best when it's used to supplement advertising, not replace it.

8

CONVINCING PEOPLE TO BUY

Do-It-Yourself Advertising

♦ *I've very little experience with advertising. What's expected of me?*

To keep costs down, home entrepreneurs frequently create their own advertising copy for fliers, classified and small display ads, direct-mail material, and sometimes catalog pages. It's not as difficult as it seems if you know how to approach it. For example, you can learn a great deal by picking the brains of the professionals. Thumb through the pages of newspapers, magazines, and catalogs. Read the sales letters that come in the mail. Take notes on the words, layout, typography, and art. All are intended to attract attention and have you perceive what's being offered as better than anything else around.

♦ *What do you mean by "perceive"?*

Products and services of competing businesses in many instances are not all that different. But selling depends upon creating in the minds of all prospective purchasers the idea or perception that a difference really does exist. That, in a nutshell, is what advertising is all about.

♦ *How is this perception created?*

There are five general guidelines for creating a good ad. Begin with a catchy headline, something that will compel prospective buyers to continue to read and get into the body of the message. Certain words and phrases always seem to work well: "Free," "new," "sale," "discount," "save," and "bargain," for example, are considered attention grabbers. Next, emphasize benefits in the body of the copy. Quality, service, economy—anything that provides reasons for making the purchase. An extra inducement to buy, a bonus, for example, helps make the sale. Then add a sense of urgency—such phrases as "as long as supply lasts" and "offer expires tomorrow" are used to move people to make up their minds more quickly. Finally, close with the action desired. "Order now," "come in," or "phone today" will direct people toward a positive response. If possible, include a money-back guarantee so a confidence level can be built between seller and buyer.

♦ *That sounds fine for large ads, but how would I get all that into a few classified lines?*

Achieving results in the limited space of a classified ad presents a copywriting challenge, but the basics still apply. For example, "How

> ## THE TWENTY-FIVE WORDS AND PHRASES USED MOST FREQUENTLY IN ADVERTISING
>
> Free, new money, sale, save, discount, now, bargain, easy, proven, results, valuable, amazing, secret, exciting, unique, how-to, announcing, introductory offer, at last, discovery, no risk, no obligation, money-back guarantee, limited supply

Ad creativity. Home-business entrepreneurs have to learn how to create small ads that have impact. What ad components are effective in grabbing attention and getting the message across? Bold type and catchy headlines, layout, graphics, distinctive borders, reverses (white text on a black background); words like "free" and "discount"; and personalized service are all response motivators.

Give ads pizazz. The ad on the left makes all the right points but is likely to go unnoticed. The two ads to the right hook the reader with big, black, bold headlines that jump out from the ad. The copy makes a logical case for the product. If the police recommend it, or, if the thieves "hate" it, the product must be good. (Reprinted with permission from *Entrepreneur* magazine, June 1991.)

to Live Debt Free" is a classified headline or lead that will cause most people to at least pause and continue to read. The persuasive value of each word has to be carefully judged. One mail-order specialist claims that the word "manual" pulls twice as many responses as the word "instruction." "Catalog" is better than "list." "Refundable," "guaranteed," and "accredited" are words likely to increase ad response. And ad money can be saved by not listing the firm's full name and address in the ad. Premium Merchandising Company, 777 Worth Avenue, Boston, MA can be run as Premium, 777 Worth, Boston, MA.

◆ *Do the same copywriting guidelines hold for direct-mail sales letters?*

Since space is less restrictive, sales letters permit the full range of copywriting techniques to describe what's being sold. "My secretarial services are available to you days, nights, and weekends—whenever you need them" is an illustration of an effective first line for a sales letter. Follow this by a "what's-in-it-for-the-customer paragraph. Next create

VENTRILIQUISM/Puppets! Catalog $1.00 (Refundable). Maher, Box 420PM, Littleton, Colorado 80160.

LEARN VENTRILOQUISM! Guaranteed Instruction, Supplies. **DUMMIES.** Information Free! Maher, Box 420-PM, Littleton, Colorado 80160.

COLLECT Military Medals. List 50¢. Vernon, Box 387 PM, Baldwin, New York 11510.

MILITARY Medals Catalogue $1.00. Subscription Yearly $6.00. Vernon, Box 136// M. N. Baldwin, NY 11510.

CATALOG FULL-SIZE FURNITURE PLANS — $1.00. Refunded with first order. Traditional, Early American, over 150! Furniture Designs, 1425 Sherman, Dept. CP-80, Evanston, Illinois 60201.

CATALOG FULL-SIZE FURNITURE PLANS - $2.00. Refunded with first order. Traditional, Early American, over 180! Furniture Designs, 1827 Elmdale, Dept. C ›-87, Glenview, Illinois 60025.

PREPARE Tax Returns - Housewife Jo Ann Netzley made $5,500 last season. Train at home. VA Approved. National Tax School, Monsey 2CM, New York 10952

PREPARE Tax Returns. Earn high fees, dignified work. Train at home. Accredited Program. National Tax Training School, Monsey, 2GU, New York 10952.

Ads that pull. Neophyte entrepreneurs can learn a great deal about advertising by studying ads that run year after year. The above ads have been run seven years apart. What has changed? The ventriloquism ad now offers "free information" instead of charging $1.00 for a catalog. "List" was changed to "catalog" in the military medal ad. The furniture plan ad remains essentially unaltered. The prepare tax returns ad continues to convey credibility ("accredited program"). It was also reduced by two words, saving the cost of a line. All the ads are keyed so the response source can be determined.

a picture in the mind of the reader by appealing to basic desires such as safety, fun, leisure, beauty, health, thrift, or popularity. Use words and phrases that stir emotions. Sell the sizzle, not the steak. Believability is important, so include testimonials or evidence plus a warranty or trial offer. Close the letter with a call for action and make it easy for someone to respond by providing an order form, reply envelope, card, or telephone number. Anything else you can do to motivate an immediate response is a plus. Act-now incentives can be in the form of coupons with expiration dates, special discounts, premiums, or free bonuses.

♦ *What about presentation of the advertising message?*

All advertising competes for attention. Layout and graphics can make the difference in whether your message gets read, and there are a number of ways ads can be given greater impact. Illustrations are a big plus. They can be line art—such as pen and ink sketches—or photographs, which tend to be more expensive. Line art can be drawn by an artist or provided by printers who have available art books containing prepared drawings of various types. Do-it-yourselfers can also purchase transfer sheets with line drawings from art stores. Layouts—the selection and arrangement of headlines, copy, illustrations, and borders—can give

Both these ads appeared the same day in the same newspaper. If you were looking for a job, which résumé service would you call? I would select the "Resumes that get results," because I'm more concerned about getting a good job quickly than saving a few dollars on résumé preparation. Also, the service promises to do more.

HOW ADVERTISING IS SOLD

◆ Newspapers: Classified advertising is sold by the line. Display advertising is sold by space—number of columns and depth. Rates may vary by category of advertising. All ads run ROP (run of paper), which means position is at the discretion of the newspaper. Preferred positions and color are available at an extra charge. Ad preparation is included in the price of the ad.

◆ Magazines: Classified advertising, where available, is sold by the line or word. Display advertising is sold by the page, by the fraction of a page, and by columns. The advertiser is responsible for delivering a completed display ad, known as a mechanical or camera-ready copy, to the publication. Deadlines usually precede publication date by several months.

◆ Radio: Spot advertising is sold on a time and frequency basis, with the rates varying by time of day. Usually the highest rates apply during the morning and evening drive to and from work, when the audience is the largest.

◆ Television: Spot advertising is sold by time and frequency. Rates vary by viewing time.

◆ Yellow Pages: Basic listing in geographical area comes free with business telephone. Additional ad space can be purchased at extra cost. Illustrations and color are available only in multicolumn ads. Other geographical regions are optional at additional expense.

advertising some distinctiveness. Color and reverses—white type on black background—may also help draw the eye of the reader.

◆ *What about using an advertising agency?*

If your business requires extensive mail order, television, radio, or sophisticated direct-mail advertising, definitely use an agency, since mistakes can be costly. But for most small ventures an agency is an unnecessary luxury in the startup phase. For some media—newspapers, Yellow Pages, and radio—help is available. They offer free assistance in the preparation of ads. That, along with what can easily be self-taught, may be all that's needed.

◆ *If I have an ad that produces results, should I change it?*

No one is ever certain that another advertising approach will not produce a better response. That's why different offers, different ads, and different media should be tested periodically.

Two versions of the same ad, one prepared conventionally, the other a reverse. Even two effective ads should be slightly altered periodically to give them a new look.

Minor changes can make advertising distinctive. Both of the illustrated ads cost the same, but the presentation makes the differences in the ad's ability to catch the eye of the ready, and therefore, to produce a response.

A simple but graphically well-balanced ad with a clear message. The type style and the border give it distinction.

CAREER SERVICES

Discounts can be effective sales motivators. If customers are asked to show the ad to receive the discount, it helps tell the entrepreneur whether the medium used is "pulling."

Ad layout. Home-based entrepreneurs should learn enough about advertising basics to rough out their own ads. Above is a rough layout of how the ad actually appeared.

A close-to-perfect ad. Shown here are three versions of an ad that over a ten-year period has remained essentially the same. The one on the left ran ten years ago, center, five years ago, and right, more recently. They contain most of the elements of a classic ad. Graphics and text are blended in a layout that's appealing to the eye. The copy is clear and concise. Words that have survived ten years—factory direct, heirloom quality, solid, West German movements—serve to create confidence in the product in the mind of the reader. A money-back guarantee response form are big pluses for stimulating action. If they awarded Oscars for small ads, the Emperor entry would almost certainly be a winner.

MARY KAY

ONE FLAWLESS REASON TO LEARN ABOUT SKIN CARE FROM MARY KAY. YOUR COMPLEXION

Mary Kay has a personalized, proven-effective program specially designed to meet your skin's individual needs. To find out the program and products best suited to your complexion, call today.

Professional Mary Kay Skin Care Consultant
Eileen Ingrassia
268-9079

Good advertising sells fulfillment of a basic desire—in this case, beauty—not products.

RECEIVING TOP DOLLAR FOR YOUR EFFORTS

Costing and Pricing Products and Services

9

♦ *How do I arrive at a price for my product or service?*

Home entrepreneurs starting a business usually underprice. All costs have to be taken into account, a fair hourly rate that compensates you for your time and talents must be charged, and a reasonable profit must be added. The owner of a home venture, like the owner of any other business, is entitled to a return for the investment and risk.

The pricing process begins with the cost determination. While cost may not itself be the basis for establishing prices, the information is needed to make certain all expenses are safely covered. Costs fall into four categories: direct material, direct labor, overhead, and selling, general, and administrative.

♦ *What goes into direct material?*

Materials or parts used in the manufacture of the product or in providing the service. For example, for a patchwork pillow craft kit, the direct material cost would be the cloth, filler, trim, and zipper. In a cooking class, any books given to attendees and the food used in the demonstrations would be considered direct material expenses.

SELLING, GENERAL, AND ADMINISTRATIVE EXPENSES

Some representative selling, general, and administrative (SG&A) expenses: advertising, promotion, office supplies, stationery, printed material, forms, postage, telephone expenses related to SG&A, professional fees (legal, accounting), insurance (liability, fire, theft, auto), bookkeeping services, telephone-answering services, office and auto equipment repairs and maintenance, depreciation of office and auto equipment, dues for business or professional association membership, subscriptions to publications, annual renewal of licenses and permits, education and training expenses, business gifts, entertainment, sales commissions, interest on loans.

◆ *What about direct labor?*

The time used in the creation of the product or service multiplied by an hourly rate constitutes direct labor. If the craft kit took a quarter of an hour to cut to size, assemble, and package, and your time was worth eight dollars an hour, or you paid that rate to an employee to do the job, the direct labor cost per kit would be two dollars.

◆ *What is overhead?*

There are always items for which costs can't easily be calculated on a unit basis. It's more practical to lump them together and apply the cost as a single figure, usually a percentage of the direct labor cost. In the illustration of product cost analysis on page 97, the overhead is 60 percent of direct labor or $1.20 per unit.

The sum of material, labor, and overhead is the cost of goods manufactured, or in a service business, the cost of services provided. To arrive at a total cost, selling, general, and administrative expenses must be added. These are costs not themselves part of the product or service but still incurred in any business operation. This category of cost must be calculated separately for each channel of distribution and method of selling. There would be significant differences in advertising and promotion costs between a business that does its own mail-order solicitation and a business that markets through mail-order catalog houses.

The total cost in a product enterprise is called cost of goods sold and in a service operation, cost of services provided.

◆ *Is a service business costed the same way as a product business?*

The method of compiling costs is similar. But since services are time-related, an hourly cost unit must be determined, which includes direct-service labor time at some value you deem appropriate plus allowances for overhead expenses and indirect activities.

◆ *What are indirect activities?*

In any business you are going to have to spend time selling your services and handling administrative chores. The only way to get paid for this is by building something into your hourly billing rate. The illustration of service cost analysis on page 100 shows you how to do this.

MANUFACTURING OR SERVICE OVERHEAD EXPENSES

Some representative overhead expenses: supplies used in the production of the product or providing the service, freight in, shipping, packaging materials, small tools, utilities (electricity, gas, water, telephone), equipment repairs and maintenance, self-employment taxes, employer's share of taxes paid for labor employed, workmen's compensation insurance paid for employees, benefits (medical plans, life insurance, pension), depreciation of equipment used in manufacturing or creating services. (A simple way of calculating annual depreciation expenses is to divide the equipment purchase cost by the number of years you expect the equipment will be used. For example, if $1,000 is spent for an electronic typewriter and the useful life is estimated to be four years, the annual depreciation expense will be $250.)

♦ *I have a pretty good picture of costing, but how do I get from there to a price?*

There are three commonly used approaches or strategies to pricing. In cost pricing all expenses are determined and a profit margin is added. Competitive pricing is matching what's being charged in the area for similar products and services. Then we have market-value pricing, which is charging what the market will bear. There is also rule-of-thumb pricing. It saves trying to come up with prices for each product. For example, a price of three times the material cost seems to work well for many craft items. Four or five times the merchandise cost is frequently used in mail order. But don't use these rates without first examining your own costs to make certain the ratios apply.

♦ *How do I select a pricing strategy?*

Pricing depends on a number of factors. Cost, competition, demand, pricing patterns in the industry, and business conditions all play a role in determining price. Then there are product and service characteristics. Features such as uniqueness, customizing, and special services permit one to charge more. Maximum profit is obtained when prices are set at what the market will bear. But this pricing strategy can only be used if there is little direct competition. And, of course, the price has to be within a range users expect to pay.

Such special services as pickup and delivery should, if possible, be added to the price of the product or service provided.

◆ *What do you mean by that?*

Everyone has preconceived ideas about what something should cost. An hour in a craft workshop may be worth five to eight dollars, sewing a skirt hem ten dollars, a special sale twelve dollars, and so on. Where something is sold can have an effect on what can be charged. You'll be able to price higher at an arts and crafts fair than at a flea market.

◆ *Suppose the product or service isn't different from what's being offered by others?*

Then you will have to use a competitive pricing strategy and come in at roughly the same price as the competition or lower if that's the only way to gain a foothold in the market. If the going rate for a double-spaced type page is $1.50 for example, it's not likely that a new secretarial service will be able to charge much more.

◆ *Is there any safe pricing approach?*

Cost pricing, that is, the cost of goods or services sold, plus a 15 percent to 25 percent markup will give you a respectable profit. In all situations, however, cost pricing by itself is the least desirable pricing strategy because it ignores the reality of the marketplace, namely competition and what people might pay. It can result in pricing your product or service out of the market or in not maximizing profit. Both are less than desirable business practices.

◆ *Is that it for pricing?*

For strategy concepts, yes. Now let's move on to setting an actual price, using the crafts kit described earlier as an illustration. Let's say, for instance, your market research indicates that similar kits retail in stores for $12.00. Since local retailers traditionally receive a 50-percent discount, your selling price to them has to be $6.00, giving you a profit of $1.33. Large chain stores and department stores expect an additional 10 percent discount, making your price to them $4.80.

ILLUSTRATION: PRODUCT COST ANALYSIS

The following costing illustration is for a patchwork pillow craft kit with anticipated production volume of 5,000 units, to be marketed through retail stores.

	UNIT COST	ANNUAL COST
Direct Material		
Material	$0.50	
Parts	$0.10	
Total direct material cost	$0.60	$ 3,000
Direct labor		
Owner (one-quarter hour of time per unit at $8.00 per hour)	$2.00	
Employees	—	
Total direct labor cost	$2.00	$10,000
Manufacturing Overhead		
Payroll taxes		$ 800
Fringe benefits		700
Supplies		850
Tools		450
Equipment maintenance		300
Inbound shipping costs		500
Packing and shipping supplies		900
Equipment depreciation		600
Auto expenses		400
Other		500
Total manufacturing overhead		$ 6,000
Overhead as a percentage of direct labor (overhead divided by direct labor)		60%
Direct Material		
Overhead unit cost (direct labor unit cost multiplied by overhead percentage)	$1.20	
Total unit costs of goods (COG) manufactured (total of material, labor, overhead)	$3.80 (variable cost)	

(Continues)

PRICING PITFALLS

Pricing right is important for any business. Unfortunately, too many novice entrepreneurs, lacking business experience, either overlook all cost factors, or don't take advantage of all pricing opportunities. Listed below are the most frequent pricing mistakes.

- Underestimating the cost of attracting and keeping customer. To play it safe, double your initial estimates for such items as promotion and selling time.
- Failure to allow for waste, inventory shortages, and damaged goods. If the business uses material and ends up with finished products, there has to be some shrinkage. Add a percentage to the cost.
- Not adjusting prices every year. Some costs are bound to increase over the year, resulting in decreased profit margins. An annual review of costs is a must.
- Ignoring the cost of replacing equipment. Everything wears out or becomes obsolete. Build some depreciation cost into product or service pricing.

(Continues)

ILLUSTRATION: PRODUCT COST ANALYSIS (CONT.)

	UNIT COST	ANNUAL COST
Selling, General, and Administrative Expenses (SG&A)		
Advertising and promotion		$ 1,200
Insurance (fire, theft, liability)		800
Office supplies, stationery		550
Travel		300
Postage		300
Professional services (legal, accounting)		600
Permits, licenses		50
Other expenses		500
Total selling, general, and administrative expenses		$ 4,300 (fixed cost)
Selling, general, and administrative expenses as a percentage of cost of goods manufactured (SG&A divided by COG)	23%	
Selling, general, and administrative unit cost (SG&A multiplied by COG)	$0.87	
Total product cost per unit (COG plus SG&A)	$4.67	

BREAK-EVEN ANALYSIS

A good business manager should always know what volume of sales is needed for his or her operation to become self-supporting. This is determined by subtracting the unit variable cost from the unit selling price and dividing the result into the annual fixed cost. Using the firm used in the illustration of product cost analysis as an example:

$$\frac{\$4,300}{\$6.00 - \$3.80} = 1,954 \text{ units}$$

This means that up to 1,954 units, or $11,724 in sales (1,954 times $6.00), the business will be losing money. Sales over 1,954 units will begin to produce profits with all revenues between the unit selling price and variable cost—$2.20—flowing to the bottom line.

Offering a package of services at special combination prices can substantially increase revenue per customer.

♦ Underpricing special services. People will usually pay more for product variations or extra services. Even though the cost may be a few pennies, that doesn't mean that's all you should charge.

♦ *But that only leaves me with a $0.13 unit profit.*

It's not a sufficient profit if you are only going to sell the larger accounts, but as an add-on to your retail store sales it can contribute greatly to the bottom line. Here's why. The cost of goods manufactured is a variable cost and increases or decreases in direct proportion to volume. Selling, general, and administrative expenses are mostly fixed costs and do not change with volume.

The illustration of the impact of sales volume on profit (see page 101) shows what happens to profits when kit volume is doubled by adding sales to chain and department stores, even at lower unit prices. Another advantage of increased volume is that it may allow you to purchase materials and parts at better prices.

♦ *How do I price various order quantities?*

By discounting percentages from the suggested list price, a pricing sheet for the craft kit might show the suggested list price at $11.99 and

ILLUSTRATION: SERVICE COST ANALYSIS

The following illustrates a method for costing service time. In the example we have a career counselor who wishes to bill for services on a time basis. The goal is to net $15 an hour, plus a profit, for the ten hours a week the individual expects to devote to the part-time venture. Of the ten hours, nonbillable administrative activities such as promoting the business will consume about two hours a week. Nonlabor overhead and administrative expenses are estimated to be $50 per week.

Labor Cost

(1)
$$\frac{2}{\text{hours or period that can't be charged to job}} \div \frac{10}{\text{total hours worked in period}} = \frac{25\%}{\text{percentage of nonbillable time}}$$

(2)
$$\frac{\$15.00}{\text{pay rate desired}} \times \frac{1.25}{\substack{\text{percentage of nonbillable time plus \$1.00}}} = \frac{\$18.75}{\substack{\text{labor cost per period to be charged}}}$$

Overhead and Administrative Expenses

(3)
$$\frac{10}{\text{hours per period worked}} - \frac{2}{\text{nonbillable time}} = \frac{8}{\text{billable hours}}$$

(4)
$$\frac{\$50}{\substack{\text{overhead and administrative costs per period}}} \div \frac{8}{\substack{\text{billable hours per period}}} = \frac{\$6.25}{\substack{\text{overhead and administrative expenses per hour}}}$$

Total Costs

labor costs per hour	$18.75
overhead and administrative expenses per hour	$ 6.25
total service cost per hour	$25.00

ILLUSTRATION: IMPACT OF SALES VOLUME ON PROFIT

	SALES: 5,000 UNITS	SALES: 10,000 UNITS
Variable cost ($3.80)	$19,000	$38,000
Fixed cost	$ 4,300	$ 4,300
Total Cost	$23,300	$42,300
Sales		
To small retailer (5,000 × $6.00)	$30,000	$30,000
To chains and department stores (5,000 × $4.80)	—	$24,000
Profit	$ 6,700	$11,700

a 35-percent discount for order quantities of two to six and a 50-percent discount for higher amounts. Large quantities, such as those that might be ordered by a department-store chain, should be given special quotes. Also, never discount one-unit orders. Nontrade customers sometimes try to make purchases this way to avoid paying retail prices.

10 AVOIDING FUTURE PROBLEMS

Business Planning

♦ *I've made a business selection, so I think we can finally get the show on the road.*

Not just yet. Let's get everything down on paper first. Experience has shown that it's much better to face problem issues in the planning stages than after they come up in the course of running the business. There is nothing mysterious about planning. It simply is a pulling together in a logical manner of the detailed steps needed to move a business from the conceptual phase to reality.

♦ *Is there a good place to start?*

Start by giving some thought to the exact nature of the business. This should include the specific products or services to be offered, how they will be produced or created, anticipated volume, and the target market, that is, the customers you intend to sell to.

Next, decide on a legal structure. There are four options here. The most popular for home business is a *sole proprietorship*. This is the simplest legal form for single-owner operations and professional setup assistance is not needed.

The other three forms of business ownership usually need the help of an attorney to set up, and this can sometimes add over $1,000 to startup costs. A *general partnership* structure is similar to a sole proprietorship in many ways but includes a relationship between two or more parties on a shared-income basis. For corporate forms of ownership there are two types—*Subchapter C* and *Subchapter S corporations*.

♦ *How do the legal structures differ?*

There are many differences, but there are two important ones: First, owners in sole proprietorships and partnerships are personally liable for any debts incurred by the business. This means if the business can't

NAMING THE BUSINESS

While selecting a name for a new venture would appear to be a simple task, it requires a great deal of thought. A name that bestows distinction and makes a positive impression will help the business achieve recognition in the marketplace.

In naming a business one might use the owner's name, a geographical name, a name that includes the product or service, initials, or something unique and catchy. Combinations are also possible. Stanley H. Kaplan Educational Services is an example. Here are some guidelines to use in naming the business.

- ♦ The name should, somehow, be related to the business but not be too limiting. This will allow the company to stretch into other products or services at a future time without a name change.
- ♦ The name should be attention-getting, easy to remember, understandable, and pronounceable.
- ♦ The name should have meaning to customers and suggest a bigger organization than a one-person startup venture. (Name consultants advise against using personal names and the word "enterprises" as part of the firm's name.)

Most important, a name should not infringe in any way on a name used by others. When an immigrant from the Philippines named her small restaurant Sony's—her lifelong nickname—the billion-dollar Sony Corporation claimed damages and sued for $2.9 million. Rather than go through the cost of fighting the suit, she changed the name.

The best way to make certain a name is legally clear is to check with the county clerk, locally, and the secretary of state, statewide. If the business is interstate, peruse trade directories in libraries to avoid selecting a name used by a major firm in the same business. If you want to be absolutely certain the name is not being used by others, use a firm such as Trademarkscan to do a computer search of all trademarks on file. This costs about $300. A logo tied to a business name should also be protected. Expect to pay $240 for registration. The search can be done over the Internet (http://training.krinfo.com/quick/solutions/4915.html/).

SHOULD YOU INCORPORATE?

In most instances, you should not incorporate.

The majority of small businesses operate as sole proprietorships—and for good reason. For a few dollars, you're in the business. No lawyers, no accountants, and chances are you'll be able to do your own taxes and pay less to the IRS than if you incorporate. The advantage of limited liability from incorporation is frequently negated by banks, which usually will lend money to a small business only if the owner personally guarantees the loan.

Incorporation for a small business is justified if there is extensive personal liability exposure: for example, if there may be product-defect claims that can't adequately be covered by liability insurance, or if the business is heavily dependent on credit. Another reason for incorporation is to raise capital. Financial sources will almost

(Continues)

meet its financial obligations, creditors can go after an individual's house, car, and bank account. In a corporate form of business, the owner's personal assets are protected.

The second major difference is the way profits are taxed. In a sole proprietorship or partnership, the proprietors simply add profits or subtract losses from the business when computing personal taxable income. In a Subchapter C corporation, profits are taxed twice, once at the corporate level and again as dividends to the owner. To avoid this double taxation on corporate income, a small business owner can choose a Subchapter S structure, which is taxed only once at the owner's level.

◆ *Which business structure is best?*

There is no best structure for all situations. For small businesses that have little debt and low risk of financial failure, a sole proprietorship is recommended. If the potential exposure can involve personal assets, a Subchapter S corporation has advantages. If you are in doubt, an exploratory session with an accountant or lawyer would be worthwhile.

DO-IT-YOURSELF INCORPORATION

If you choose a corporate form of business you can save many hundreds of dollars by incorporating without the services of an attorney. The necessary forms—the articles of incorporation and the like—and corporation kit can be purchased at large stationers. You first should check out your choice of a business name with the state's secretary of state to make certain it does not closely resemble the name of another corporation in the jurisdiction. In completing the forms you must state a corporate purpose. This should be written to give the business as much latitude as possible, so that if you decide to change direction later on, you'll be able to do so.

The package of material must be sent to the appropriate state agency with a fee, and if this is done properly, you will receive notification of the corporate formation in several weeks. The business then must hold a meeting at which bylaws are adopted, directors and officers elected, and stock issued. The proceedings must be recorded in official minutes. All the procedural details can be found in books available in libraries and stores. One of the most popular publications covering the subject is *Inc. Yourself* by Judith McQuown (Macmillan).

SUMMARY OF MAJOR DIFFERENCES BETWEEN VARIOUS LEGAL FORMS OF BUSINESSES

	Sole Proprietorship	General Partnership	Subchapter C Corporation	Subchapter S Corporation
Owner(s) personally responsible for business debts	Yes	Yes	No	No
Business pays taxes on profits	No	No	Yes	No
Ease of starting	Can be done by entrepreneurs	Simple arrangements can be handled by entrepreneur	Usually requires professional assistance	Almost always requires professional assistance
Cost to form business	Under $100	$100–$1,000	$500–$1,700	$500–$1,700
Continuing professional costs per year	$150–$250	$300–$500	$500–$1,000	$500–$1,000

never lend to or invest in a sole proprietorship. Many small firms start out as sole proprietorships and incorporate later. As a general rule, this is a good path for novice entrepreneurs to follow.

♦ *Can insurance give me personal protection?*

You will need some forms of insurance, but no policy is available to cover liability from business failure.

♦ *What insurance coverage do I need?*

At the minimum a rider should be added to your homeowner or apartment-dweller's policy that covers injury on your property to business-related visitors. This same rider will also give you $5,000 to $7,000 of protection on business property. The rider costs about $75 a year. For $400 to $600 a year, you can acquire small business coverage which includes $1 million in general and product liability for errors and omissions. It will also compensate you for loss of earnings due to business interruption and provide $50,000 in property protection. If you have an extensive investment in computer equipment but don't need all the small business coverage, it's cheaper just to take out special computer insurance. For about $175 you can get about $15,000 in coverage. An insurance broker can best advise you what combination of household and business insurance will give you the coverage needed.

◆ *Let's get down to the nitty-gritty of the business plan. What details does it have to cover?*

A business plan contains four parts. In the marketing segment the business scope is clearly defined, channels of distribution determined, prices established, the most appropriate advertising and promotional technique selected, and suitable selling methods chosen. Steps needed to create the product or service are covered in the *technical* plan. The *administrative* section of the business plan deals with items such as clearing legal hurdles and operating the business on a day-to-day basis—receiving orders, paying bills, keeping records, and so on. The checklists below provide a working framework for preparing the business plan. Obviously, not all the items mentioned will apply to every home business. The best way to handle the planning process is to jot down each action step on a three-by-five card and organize the cards in a logical time priority order. This will enable you to identify and give priority to activities that can delay business startup, such as zoning.

MARKETING PLANNING CHECKLIST

◆ Define the exact nature of the products or services to be offered.
◆ Decide on what market research and testing techniques are needed to define target market, marketability of product or service, and competitive factors.
◆ Identify distribution channel that can best reach target market by demographics and geography.
◆ Establish pricing structure by channel of distribution. Determine policies on volume discounts, credit, advertising allowances, shipping costs, and warranties.
◆ Analyze various advertising and promotion methods and decide which are the most appropriate for startup and for later stages.

◆ Determine selling methods and list items to be ordered (e.g., point-of-purchase display racks).

TECHNICAL PLANNING CHECKLIST

◆ *Priority:* Acquire skills necessary to carry out business (e.g., attend craft workshop, get job experience).
◆ Decide how the product or service will be created.
◆ Determine space and location in home needed to operate business. Allow for furniture, equipment, work area, customer waiting area, storage of raw materials and finished product, and so forth.
◆ Detail steps that must be taken to prepare space (e.g., renovate room; section off work area; finish basement, garage, attic; install lighting, heat, air-conditioning; bring electric, water, and gas lines to area, and so forth).
◆ List equipment, furniture, and transportation needs and survey vendors for best price, availability, and credit terms.
◆ Identify suppliers of raw materials, merchandise supplies, and tools. Compare quality, prices, volume discounts, credit terms, and delivery.
◆ If outside labor—employees or contractors—will be needed, determine how it will be recruited.
◆ Decide on best method of delivery for product to reach customer (e.g., Postal Service, UPS).

ADMINISTRATIVE PLANNING CHECKLIST

◆ *Priority:* Apply for patents, copyrights, trademarks.
◆ *Priority:* Apply for zoning permit or variance.
◆ *Priority:* Apply for occupational license.
◆ Choose company name and legally clear use.
◆ Evaluate various forms of ownership, using professional services if necessary.
◆ Check government agencies and determine what business permits are needed to operate.
◆ Decide on appropriate record-keeping system. Consult accountant if necessary.

◆ Discuss types of insurance needed with agent and decide on appropriate coverage.
◆ Determine who will be the suppliers and attempt to establish credit.
◆ Decide on a bank for business checking and savings accounts. See what's needed to accept credit-card charges if in retail business.
◆ Decide on telephone service—personal phone or business phone. Investigate advantages of answering machines and answering services.
◆ Decide on business address—home, postal box, or mail drop.
◆ Get forms for obtaining postal bulk-rate permit if needed for mailings.
◆ List office and stationery supplies needed.
◆ After determining the investment amount, check into obtaining money through friends, relatives, or bank if needed to start business.

◆ *What's the fourth planning component?*

The fourth planning component is *financial*. Completing this segment of the planning process involves putting dollar amounts on all the action steps. The financial plan is critical to the success of the home venture. Don't pull numbers out of the air. For major cost items contact the providers, such as suppliers and professionals, and request quotations. Rough estimates can easily be acquired by phone.

◆ *What cost items are related to startup?*

Worksheet A (see pages 109–110) lists the costs most often associated with startup. There are the one-time expenses, such as equipment, furniture, and professional fees that might be incurred in organizing the business. Then there are special startup costs. For example, a business might have unusually heavy advertising and promotion expenditures in the first couple of months. If the operation requires merchandise, some early purchasing in volume may be needed.

You also have to allow for some working capital. To arrive at this figure, monthly expenses must be multiplied by a factor that can range from two times (for payments that may be deferred, such as credit purchases) to four times (where timely remittances are law—taxes, for example).

If you're dealing in credit, expect some deadbeat accounts. An allowance of 3 percent of total sales is typical. Also add a contingency percentage—10 percent is reasonable—for unanticipated expenses.

After you've completed the startup cost analysis, go on to making a twelve-month profit-and-loss forecast and cash-flow projection.

WORKSHEET A:
STARTUP CAPITAL REQUIREMENTS

ONE-TIME COSTS

	Total
Renovations	$_____
Equipment	_____
Furniture	_____
Licenses and permits	_____
Legal fees	_____
Accounting fees	_____
Deposits with utilities	_____
Utility installation	_____
Tools	_____
Other	_____
Subtotal (1)	_____

SPECIAL STARTUP COSTS

	Total
Advertising and promotion	$_____
Startup inventory	_____
Insurance prepayments	_____
Printing, stationery, forms	_____
Startup cash	_____
Other	_____
Subtotal (2)	_____

(Continues)

BEWARE OF EASY MONEY

Entrepreneurs needing money sometimes are attracted to small ads offering loans based on the "creditworthiness of the individual." While most of these lenders are legitimate loan brokers, the Better Business Bureau warns that others may be operating advance-fee schemes. In some instances a loan is promised within two weeks, but an up-front fee of $750 is required, plus $150 to process the loan. After payment the "broker" is not heard from again. Other scam artists stay within the law by providing the names of an agreed number of potential lenders, none of whom will lend money. They then withhold the refund for a variety of reasons, or point out the fine print in the contract that indicates there was no assurance of funding.

Always investigate a loan broker that requests an advance fee. How long has the firm been in business?

(Continues)

WORKSHEET A:
STARTUP CAPITAL REQUIREMENTS (CONT.)

MONTHLY OPERATING COSTS
(FOR CALCULATING WORKING CAPITAL REQUIREMENTS)

		Multiplication Factor	
Advertising and promotion	$_____	_____	$_____
Materials	_____	_____	_____
Product/service supplies	_____	_____	_____
Wages/salaries	_____	_____	_____
Payroll taxes	_____	_____	_____
Benefits	_____	_____	_____
Freight	_____	_____	_____
Postage	_____	_____	_____
Auto expense	_____	_____	_____
Telephone	_____	_____	_____
Utilities	_____	_____	_____
Professional fees	_____	_____	_____
Insurance	_____	_____	_____
Office Supplies	_____	_____	_____
Loan payments	_____	_____	_____
Bad Debts	_____	_____	_____
Other	_____	_____	_____
Subtotal (3)			_____
(total of 1, 2, and 3)			
Contingency factor			_____
Startup capital requirements			_____

◆ *Why do I need both profit-and-loss and cash-flow projections? Aren't they the same?*

No. In any new venture credits are likely to demand cash with the order while customers may take up to ninety days to pay. This cash lag can cause problems. It is not unusual for a business to be profitable on paper and at the same time not able to meet current obligations.

♦ *How do I go about preparing the profit-and-loss forecast and cash-flow projection?*

Worksheets B (page 112) and C (page 113) are provided to guide you through the process. Start by going back to your costing analysis, which contained sales projections and a breakdown of fixed and variable costs. Then plug the right numbers into the worksheets.

What banks have provided loans through him? Make certain the refund policy is not conditioned by "after accounting expenses."

♦ *Some information is hard to come by. For example, how do I know how long customers are going to take to pay or how much time creditors will give me?*

Good question. Sometimes it's better to prepare two cash-flow scenarios—a most likely and a worst case. If both cash flow projections come out positive, you know it's safe to proceed. However, if the worst-case scenario is not favorable, daily cash flow will have to be closely monitored.

♦ *What do I do if the analyses show more money is needed than I can muster up?*

One possibility is to get a loan from relatives, friends, or a bank. Another is to reduce expenditures. Buy used instead of new equipment, or lease instead of purchase. Postpone remodeling and get by with

BORROWING MONEY FROM A BANK

A business loan requires the completion of a loan application with a detailed description of the operation and market. The bank will also want to know the amount of money you need, how and when it will be spent, how much you plan to invest yourself, monthly projections of sales and profit or loss, and personal information regarding your qualifications and financial status. On a twenty-four-month loan, monthly payments for each $1,000 borrowed are $47 if the interest rate is 12 percent and $49 at 16-percent interest.

Self-employed people without a credit history may find bank borrowing difficult when the money is needed for expansion. To avoid this problem some experts suggest taking out small personal loans at several banks even when the money is not needed for the business, then paying the loan back quickly. Once your credit history is established, you'll be considered a good risk and chances are the money will be available at the right time.

WORKSHEET B: PROFIT AND LOSS FORECAST

MONTH	1	2	3	4	5	6	7	8	9	10	11	12
1. Anticipated sales	—	—	—	—	—	—	—	—	—	—	—	—
Product costs												
2.1 Materials	—	—	—	—	—	—	—	—	—	—	—	—
2.2 Labor	—	—	—	—	—	—	—	—	—	—	—	—
2.3 Overhead	—	—	—	—	—	—	—	—	—	—	—	—
2. Total product cost (total of 2.1, 2.2, 2.3)	—	—	—	—	—	—	—	—	—	—	—	—
3. Gross profit (1 minus 2)	—	—	—	—	—	—	—	—	—	—	—	—
4. Selling, general, and administrative expenses	—	—	—	—	—	—	—	—	—	—	—	—
5. Net profit before taxes (3 plus 4)	—	—	—	—	—	—	—	—	—	—	—	—
6. Cumulative net profit (add net profit each current month to cumulative net profit of previous month)	—	—	—	—	—	—	—	—	—	—	—	—

what you have. The old bridge table may work almost as well as a new desk. Also, initially, buy in smaller quantities. It's more costly but it helps to keep down current cash needs. Another option is to tighten your own credit policies so incoming money is speeded up. Another approach is to offer early remittance discounts. For some types of businesses "bootstrapping" can be used—that is, the home business can partially finance itself by requiring down or advance payments on custom-ordered items. With credit obtained from suppliers the products can be completed and sold before the payment is due. If expenses can't be brought in line with revenue, you'll have to give up the business idea and move on to something requiring a smaller investment.

WORKSHEET C: CASH FLOW PROJECTION

MONTH	1	2	3	4	5	6	7	8	9	10	11	12
1. Cash beginning of month	—	—	—	—	—	—	—	—	—	—	—	—
2. Monthly cash income from cash sales, receivable collections, and other sources	—	—	—	—	—	—	—	—	—	—	—	—
3. Total cash available during month (1 plus 2)	—	—	—	—	—	—	—	—	—	—	—	—
4. Cash disbursements during month	—	—	—	—	—	—	—	—	—	—	—	—
5. Cash balance at end of month (3 minus 4)	—	—	—	—	—	—	—	—	—	—	—	—

◆ *I won't give up that easily. Aren't there other things I can do?*

Some entrepreneurs use personal credit cards to purchase office machines, stationery, and advertising space. This provides you with buying power, but at a high interest rate. A better idea is to barter products or services. One individual exchanged a crocheted sweater for public relations services, which helped successfully launch the business.

11 OPEN FOR BUSINESS

Starting Up and Managing the Day-to-Day Operations

♦ *I've completed the business plan. Now what?*

Start implementing the plan in priority sequence. Typically the first steps will be:

1. Acquire zoning approval from the local municipal authorities, if necessary.
2. Obtain any occupational and special health and safety permits or licenses if required for your type of business. These come from the appropriate governmental agency.
3. Obtain a local building permit if permanent renovations are going to be done to any part of the home.
4. Decide on the business legal structure. If you are not going to incorporate or use your own name as part of the company name, you'll need to obtain a *fictitious name statement*, or as it is also known, a DBA—"doing business as." The forms are available at any stationer and are to be filed with the county clerk or state tax office. In some areas, a DBA notice must be published in the local newspaper. The one-time registration costs run about $50 to $100. If you decide on a corporation, see an attorney, or try to incorporate yourself.

5. Trade register the business name with the county.
6. Obtain a *business license*. Many municipalities or states require a permit to conduct business. The fee is usually based on gross sales, but volume from most part-time ventures falls below the minimum tax level, so, at least initially, it won't be costly.

X 201—Certificate of Conducting Business under an Assumed Name
For Individual

JULIUS BLUMBERG, INC., LAW BLANK PUBLISHERS
80 EXCHANGE PL. AT BROADWAY, N. Y. C. 10004

Business Certificate

I HEREBY CERTIFY *that I am conducting or transacting business under the name or designation*

of

at

City or Town of   County of   State of New York.

*My full name is**

and I reside at

I FURTHER CERTIFY *that I am the successor in interest to*

the person or persons heretofore using such name or names to carry on or conduct or transact business.

IN WITNESS WHEREOF, *I have this*   day of   19   , made

and signed this certificate.

....

* Print or type name.
* If under 18 years of age, state "I am .... years of age".

STATE OF NEW YORK
COUNTY OF   } ss.:

On this   day of   19   , before me personally appeared

to me known and known to me to be the individual   described in and who executed the foregoing
certificate, and   he   thereupon   duly acknowledged to me that   he   executed the same.

Fictitious name statement. A sole proprietorship business that operates under a name other than the owner's must register with the county or state.

7. Get a *resale tax certificate* or *state sellers permit* if the operation will involve purchasing items for resale. This exempts the business from paying sales tax on some of its purchases.

Form ST-3 (Rev. 5/82)
RV 01001-03

Minnesota Department of Revenue
Sales and Use Tax Division
CERTIFICATE OF EXEMPTION

I, the undersigned purchaser, hereby certify that I am engaged in the business of _____

_____

(Describe nature of business activity)

and that the tangible personal property described below which I shall purchase, lease or rent from

Name of Seller	
Address	

is exempt for the following reason:

☐ The purchaser is an organization organized and operated exclusively for educational or religious purposes.

☐ The property is for use or consumption in agricultural or industrial production of property intended to be sold ultimately at retail. This exemption does not cover machinery, equipment, implements, tools (except qualifying detachable accessory tools), accessories, appliances, contrivances, furniture and fixtures; neither does it apply to purchases over $100,000 in any calendar year of paper and ink products by a publisher for use in an exempt publication.

☐ The property is packing materials used to pack and ship household goods to destinations outside Minnesota, and material designed to advertise and promote the sale of merchandise or services, purchased and stored for the purpose of subsequently shipping or otherwise transferring outside the state by the purchaser for use thereafter solely outside Minnesota.

☐ The property is rolling stock purchased by a railroad, taconite railroad, freight line, sleeping car or express company, taxed on gross earnings under Minnesota Statutes, Chapters 294 and 295. Rolling stock includes engines, cars, tenders, coaches, sleeping cars and parts necessary for the repair and maintenance of such rolling stock.

☐ The property is telephone central office telephone equipment used in furnishing intrastate and interstate telephone service to the public.

☐ The property is mill liners, grinding rods, and grinding balls purchased by a company taxed under the in lieu provisions of Minnesota Statutes, Chapter 298, and is substantially consumed in the production of taconite, the material of which primarily is added to and becomes a part of the material being processed.

☐ The property is airflight equipment purchased by an airline company taxed under Minnesota Statutes, Sections 270.071 through 270.079. Air flight equipment includes airplanes and parts necessary for the repair and maintenance of such air flight equipment and flight simulators.

Detailed description of property for which exemption is claimed: _____

_____

Check applicable box: ☐ Single purchase certificate   ☐ Blanket certificate

If blanket certificate is checked, this certificate continues in force until cancelled by the purchaser. If the purchaser uses this property for other than exempt purposes, and fails to file a sales or use tax return declaring the taxable use of such property, with the intent to evade the tax, the purchaser will be subject to the full penalty of the law.

Signature of Authorized Purchaser	Title	Date

Purchaser's Business Name _____

Address	City	State	Zip Code

Purchaser's Sales and Use Tax Account Number _____

If you have no number, give reason: _____

NOTE: Sellers must keep this certificate as a part of their records. Incomplete certificates cannot be accepted in good faith.

Sales tax exemption. A business is exempt from paying sales taxes on merchandise used for products that will be resold.

8. If you don't have a Social Security number or you intend to hire employees, obtain a *federal employee identification number* from the local IRS office. If the business is not a corporation this identification or

Form **SS-4** (Rev. February 1998) Department of the Treasury Internal Revenue Service	**Application for Employer Identification Number** (For use by employers, corporations, partnerships, trusts, estates, churches, government agencies, certain individuals, and others. See instructions.) ► Keep a copy for your records.	EIN OMB No. 1545-0003

Please type or print clearly.

1	Name of applicant (legal name) (see instructions)		
2	Trade name of business (if different from name on line 1)	3	Executor, trustee, "care of" name
4a	Mailing address (street address) (room, apt., or suite no.)	5a	Business address (if different from address on lines 4a and 4b)
4b	City, state, and ZIP code	5b	City, state, and ZIP code
6	County and state where principal business is located		
7	Name of principal officer, general partner, grantor, owner, or trustor–SSN or ITIN may be required (see instructions) ►		

8a Type of entity (Check only one box.) (see instructions)

Caution: *If applicant is a limited liability company, see the instructions for line 8a.*

☐ Sole proprietor (SSN) _____
☐ Partnership   ☐ Personal service corp.
☐ REMIC   ☐ National Guard
☐ State/local government   ☐ Farmers' cooperative
☐ Church or church-controlled organization
☐ Other nonprofit organization (specify) ► _____ (enter GEN if applicable) _____
☐ Other (specify) ►

☐ Estate (SSN of decedent) _____
☐ Plan administrator (SSN) _____
☐ Other corporation (specify) ► _____
☐ Trust
☐ Federal government/military

8b	If a corporation, name the state or foreign country (if applicable) where incorporated	State		Foreign country

9 Reason for applying (Check only one box.) (see instructions)

☐ Started new business (specify type) ► _____
☐ Hired employees (Check the box and see line 12.)
☐ Created a pension plan (specify type) ►

☐ Banking purpose (specify purpose) ► _____
☐ Changed type of organization (specify new type) ► _____
☐ Purchased going business
☐ Created a trust (specify type) ►
☐ Other (specify) ►

10	Date business started or acquired (month, day, year) (see instructions)	11	Closing month of accounting year (see instructions)

12	First date wages or annuities were paid or will be paid (month, day, year). **Note:** *If applicant is a withholding agent, enter date income will first be paid to nonresident alien. (month, day, year)* . . . . ►			

13	Highest number of employees expected in the next 12 months. **Note:** *If the applicant does not expect to have any employees during the period, enter -0-. (see instructions)* . . . ►	Nonagricultural	Agricultural	Household

14 Principal activity (see instructions) ►

15	Is the principal business activity manufacturing? . . . . If "Yes," principal product and raw material used ►	☐ Yes	☐ No

16	To whom are most of the products or services sold? Please check one box. ☐ Public (retail) ☐ Other (specify) ►	☐ Business (wholesale) ☐ N/A

17a	Has the applicant ever applied for an employer identification number for this or any other business? . . . . ☐ Yes ☐ No **Note:** *If "Yes," please complete lines 17b and 17c.*

17b If you checked "Yes" on line 17a, give applicant's legal name and trade name shown on prior application, if different from line 1 or 2 above.
Legal name ►   Trade name ►

17c	Approximate date when and city and state where the application was filed. Enter previous employer identification number if known. Approximate date when filed (mo., day, year)	City and state where filed	Previous EIN

Under penalties of perjury, I declare that I have examined this application, and to the best of my knowledge and belief, it is true, correct, and complete.	**Business telephone number (include area code)**
	Fax telephone number (include area code)
Name and title (Please type or print clearly.) ►	

Signature ►		Date ►	

Note: *Do not write below this line. For official use only.*

Please leave blank ►	Geo.	Ind.	Class	Size	Reason for applying

Federal employer identification numbers. Entrepreneurs who are sole proprietors and don't employ others can use their Social Security number for federal identification purposes. All others must file for a federal employer identification number.

Social Security number will be needed before a bank account can be opened.

9. After checking around to see which bank offers the most advantageous minimum balance and checking fee schedule for your type of business, open a bank account.

10. Assemble the basic business stationery package of everyday supplies and equipment.

11. Order any equipment or supplies that have excessively long delivery times.

12. Set up an appropriate record-keeping system to account for all business-related expenses and revenues. This is important for managing the business as well as for IRS documentation.

◆ *Is there any particular record-keeping system I should use?*

Choose the bookkeeping system that will provide enough financial information for you to effectively operate the business and, of course, meet IRS requirements.

◆ *What information might that be?*

Any entrepreneur will want to know how much cash is on hand and in the bank. If it begins to run dangerously low, take steps to conserve or increase it quickly by delaying paying some bills, reducing ordering quantities, and moving merchandise by promotion and discounting.

Accounts receivable data is essential. How much is owed to the business, by whom, and for how long? This information helps focus the entrepreneur's attention on delinquent payers. Just as important for control is *accounts payable*. To whom does the business owe money? Will continued nonpayment affect credit standing?

How much money is tied up in material and finished merchandise *inventory*? If it's too high, the entrepreneur should reevaluate product manufacturing or purchasing in relation to sales. Obsolete items should be disposed of and written off. The *sales* and *expense* numbers, which determine the *profit*, are obviously critical bits of information for a business. What products or services are profitable? Losers? The figures must be looked at monthly to determine trends that may require that action be taken.

♦ *What system choices do I have?*

The most simple bookkeeping system is a *cash system*, which requires only a checking account for recording receipts and expenditures and some sort of sales or billing procedure. Still relatively easy to use but a bit more detailed is the *single-entry system*, which involves listing daily transactions by date, amount, and purpose in an account book and summarizing the information monthly in a ledger. (The simplicity of this system is illustrated in the box on page 120.) Then there is the *double-entry system*, which is similar to conventional accounting used by large businesses. It requires entering data in journals twice, once as debit and once as a credit. The theory here is that every transaction really affects two accounts. For example, if merchandise is sold, cash increases while inventory is reduced.

♦ *Suppose I sell something but don't get paid for it immediately. How does it get recorded?*

Transactions in the single- or double-entry bookkeeping systems can be recorded under a *cash* or *accrual* method. In the cash method income is reported only when money is received and expenses only when bills are paid. Under the accrual method both income and expenses are recorded when they are incurred. Use the cash method if the business isn't involved much in credit sales or purchases.

However, if the business deals in material purchasing and inventories in quantity, the accrual method will more accurately reflect the true profit or loss at any time and is, therefore, preferred by the IRS.

♦ *Which is the best system for my business?*

If you have a low-activity enterprise and plan to stay small, a cash system will prove more than adequate. However, for most businesses the single-entry system is recommended. It contains many of the best features of the double-entry method, such as summarizing transactions

RECORDING TRANSACTIONS IN A MODIFIED SINGLE-ENTRY BOOKKEEPING SYSTEM

CASH RECEIPT/PAYMENTS JOURNAL

Date	Transaction	Check No.	Acct.	Amt. In	Amt. Out	Cash Balance
5/1	Cash at beginning of month	—	—	—	—	$1,700
5/3	Merchandise sale	—	01	$150	—	$1,850
5/5	Product purchase	221	03	—	$131	$1,719
5/7	Advertising	222	04	—	$ 50	$1,669
5/8	Merchandise sale	—	01	$100	—	$1,779
5/9	Wages paid	—	05	—	$ 75	$1,704
5/13	Office Supplies	—	06	—	$ 35	$1,669

MONTHLY SUMMARY LEDGER

	Revenues		Expenses			
	Sales	Other	Product Purchase	Advtg.	Wages	Office Supplies
Month	01	02	03	04	05	06
May	$1,300	0	$650	$150	$250	$ 35
June	$1,100	$ 75	$400	$ 95	$125	0
July	$ 975	0	$275	$ 75	$ 50	0

monthly into income and expense ledgers as well as balance sheet categories—assets, liabilities, and net worth—and yet is relatively easy for a neophyte entrepreneur to understand and maintain without the help of an accountant. Ready-made supplies are available from stationers and are inexpensive.

A variation of the single-entry method is a "one-book" or "one-write" system. The checks and receipts are overlaid and the information is transferred via carbon paper, automatically creating an accounting record when a check is written. It saves time and reduces the chance for error. As business complexity and volume grow, convert to a double-entry system, which has built-in checks and balances and is capable of providing more detailed information needed for control.

♦ *What other business procedures must I set up?*

Organize a good alphabetical filing system for legal papers, insurance policies, correspondence, canceled checks, bank statements, tax-related documents, purchase orders, bills of lading, expense receipts, personnel records, labor time sheets, and general information such as suppliers' catalogs and advertising data. Also create an index file for frequently used names, addresses, and telephone numbers.

Since writing checks for small amounts is impractical, you'll need a procedure for handling petty cash. Every time money is removed it should be supported by an actual receipt or completed petty cash slip. Documentation is important for tax purposes.

For any business dealing with raw materials, supplies, finished products, and merchandise, accurate inventory records are essential for knowing what and when to reorder, as well as for accounting data.

Home operations buying on credit need a simple purchase-order system. Standard forms available in duplicate can be purchased from stationery and office-supply mail-order firms. The original order goes to the supplier while the copy goes into the office file.

Selling on credit usually requires a triplicate-form billing system as well as a credit policy. The original billing invoice and copy go to the buyer, and you hold on to the third copy.

♦ *What sort of credit policy is suitable for a home business?*

In dealing with other firms your credit policy will normally have to follow industry practices. Frequently this will be full payment in thirty days, or "net 30." Sometimes a 2-percent discount is offered as an incentive for prompt payment, say within ten days. If you wish to use these terms, your invoice should indicate "2–10, net 30." Credit to individual customers is usually offered through the acceptance of credit cards. Most banks can provide you with the imprinting, the machine, and credit forms. Payment is processed through the bank and is assured if the right procedures are followed. But it will cost the business a fee of 3 percent to 4 percent of the sales amount.

If you're in a retail business that requires the acceptance of credit cards and checks from the public, especially transients, be careful. For large credit-card purchases, verify the validity of the card number with the credit-card company. As far as purchases made by check,

---

DID YOU KNOW. . .

. . . physicist Chester Carlson believed the use of powder and static electricity could result in an efficient paper copy process. In 1935 he set up a makeshift laboratory in an apartment over a bar in Queens, New York. Three years later the "electrophotograph" system was ready. But major firms didn't think much of the idea. IBM, Kodak, RCA, and others all turned Chester down. Only the Battelle Research Institute thought the process had commercial potential and paid for additional development. Later on, a Rochester, New York, company, Haloid, began marketing machines using the copying process, now called xerography. Haloid later changed its name to Xerox.

SECURING MERCHANT STATUS

1. Shop around, fees charged vary.
2. Before signing any merchant status agreement on the spot, check to see if the independent sales organization (ISO) is a member of the Electronic Sales Association (1-800-695-5509) and get written acceptance before commiting to an equipment lease.
3. If you have an American Express card, check with them first. They might approve your merchant status application immediately and sell you a terminal for under $600, or rent it to you for about $20 a month.

make sure any check you accept is a bank check and is filled in completely and accurately—date, amount, and signature. Also ask the customer to provide two types of identification and to write his or her name, address, and telephone number on the back of the check.

♦ *Credit cards are great for making sure I don't get stuck by consumers, but what do I do if one of my business customers doesn't pay within a reasonable time?*

Unfortunately such problems are not unusual, and they can be serious for small home businesses operated with marginal capital. Overdue invoices can be kept to a minimum by a good collection procedure. Within a week after payment is due follow up with a polite letter and then a phone call. This "squeaky wheel gets the grease" approach will be successful for most accounts. For those that don't pay, your last resort is a collection agency or an attorney. These will charge hefty fees—33 percent to 40 percent of the outstanding amount owed. The thing to remember is not to stretch credit for any one customer to a point where it can jeopardize your whole business in the event the receivable goes bust.

CREDIT CARD APPROVAL

About one-third of the sales made today use credit cars and their use can be important since it affords an emerging small business the opportunity to grow in volume without the risk of extending credit. But when it comes to home-based businesses getting banks to approve merchant status—the right to accept MasterCard and Visa credit cards—the answer is more likely to be no than yes. The banks say they've been burned in the past by home-based businesses and as a result have tightened their regulations. While achieving merchant status approval is difficult for home entrepreneurs, it's not impossible. Here are some options when your local bank turns you down.

♦ If you have personal deposits at the bank, discuss the possibility of setting up a cash reserve account to protect the bank against losses.
♦ Look into nonbank transaction processors—computer companies linked to banks.
♦ Independent sales organizations (ISOs) representing various banks may also provide merchant status to home-based businesses. But be careful—some overcharge for the point-of-sale terminal.

♦ *Will suppliers permit me to buy on credit?*

Don't feel hurt if they decline to give you credit initially. That's just normal business practice. After you've been in business for a while and have developed a good relationship, you'll be able to get credit just by asking.

♦ *Do I need a business phone?*

If the phone is not an important part of the operation, the answer is no. Use your residential line, possibly adding an extension into the home-business work area. Unfortunately, a residential line will entitle you only to a White Pages listing under your own name. For a Yellow Pages listing in a business category, you'll have to install a business phone. A business phone sometimes is also preferable for tax purposes, as the expense is less likely to be challenged by the IRS.

Don't skimp on phone service. Customers don't like busy signals. If phone activity is on the heavy side and you'll be working with others who will be making or receiving calls, install a multiline telephone set. Also, a business with a substantial volume of long-distance calling should consider reduced-rate WATTS-type service.

♦ *What happens if I'm not always home to answer the phone?*

This is not an unusual problem for part-time home businesses. You can purchase an answering machine to record messages for $50 to $250. Or you can use a telephone-answering service, which means a recurring monthly cost of $12 to $35.

♦ *Sounds like the machine makes more sense.*

For some enterprises, yes. For obvious one-person businesses, such as bookkeeping or tutoring, machine responses are not unusual. However, if you want the operation to be perceived as a big business, an answering service is preferable.

♦ *Should my home address be used for business correspondence?*

There isn't one yes or no answer to this question. For a legally operated business depending on customer visits, the answer is definitely

---

SUCCESS TIP

MAKING SURE YOU GET PAID

If you don't get paid or don't get paid promptly for your products or services, the business won't last very long. Here's how to minimize losses and overdue accounts.

♦ For a new account, attempt to get credit references or prepayment, possibly by offering a discount or free shipping.

♦ If you wish to take a chance, limit the amount of the credit on the first few orders.

♦ If payment is late follow a formal collection procedure. Send a reminder letter after thirty days and follow up with courteous phone calls two weeks apart. Pin down a commitment: When will a check arrive and for how much? If promises are continually made and not kept, turn the account over to a collection agency.

♦ If you're dealing with credit-card phone orders always call for verification of account number, expiration date, and credit balances. Make sure the name of the person ordering is the same as the ship-to name and the merchandise is addressed to a street address, not a box number.

SUCCESS TIP

SETTING UP A BUSINESS OFFICE AT HOME

The cost of setting up a home office complete with computer, telephone, and furniture can easily approach $6,000 or $7,000. There are ways to save money but also times when the more expensive alternative will buy more value.

- ◆ Appearances are important if you're in a business that brings customers into your home office. Don't skimp so much on furniture that the place looks as if it was furnished with leftover war surplus.
- ◆ Spring for a chair that costs $75 to $125 more but will bring you hours of comfort, not a backache. Fatigue will cut the time you spend in home-business activities.
- ◆ A computer, while costing three to four times more than a typewriter, can save you money in the long term by efficiently producing standard letters, running mailing lists for sales promotion, doing billing, and keeping accounting records. Unless you're computer knowledgeable, purchase equipment locally so instruction will be readily available to you.

(Continues)

DELIVERY SERVICES

Entrepreneurs should be aware of the types of delivery services available. For correspondence and direct-mail advertising the Postal Service provides convenience. First class is the simplest but most expensive method of reaching anyone in the continental United States within three to four days. First class is limited to items weighing up to twelve ounces and has the advantage of automatic mail-forwarding and the return of undeliverable mail. Postcards cost a few cents less and are effective for advertising—reminders, special-event announcements, and one-time offers. Standard Mail A mail under sixteen ounces can be single-piece or bulk mailings of at least 200 pieces, which require sorting by zip code. Bulk rate offers discounts of up to 50 percent over first-class rates and should be used for promotional information.

Merchandise up to seventy pounds in weight can go Standard Mail B, a USPS service, or United Parcel Service (UPS). UPS charges a small fee for pickup service and allows you to open an account, a business convenience. Both USPS and UPS make available cash on delivery (COD) and express mail services.

Express mail services are provided by USPS and UPS and also by Federal Express, Emery Worldwide, Airborne Express, and DHL Worldwide Express. Overnight delivery is expensive but reliable. Discounts are available for those willing to accept second-day delivery, using collection points such as service centers or drop boxes, and for those who have high volume.

yes. Many home businesses prefer the anonymity of a post office box, but others claim this has a negative, fly-by-night connotation. An alternative is a private postal drop.

In some communities prestige addresses, such as The Empire State Building, add credibility and could increase mail-order responses. Through a telephone feature known as call-forwarding, a business can even have a city telephone area code and still operate from a suburban home or vice versa. Small operations, by using postal drops, call-forwarding, and quality letterheads, can avoid a home-business appearance.

◆ *Are there any tax advantages to operating a home business?*

Yes. Homeowners may take tax deductions on the prorated portion of their home expenses used for the business. These would be for mortgage interest, property taxes, depreciation, utilities, insurance, maintenance, and repairs. Otherwise, these items are nondeductible personal expenses. Renters are also allowed to prorate deductions. Auto expenses and depreciation are deductible as long as business travel is carefully logged.

Tax deductions for equipment purchases are allowed up to a maximum for the year purchased. Some entrepreneurs have taken advantage of this to acquire items, such as computers, that have business application. Self-employed people can put a child on the payroll, making the salary a business expense. The income thereby gets passed along to someone in a lower tax bracket. Those working for themselves can also set up a Keogh retirement plan, with the contributions tax deductible.

You must also be sure that Uncle Sam doesn't view you as dabbling in a hobby and representing it as a business. You're expected to make a profit in three out of five years.

♦ *Are there any other tax breaks for home businesses?*

A sideline home venture is viewed like any other self-employment business and owners are responsible for paying the same taxes. Also, if other people are employed the business has to obtain workmen's compensation insurance from a private carrier to cover job-related injuries to full-time employees.

♦ Machines that don't require much service (answering machines, telephone, facsimile machines, typewriters, small personal copiers) can be purchased at discount retailers and by mail order. If possible, buy brands that have near-home carry-in authorized service for lower repair costs and faster turnaround. Larger machines, such as standard copiers, should be bought locally for on-site service.

♦ Before making office-equipment decisions, read up on the pros and cons of each type in such publications as *Consumer Reports*, *Buyers Laboratory*, and *Datapro Research*. They are available at some libraries.

HOME USE AS VIEWED BY THE IRS

The IRS recently tightened some loopholes that affect those who work at home. In order to take tax deductions, entrepreneurs must be able to prove that part of the home is used regularly and exclusively for the business. This means ten to twelve hours a week at least should be devoted to the business with no other activities occurring in the business area of the home. In addition, if challenged, the business must meet one of these three tests:

1. The space is the primary location for the business.
2. It is used in meeting and dealing with patients, clients, or customers in the normal course of doing business.
3. It is a separate structure used in connection with the business, such as a garage or barn used for storage.

BUSINESS TAXES

Here is a summary of the taxes you may be responsible for if you operate a business.

◆ Business income taxes: Every firm is required to report annual income on a federal tax return. For sole proprietorships, this filing can be included on Schedule C of an individual's regular Form 1040 tax return. Many states and some local municipalities also levy income taxes.

◆ Estimated taxes: Self-employed individuals generating significant income through a business are required to pay taxes on this income in quarterly installments. This pay-as-you-go system is also required by some state and local municipalities.

(Continues)

Form MBA (Rev. 1/81)
RV-01676-02

MINNESOTA DEPARTMENT OF REVENUE
APPLICATION FOR TAX IDENTIFICATION NUMBER

For Department Use

Acct. No.

See instructions before filling out   Please complete all items   Please print or type

1. This application is for:
   $1.00 fee
   ☐ Sales Tax Permit
   Date of first taxable sale:

   No fee
   ☐ Employer's Withholding
   Date of first taxable wages:
   ☐ Information Return M-9/M-10
   ☐ Bank/Corp. Estimated Tax
   ☐ Other (explain in item 16)

2. Reason for applying:
   ☐ Starting a new business
   ☐ Purchasing a going business
   ☐ Change of Legal organization
   ☐ Other (explain in item 16)

   SIC Code

3. Name of Owner Partner or Corporation

4. Name and Address to which forms are to be mailed (if different from #3)
   Name

Business Name   Business Name

Address at Business Location   Address

City or township of: State   Zip Code   County   City   State   Zip Code

5. List all owners, partners, or principal officers below. Persons listed below may be held personally responsible for taxes due.

Name	Title	Social Security Number	Home Address

6. Type of Legal organization
   ☐ Individual   ☐ Minnesota Corporation   ☐ Bank   ☐ Fiduciary   ☐ Other (explain)
   ☐ Partnership   ☐ Non-Minnesota Corporation   ☐ Insurance   ☐ Exempt Organization

7. Principal Business Activity (check only one)
   ☐ Agricultural Production Forestry/Fishing   ☐ Construction   ☐ Transportation   ☐ Wholesale Trade   ☐ Finance/Insurance/ Real Estate   ☐ Public Administration
   ☐ Mining   ☐ Manufacturing   ☐ Utilities/ Communications   ☐ Retail Trade   ☐ Services   ☐ Other (explain in item 16)

8. List principal products or services

9. Will your business be open all 12 months of the year?   ☐ Yes   ☐ No
   If no, list months business will be open

10. Will you be making taxable sales from more than one location?   ☐ Yes   ☐ No
    If yes, do you want to file a Sales Tax Consolidated Return? (see instructions)   ☐ Yes   ☐ No

11. What is the last month of your accounting year?

12. What is your Federal Employer's Identification Number?

13. If business was previously operated by another owner, please fill in below
    Previous owner name   Previous business name   Previous Minnesota Tax ID Number (if Known)

14. Do you now have a Minnesota Tax Identification Number?   ☐ Yes   ☐ No
    If yes, what is the number?
    What is the Number used for?   ☐ Sales   ☐ Withholding   ☐ Information Return M-9/M-10   ☐ Corporation Estimated Tax
    Should this number be cancelled?   ☐ Yes   ☐ No

15. Is your business a branch or division of a company?   ☐ Yes   ☐ No
    If yes   Name and address of parent company   Minnesota Tax ID No. of parent company

16. Use this space to explain any items above.

If you have any questions about this application
Call: Twin Cities (612) 296-2863
        Elsewhere in Minnesota (toll free) 1-800-652-9747
        ask for Master Business Unit

YOU MUST ENCLOSE
$1.00
WITH EACH SALES TAX APPLICATION

DO NOT SEND CASH
Make check payable to:
"Commissioner of Revenue"

I declare under the penalties of perjury and criminal liability for willfully making a false statement that this application is to the best of my knowledge and belief true, correct, and complete.

Signature of owner, partner, or principal officer   Title   Date   Phone No

Mail this application to: Minnesota Department of Revenue   Centennial Office Building   St. Paul, MN 55145

Sales taxes. A business that sells products may have to charge sales taxes. State registration is required.

SCHEDULE SE
(Form 1040)
Department of the Treasury
Internal Revenue Service   (0)

Social Security Self-Employment Tax

▶ See Instructions for Schedule SE (Form 1040).
▶ Attach to Form 1040.

OMB No. 1545-0074

199
Attachment
Sequence No. **17**

Name of person with **self-employment** income (as shown on Form 1040)

Social security number of person with **self-employment** income ▶

Who Must File Schedule SE

You must file Schedule SE if:

- Your net earnings from self-employment were $400 or more; **OR**
- You were an employee of an electing church or church-controlled organization that paid you wages (church employee income) of $100 or more;

    AND

- Your wages (subject to social security or railroad retirement tax) were less than $51,300.

Exception: If your only self-employment income was from earnings as a minister, member of a religious order, or Christian Science practitioner, AND you filed **Form 4361** and received IRS approval not to be taxed on those earnings, DO NOT file Schedule SE. Instead, write "Exempt–Form 4361" on Form 1040, line 48.

For more information about Schedule SE, see the Instructions.

Note: *Most people can use the short Schedule SE on this page. But, you may have to use the longer Schedule SE on the back.*

Who MUST Use the Long Schedule SE (Section B)

You must use Section B if ANY of the following apply:

- You elect the "optional method" to figure your self-employment tax (see Section B, Part II, and the Instructions);
- You are a minister, member of a religious order, or Christian Science practitioner and you received IRS approval (from **Form 4361**) not to be taxed on your earnings from these sources, but you owe self-employment tax on other earnings;
- You had church employee income of $100 or more that was reported to you on Form W-2;
- You had tip income that is subject to social security tax, but you did not report those tips to your employer; OR
- You were a government employee with wages subject ONLY to the 1.45% Medicare part of the social security tax (Medicare qualified government wages) AND the total of **all** of your wages (subject to social security, railroad retirement, or the 1.45% Medicare tax) plus **all** your earnings subject to self-employment tax is **more** than $51,300.

Section A—Short Schedule SE (Read above to see if you must use the long Schedule SE on the back (Section B).)

1 Net farm profit or (loss) from Schedule F (Form 1040), line 36, and farm partnerships, Schedule K-1 (Form 1065), line 15a	**1**	
2 Net profit or (loss) from Schedule C (Form 1040), line 29, and Schedule K-1 (Form 1065), line 15a (other than farming). See Instructions for other income to report.	**2**	
3 Combine lines 1 and 2. Enter the result	**3**	
4 Multiply line 3 by .9235. Enter the result. If the result is less than $400, **do not** file this schedule; you **do not** owe self-employment tax . . . . ▶	**4**	
5 Maximum amount of combined wages and self-employment earnings subject to social security or railroad retirement (tier 1) tax for 1990	**5**	
6 Total social security wages and tips (from Form(s) W-2) and railroad retirement compensation (tier 1). **Do not** include Medicare qualified government wages on this line	**6**	
7 Subtract line 6 from line 5. Enter the result. If the result is zero or less, **do not** file this schedule; you **do not** owe self-employment tax . . . . ▶	**7**	
8 Enter the **smaller** of line 4 or line 7	**8**	
9 Rate of tax	**9**	
10 **Self-employment tax.** If line 8 is $51,300, enter $7,848.90. Otherwise, multiply the amount on line 8 by the decimal amount on line 9 and enter the result. Also enter this amount on Form 1040, line 48 **Note:** *Also enter one-half of this amount on Form 1040, line 25.*	**10**	

For Paperwork Reduction Act Notice, see Form 1040 Instructions.

Schedule SE (Form 1040) 1990

Social Security taxes, in the form of self-employment taxes, must be paid by those engaged in their own business.

- ◆ **Self-employment taxes:** This is equivalent to Social Security taxes for people who are self-employed and therefore do not have taxes withheld from income.
- ◆ **Employment taxes:** If other people are employed, the business is obligated to pay Social Security, unemployment taxes, and disability insurance for them. In addition, income taxes, Social Security, and unemployment taxes must be withheld from employee wages as their contribution.
- ◆ **Sales tax:** Many states and some municipalities require business owners to collect sales tax on anything sold retail. Some products and services also have a special excise or luxury tax, and the IRS can advise you where this applies.

SCHEDULE C
(Form 1040)

Department of the Treasury
Internal Revenue Service (0)

Profit or Loss From Business
(Sole Proprietorship)
Partnerships, Joint Ventures, Etc., Must File Form 1065.
▶ **Attach to Form 1040 or Form 1041.**   ▶ **See Instructions for Schedule C (Form 1040).**

OMB No. 1545-0074

199

Attachment
Sequence No. **09**

Name of proprietor

Social security number (SSN)

A Principal business or profession, including product or service (see Instructions)

B Enter principal business code
(from page 2) ▶

C Business name and address
(include suite or room no.) ▶ ....

D Employer ID number (Not SSN)

E Accounting method: (1) ☐ Cash   (2) ☐ Accrual   (3) ☐ Other (specify) ▶ ....

F Method(s) used to
value closing inventory: (1) ☐ Cost   (2) ☐ Lower of cost or market   (3) ☐ Other (attach explanation)   (4) ☐ Does not apply (if checked, go to line H)

Yes | No

G Was there any change in determining quantities, costs, or valuations between opening and closing inventory? (If "Yes," attach explanation.)
H Are you deducting expenses for business use of your home? (If "Yes," see Instructions for limitations.)
I Did you "materially participate" in the operation of this business during 1990? (If "No," see Instructions for limitations on losses.)
J If this is the first Schedule C filed for this business, check here .... ▶ ☐

Part I   Income

1	Gross receipts or sales. *Caution: If this income was reported to you on Form W-2 and the "Statutory employee" box on that form was checked, see the Instructions and check here* ▶ ☐	1
2	Returns and allowances	2
3	Subtract line 2 from line 1. Enter the result here	3
4	Cost of goods sold (from line 38 on page 2)	4
5	Subtract line 4 from line 3 and enter the **gross profit** here	5
6	Other income, including Federal and state gasoline or fuel tax credit or refund (see Instructions)	6
7	Add lines 5 and 6. This is your **gross income** ▶	7

Part II   Expenses

8	Advertising	8	21	Repairs and maintenance	21
9	Bad debts from sales or services (see Instructions)	9	22	Supplies (not included in Part III)	22
			23	Taxes and licenses	23
10	Car and truck expenses (attach Form 4562)	10	24	Travel, meals, and entertainment:	
11	Commissions and fees	11	a	Travel	24a
12	Depletion	12	b	Meals and entertainment	
13	Depreciation and section 179 expense deduction (not included in Part III) (see Instructions)	13	c	Enter 20% of line 24b subject to limitations (see Instructions)	
14	Employee benefit programs (other than on line 19)	14	d	Subtract line 24c from line 24b	24d
15	Insurance (other than health)	15	25	Utilities	25
16	Interest:		26	Wages (less jobs credit)	26
a	Mortgage (paid to banks, etc.)	16a	27a	Other expenses (list type and amount):	
b	Other	16b			
17	Legal and professional services	17			
18	Office expense	18			
19	Pension and profit-sharing plans	19			
20	Rent or lease (see Instructions):				
a	Vehicles, machinery, and equip.	20a			
b	Other business property	20b	27b	Total other expenses	27b

28	Add amounts in columns for lines 8 through 27b. These are your **total expenses** ▶	28
29	**Net profit or (loss).** Subtract line 28 from line 7. If a profit, enter here and on Form 1040, line 12. Also enter the net profit on Schedule SE, line 2 (statutory employees, see Instructions). If a loss, you MUST go on to line 30 (fiduciaries, see Instructions).	29
30	If you have a loss, you MUST check the box that describes your investment in this activity (see Instructions).	30a ☐ All investment is at risk.
	If you checked 30a, enter the loss on Form 1040, line 12, and Schedule SE, line 2 (statutory employees, see Instructions). If you checked 30b, you MUST attach Form 6198.	30b ☐ Some investment is not at risk.

For Paperwork Reduction Act Notice, see Form 1040 Instructions.

Schedule C (Form 1040) 1990

Earning from an individually owned business must be reported to the federal government on IRS Form 1040—Schedule C.

TURNING A PROFIT THE FIRST YEAR AND THEN EXPANDING

12

A Blueprint for Success

♦ *It would be helpful if some of the key elements for success in a home business could be pulled together into a sort of summary.*

Entrepreneurs who have made it provide similar what-to-do-advice even though their businesses ranged from crafts to high tech. Here are ten components of a winning formula for those working at home. Use the information to guide your own entrepreneurial career.

1. Choose a business with activities that make you comfortable and reflect personal interests. You'll almost never find the time to work at something you don't like.
2. The business's products or services should respond to needs. Frivolous or fad items dependent on impulse buying are risky and usually not long-term revenue producers.
3. The business should generate continuous revenues from the same customers. Repeat sales mean lower per-unit marketing costs and higher profits.
4. Find a market niche. Create distinctive products or services that will appeal to particular segments of a market. Give customers some reason for choosing you over the competition.

5. Make certain the products or services chosen can pass two basic marketing tests: First, the targeted buying groups should be readily identifiable, and second, they should be reachable through affordable means. If there is any difficulty nailing down both of these, the business will be starting on shaky grounds.

6. Create a broad enough business package—patchwork or related products and services—to assure profitable volume levels in your market. As the business grows, cut back on the less profitable activities, or hire people to do the work.

7. Acquire as much knowledge about the business as possible before starting, and focus especially on marketing. Read whatever books and magazine articles are available on the subject, attend classes and seminars, talk to people in the trade, and if you can, work for someone in a similar activity for a period of time. All this can help you hit the ground running.

8. Develop some sort of business plan. Home-based entrepreneurs are notorious for plunging into businesses unprepared. A well-thought-out game plan will bring potential problems to the surface before they occur and get the operation up to speed with little lost time, effort, or money.

9. Make conservative financial projections and manage cash flow. Experience has shown that sales almost always develop more slowly than anticipated, while expenditures tend to exceed

---

UNIQUE PRODUCT EQUALS MARKET NICHE: SUNFEATHER HERBAL SOAP

There are success stories and there are success stories. Sandra Maine started her soap company in 1980 in the kitchen of a farmhouse at the end of a dirt road in the Adirondack Mountains of upstate New York. Her home at the time lacked electricity and a telephone. Sandra invested $25 on herbs, oils, and other ingredients to make country-style handcrafted herbal soap bars, which she sold at craft fairs. First-year sales were $900. In five years volume hit $100,000.

SunFeather has since moved to a factory, a clapboard farmhouse, and opened a gift store in Potsdam, New York. National retail accounts, which include Walt Disney World, number over 2,000. And annual sales now exceed a quarter of a million dollars. Sandra credits her success to her market intuition: creating something unique when "people began to desire earthy, natural products."

estimates. It's essential that costs and available cash be kept in balance during the startup phase.

10. Commit yourself to strict work discipline. While there can be some flexibility in working hours, blocks of time still must be set aside for the business. Also, the area used should be away from the hubbub of family activities. A work-at-home enterprise must be run like an off-premises business even though the kitchen and living room may only be a few feet away.

```
             PAPERWORK    UNLIMITED,    INC.

                   A N N O U N C E S

             QUALITY    SERVICES    THAT
                  C O M E    T O    Y O U


    FOR SMALL BUSINESSES WE CAN:

                        Maintain Cash Receipts Register
                        Compile Customer Mailing List
                                Make Bank Deposits
                        Process Bills for Timely Payment
                                     Draw Checks
                                     Do Payroll
                        Do Monthly Bank Reconciliation
                        Provide Monthly Expense Statement
                        Provide Monthly Income Statement
                        Prepare Quarterly Sales Taxes
                        Prepare Quarterly Payroll Taxes

            ANY SERVICE IS AVAILABLE INDIVIDUALLY OR WE
        CAN TAILOR A SERVICE PACKAGE TO SUIT YOUR NEEDS


     FOR THE HOME WE CAN:

                        Do Monthly Bank Reconciliations
                                     Write Resumes
                        Fill Out College Applications
                        Fill Out Student Loan Applications
                        Fill Out Student Financial Aid Forms
                    Proofread and Type Manuscripts and Reports
                                     Write Letters


            ALL SERVICES INCLUDE PICK-UP AND DELIVERY


            IF IT'S PAPERWORK--WE PROBABLY DO IT!
        QUOTATIONS FOR SPECIFIC SERVICES NOT LISTED ARE AVAILABLE
                        UPON REQUEST

        FOR FURTHER INFORMATION CALL (914) 354-8977
```

A home venture that provides a range of revenue-generating products or services has a much better chance of quickly turning the profit corner.

◆ *Let's suppose that everything goes well. What sort of profit can I anticipate?*

Assuming you're typical of newly established home businesses, with you, the owner, both creating the product or service, and solely responsible for the selling, profits are likely to be modest. Real growth comes only when the marketing efforts are broadened. This can be achieved in four ways.

The first step toward achieving growth is to *fine-tune the existing sales effort*. Make sure word on the business is getting out through friends, relatives, neighbors, and co-workers. If you haven't already done so, ask retailers you patronize to display window signs or place business cards on the counter. Include promotional inserts with mailings of religious or social groups you're associated with. Offer incentives, such as discounts or gifts, for referrals. Expand your advertising coverage so customers are drawn from a larger area. Push higher-profit items and extra services. While typing a résumé may be profitable, for instance, typing it and duplicating it, preparing individualized application letters, and providing mailing services can be much more so. Personalizing products and offering volume discounts are also ways average sales revenue per customer can be increased.

The second step toward growth is to *multiply your own marketing efforts*. Make more sales calls through the use of the telephone and direct mail. While not as effective as face-to-face selling, they still can result in greater sales for the right product or service.

Group sales promotion is another way of making more sales. A tax specialist can develop business by speaking to the local chamber of commerce, while a cooking instructor is likely to attract class enrollers by lecturing at women's group luncheons. Trade show, convention, and exhibit participation are also ways for a home entrepreneur to receive multiple exposure.

◆ *What about adding new products and services?*

Diversification is the third growth step. Sell accessories, complementary items, or services related to the business or market. A hair stylist might carry personal-care items to sell to existing customers. Craft supplies and kits are natural add-ons to a handicrafts business. An instructor in candy making can offer a line of cooking utensils and ingredients to students. Cosmetic distributors can add income by selling jewelry. Also consider marketing your skills in other areas. Some calligraphers develop product lines such as greeting cards and scrolls. Craftspeople earn extra dollars by conducting workshops.

But there are obvious growth limits for any business whose products or services are personally marketed directly to the consumer by the entrepreneur. Big volume can only come about by *increasing the channels of distribution*—the fourth growth step. If your product is suitable for direct mail or mail-order promotion, you can easily reach out to a larger audience. Every retail store outlet opened up multiplies sales potential. Using wholesalers, distributors, and jobbers will allow you to deal with relatively few firms but still achieve volume through their distribution networks. Mail-order catalog houses are always looking for something new, so try to interest them in handling your product. Agents, brokers, and representatives provide an excellent conduit to buyers at affordable commission rates.

Inexpensive display booths are available for trade-show exhibits.

◆ *Is the business opportunity route a way to expand a home business?*

Not all products or services lend themselves to franchising or can be marketed as a business opportunity. But if yours can be, by all means discuss it with a franchise consultant. In fact, one of the megasuccessful firms profiled in this book, Diet Center, turned a small local weight loss clinic into a $160 million company with 2,000 franchised units. In another similar case, a craftsman who operated from a garage franchised a patented process that simulated stained glass. The company, Stained Glass Overlay, had seventy franchises when the entrepreneur sold it to an investment group a few years later for $1 million.

As my business activity increases, won't I have to hire people?

Not necessarily. Some firms expand by subcontracting work. This eliminates the bother of withholding taxes and preparing tax returns. When an independent subcontractor is used, IRS regulations require only the filing of a single form, 1099, if the contractor's annual earnings are $600 or more. But not everyone who does work for you can legally be classified as an independent contractor. So check the regulations for conformance.

FAILURE: HOW TO AVOID IT

There is no sure thing in business, but entrepreneurs who are aware of the pitfalls can take extra precautions. Here are the three most frequent reasons for home business failure and ways the problems can be avoided:

1. Market insufficient to support the business: This can be because of (1) no demand for the product or service, (2) the competition, or (3) a market that is too thin. No demand is something preliminary market research should be able to identify. Creating or finding a market niche helps a business run around the competition. Thin markets can be dealt with by offering an array of products or services so revenues are derived from a number of sources.
2. Running out of money: Cash-flow problems can be caused by planning miscalculations, overspending, or growing too fast. There's no substitute for realistic business plans and asset management.
3. Lack of motivation: Some entrepreneurs enthusiastically charge into a new venture but run out of steam after a time when they discover how much effort is required to get and keep it going. Total commitment is an essential element of successful entrepreneurship. Don't start a business without it.

♦ *What about space—won't I have to move out of my home as the business grows?*

Probably not in the initial growth stages. For example, you can easily add storage space by renting space in a self-storage facility. Space is available on a monthly basis and inexpensive—$200 to $300 a month for a ten-by-thirty-foot garage area. Commercial warehouse space is another option, and some will provide pick-and-pack services. All a business has to do is provide them with shipping orders and labels. When it comes to manufacturing services, consider using handicapped "sheltered" workshops. There are about 4,000 in the country and they're usually very cost competitive. Also, check with your material suppliers. Some may provide product assembly and shipping services for a reasonable fee.

♦ *As the business grows, won't I need more money?*

Most likely, yes. Once you've established a business track record and can produce financial statements, money becomes much easier to acquire than when you were starting the home-based venture. A bank loan is the most common source of funds for a small business. This can come directly from a bank in the form of a standard commercial loan or a loan guaranteed by the Small Business Administration (SBA).

♦ *What's the difference between the two?*

Banks don't always like to lend money to small businesses on terms considered acceptable by the entrepreneur. The SBA was created to overcome this problem by providing guarantees up to 90 percent of a loan. The money still comes from the bank.

♦ *Can't I just short-cut the whole process by going first to the SBA?*

No. You'll only be considered for a loan if three banks reject your request.

♦ *Is an SBA-guaranteed loan easy to get?*

It's a lot easier if you go to a preferred lender bank—a bank that the SBA has contracted with to handle its processing. They can give you an answer on your loan within a week.

BARTERING

Don't be shy about offering your business's products or services in bartering arrangements. What to bargain for? Legal, accounting, and printing services, advertising space in community newspapers, and display areas at local merchants are some possibilities. If you do local mailings, offer to carry promotional material of others in exchange for their products or services— or have them include your advertising in their mailings. Personal things—dining, dry cleaning, food and drug purchases at small merchants— lend themselves to bartering.

MINORITY ENTREPRENEUR-SHIP

The Small Business Administration (SBA) licensed private sector organizations to provide debt financing and equity capital specifically for minorities to encourage entrepreneurship. It's called the Small Business Investment Company/Minority Small Business Investment Company program (SBIC/MSBIC for short), and the local SBA office can supply information on getting financing.

NONBANK MONEY SOURCES

While most businesses will resort to bank loans for growth capital, other sources should also be investigated.

- ◆ Borrow money from or sell an equity interest in the firm to another company associated with the business. Sometimes suppliers familiar with the prospects of a company will provide needed capital when a bank will not.
- ◆ Seek out venture capital companies. These firms specialize in providing risk capital in exchange for a share of the business. Venture money is not easy to acquire—only one or two of one hundred applicants receive approval—and the minimum investment will be $100,000. If you go this route the business will have to be grossing half a million dollars or more.
- ◆ Sell an equity interest privately. This type of transaction usually isn't subject to SEC regulations so the process is simpler and far less expensive than a public placement.
- ◆ Make a public stock offering. This is an effective way to raise capital. Six of the megasuccessful firms profiled in this book used this path to fund expansion. But it's a complex and costly legal process.

◆ *How would I find a preferred lender bank?*

Contact the local SBA office. Ask them to provide you with a list of banks and small business investment companies that are authorized to make SBA loans.

◆ *Can I borrow as much as I want?*

The SBA will consider applications for as little as $5,000 to six-figure amounts at maximum interest rates that go from 2.25 percent to 2.75 percent above the going prime rate. The SBA doesn't stop you from negotiating lower rates with the bank. But don't get the idea the SBA is a pushover when it comes to getting a loan. They look at the same things a bank looks at.

◆ *Like what?*

The SBA looks at the financial status of the business, reasonableness of the use of the money, and the quality of management. And they expect the borrower to put up 30 percent of the capital needed. Most of

WELCOME TO THE "REAL WORLD" OF BUSINESS

If you're entering the business world for the first time, be prepared. Some people don't play by the rules:

In 1985, when Price Waterhouse management consultant Howie Gerver was on assignment in New York City, he observed that many women wore sneakers to work, carrying their shoes, newspaper, lunch, and whatever in a flimsy plastic bag. Why not a tote? Even without design experience Howie was able to put together a paper version of a tote and book it to a sewing manufacturer. He named the product (and company) Attashoe, a combination of the words attaché and shoe. Patent and trademark protection was costly, but he decided to go ahead with it anyway. It turned out to be a good decision.

The product was offered to forty-eight mail-order catalog houses and two—Williams Sonoma and Joan Cook—followed up with orders. Publicity caught the attention of the March of Dimes, which purchased a quantity to use as a premium. Attashoe was on its way, or so Howie thought.

About six months after the first sale Howie noticed a copy of his tote being promoted by a mail-order firm he did not sell to. Then he saw it in another catalog and another. Three of the mail order catalog houses that initially expressed no interest in Attashoe had "knocked off" (copied) the product and were having it imported. Since it was being sold at half the price of the original, Howie's customers quickly dropped the higher-priced Attashoe from their catalogs.

Howie, enraged, decided to sue for patent infringement. He picked the largest mail-order house as the target since it would most likely have the most sales and, therefore, the greatest damage award. But Attashoe didn't have its day in court. A few months later the case was settled for an undisclosed amount, at least enough for Howie to break even on his entrepreneurial venture.

SBA "ANGELS"

The Small Business Administration is using the Internet to bring together entrepreneurs seeking capital and angels—investors ready to finance business ventures. There's an estimated 250,000 angel investors currently active. Both entrepreneurs and angels are required to pay a fee to be listed on the SBA's password-protected Web site, Angel Capital Electronic Network, or Ace Net for short. Angels have to have a minimum net worth of $1 million to qualify. The Web site address is http://ace-net.unh.edu/.

---

all, they'll be looking at your ability to repay it. So if poor financial data is the reason a bank turned down your application, you can be certain the SBA will also hesitate.

♦ *Are there other ways to finance business expansion?*

Businesses with national growth potential can sometimes find money from sources other than banks. Frequently it will be in the form of equity funding, meaning you'll have to give up part of the business. Successful entrepreneurs are almost always faced with a major decision—do they want to have a smaller share of a large company or 100 percent of a small company?

◆ *What about using personal assets to raise capital?*

Home equity financing will allow you to borrow up to about 80 percent of your equity in your home. But betting your home on business success is a little risky, as is borrowing against the cash value of your life insurance, another money option. Your safest recourse is an unsecured loan even at the 4 percent to 6 percent higher interest rates. And if you can't bankroll the business on your terms, it may be wiser to slow the pace of your expansion. Remember, there's no sure thing in business.

MAKE YOUR HOME A REAL OFFICE   13

The Electronic Cottage

F ew developments over the past century have had as much impact on the work-from-home industry as electronic technology. This has made possible self-contained work stations of computers, telephones, answering devices, facsimile equipment, and copying machines. Author Alan Toffler has given the home office a name—the electronic cottage. The affordable and easy-to-use equipment, combined with advances in telecommunications, have created many new business opportunities. Those seeking a home-based career should have some familiarity with the technology, its applications and, in general, the right way to set up a home office that creates a productive environment.

PERSONAL COMPUTER

Basics

The key components of a computer system for home use are:

♦ *Central Processing Unit (CPU):* A microprocessor that contains the computer chip. The chip does the actual computing by processing instructions and making calculations. It comes in different speeds, with speed measured in megahertz (MHz), or millions of cycles per second.

The faster your machine, the better it will perform before the latest software overwhelms it. *Even though the fastest chip available isn't needed to perform the most common computer tasks, it still should be a model advanced enough to support multimedia programming.*

◆ *Memory:* Also known as random access memory (RAM), it provides the capacity for material the computer is working on at any one moment. It's measured in megabytes (MB) of RAM. The more memory, the larger the software program or number of programs that can be run simultaneously. *Since new programs suck up more memory, this is not the area to save bucks.*

◆ *Hard Disk Drive:* This is the computer's electronic file cabinet—a long-term repository for programs and documents. Disk space is measured in megabytes (MB), or gigabytes (GB), which is 1000 MB. *When buying a system keep in mind software keeps swelling in size, eating up more disk space.*

◆ *CD-ROM Drive (Compact disk read-only memory):* This device accepts disks resembling audio CDs and stores programs, graphics, video, and audio. Speed is measured in multiples of the speed of the first generation of drives. So an 8× drive is eight times as fast as the original generation.

◆ *Modem:* Allows computers to communicate data, measured in kilobits per second (Kbps), over standard telephone lines. *Speed is critical for businesses with on-line activity.*

◆ *Monitor:* The televisonlike screen displays the information in color. Frequently it is sold apart from the computer bundle, permitting buyers to acquire models with larger screens than the 15-inch standard.

◆ *Printer:* The device that provides the hard copy. Ink-jet printers capable of producing color graphics and black-and-white text are the most popular. Laser printers cost a little more and don't produce in color. However, they offer better quality and a lower cost per page.

How to Go About Buying a Computer System

Rapid changes in computer technology make it almost impossible to recommend a system today and have that same advice be valid tomorrow. So here are some suggestions that can help guide you through the selection process.

MEGASUCCESS—PIONEER ON-LINE RETAILER COMPUTER EXPRESS

Phil Schier's diversified job path—racing-car builder and some years in the entertainment business—didn't exactly prepare him for an entrepreneurial career in retailing. But in the late 1970s Phil developed an interest in personal computers, and as they became increasingly popular, he recognized their potential in a retail-selling network. The concept was electronic mail, later dubbed E-mail, and in 1985 Phil and his wife started Computer Express from their California home. They later moved the operation to Sudbury, Massachusetts, but continued to operate it from home.

Computer Express sold computer-related merchandise through on-line networks, such as CompuServe and Prodigy. Customers ordered electronically by entering product data and credit-card numbers on their computer, and transmitted the information over phone lines to Computer Express headquarters. The company didn't have much room for storage, so when an order came in, they had it shipped to them from the manufacturer or distributor. They quickly reached a million dollars in sales and in 1989, had to lease space in a commercial building. The company now does most of its business over the Internet.

1. Determine the computer needs of the business in terms of features that might make an operating difference, and hardware requirements for programs that will be used. For example, if the business depends on communication with the Internet, a fast modem that reduces downloading time is essential. Desktop publishing requires a system with extensive graphics capability, and a monitor size 17-inches or larger. On the other hand, a word-processing service usually can get by with an older computer system without the bells and whistles.

2. Consider future growth. Maybe you don't currently have the big bucks to shell out for a cutting-edge machine, but that doesn't mean the system shouldn't be easy to upgrade. Empty expansion bays, extra expansion slots for plug-in cards, unused memory sockets—all permit easy-to-do system enhancements two or three years later.

3. There's no such thing as a best computer for everyone. Individuals dif-fer, some having familiarity with personal computers, others buying for the first time. Many dealers will try to talk buyers into purchasing their own proprietary system for a few hundred dollars less than name-brands. Hardware-wise they may be just as good, but for non-techies running into problems, knowing where and how to get the system running again has advantages. Name-brand manufacturers provide this type of service nationally, and you won't have to worry about support if the retailer goes out of business.

4. Avoid spending money on personal-computer frills like elaborate speakers and telephone-answering functions. Put the money on things that can add a few more years to computer life.

Shopping for Bargains

Acquiring a computer system directly from a mail-order company can save about 30 percent from equivalent store-bought models. But it's best to stay with established mail-order companies with proven customer sup-port. Late, but discontinued models and refurbished systems can save 25 to 50 percent off the sticker price. These one generation–behind machines can be a good value for many home-business applications that can get by with smaller hard drives or slower processors. New equipment comes with a ninety-day warranty, while refurbished models are usually limited to thirty days. Don't buy a used computer from a firm that doesn't offer a minimum seven-day unconditional return or exchange option.

Computers are a notoriously low-profit margin item for most retailers, so they push extended warranties. The cost is $100 to $400 and can add as much as 20 percent onto the cost of a typical PC package. Should you buy? Probably not. Most computer warranties cover parts and labor for a year, and that time period is when something is likely to go wrong if it's going to go wrong.

There's no doubt money buys more flexibility and the promise of a longer useful life. If you can afford to spend the extra thousand dollars get an advanced computer system that is likely to run software three or four years into the future. But buying less doesn't mean you'll have to junk the system you have. It still may be very adequate for all your home-business

---

POPULAR HOME BUSINESS SOFTWARE PACKAGES

- Core office programs for word processing, spreadsheets, database, and presentation. These are sold individually or in discounted "suite" bundles.
    - Microsoft Office
    - Lotus SmartSuite (IBM)
    - WordPerfect Suite (Corel)
- Financial Software
    - Basic bookkeeping—Quicken Deluxe, Microsoft Money
    - Accounting/Financial Management—Peachtree First Accounting, Microsoft Small Business
- Software Management
    - Microsoft Windows (latest version)
- Antivirus (scans incoming and hard-disk files for "viruses" that corrupt data)
    - VirusScan (McAffee)
    - Norton Antivirus (Symantec)

---

needs. What's likely to happen though, is the system will prevent you from taking full advantage of future software refinements.

Before walking down the aisle of a computer superstore make sure you've talked to friends and read up on system comparisons available in publications. Libraries maintain back issues that rate the different computer systems as they are released. Comparison shop and make sure you know what you're getting. The warranty period, service arrangements, and returns policy should be clear and in writing. Get answers to questions like: Is technical support without charge and available evenings and weekends through a toll-free number? Make the purchase with a gold or platinum credit card that offers an extended warranty or buyer protection plan that covers computer equipment. Finally, keep all the packing materials just in case you have to return the merchandise. It happens.

OTHER HOME OFFICE EQUIPMENT

Telephone

There are features beyond the basic single-line phone that may improve home-office operations. Entrepreneurs shopping for phones should seek to purchase models with the features built in to avoid paying the phone company monthly for services.

Key system: A multiline button-phone system that allows holding, intercom, and paging function from any part of the home.

Voice mail: Responds to multiple callers, lets them choose from a menu of options, and takes messages.

Call Waiting: On single-line phones, allows the taking of a second call without disconnecting the first call.

Call Forwarding: Permits the transfer of incoming calls to another number. Another feature gives the subscriber the option of changing the forwarding number remotely. An alternative to subscribing to call-forwarding services is a device called a call diverter that intercepts calls and automatically redials them to another number.

Remote Access: Lets a business located in an area establish a telephone number in another, complete with a listing in that area's directory.

Conference Call: Permits conversation with several people on a single-line phone.

Automatic or last-number redial: Redials last number punched in. Some phones will redial automatically, which can be a time-saver if dealing with busy exchanges.

Autodialer: Stores phone numbers for speed dialing.

Toll-free Access: Allows customers living outside an area to call at no cost to them by dialing 800 or 888. Receiver pays for call.

Caller ID: Lets a call receiver see who's calling by looking at a LCD display. This permits the picking up of calls before they go to an answering machine or voice mail.

◆ For the basic home business: A two-line (minimum) telephone with speaker-phone capability, digital answering with maximum recording time and multi-outgoing messages and incoming mailboxes features.

Facsimile (Fax) Machine

Fax machines allow the transmission of documents to another machine by converting hard copy into electronic signals that are sent over phone lines.

A page takes about 18 seconds and the cost is that of a telephone call. Fax machines can be used with both multiuse and separate phone lines. Cheaper models use thermal paper, instead of plain paper. The delayed-transmission option allows documents to be sent at any time and saves on long-distance charges. The autodialing feature option is for memorized dialing for frequently used numbers. Fax machines can also be used as conventional telephones.

♦ For the basic home business: The lowest priced plain-paper machine. The thermal paper fades over time and costs twice as much per copy.

Photocopiers

Small, moving platen desktop copiers can be purchased for about $300 to $400. Flat-bed copiers that require a cabinet go for $600 to $800. The larger models offer various features—choice of paper size, reduction and enlargement, automatic feeding, and copying on both sides of the paper.

♦ For the basic home business: A low-end traditional copier that can reduce or enlarge originals, and copy books.

Combination Machines

Some machines offer a combination of functions—fax, copier, computer printer and scanner, telephone, answering device—all in one machine. It's compact and frees up desk space.

♦ For the basic home business: Avoid the multifunction machine if you have the space for separate components. There's a performance compromise with the combination and putting all your eggs into one basket is risky.

Special Services

The personal computer combined with telecommunications allows home-based businesses to utilize the Internet's electronic mail, or E-mail, features. This is the sending and receiving of electronic messages via the computer. It is becoming the dominant way businesses communicate. This same computer-telecommunications combination also enables businesses operated out of the home to participate in the World Wide Web's system of electronic commerce.

SETTING UP A PRODUCTIVE HOME OFFICE

Creating an office centered around a personal computer requires intelligent planning if it's going to function successfully as a business. Here are some things to consider.

1. Even if the "office" is only the corner of a room, the work space has to be separate from home space. Co-mingling the two creates a workaholic-prone environment, historically a problem for those working from home.

2. Work surfaces are needed not only for the computer, but also for regular office activities. An L-shaped work area, combined with a swivel chair, is usually the most efficient.

3. If you intend to go on-line or depend heavily on faxes, a second business phone line is essential.

4. Invest in an uninterruptible power supply (UPS). It will permit safe shutdown of the computer system in case of a power outage. Connect only the computer to the UPS.

5. Extensive computer time requires a comfortable, adjustable-height chair and a monitor positioned to avoid excessive glare from lights and windows. But the office should be able to "borrow" light from a large window. No-strain computer keyboard activity requires lower than workstation height. It's best to bolt it to the underside of the desk.

6. Avoid putting the computer on circuits containing motors that cycle on and off. Voltage surges (spikes) can cause malfunctions and damage sensitive electronic equipment.

7. Copying machines and laser printers require high amps. They, along with air conditioners and space heaters, should be on a separate electrical circuit.

COMPUTER-RELATED BUSINESSES SUITABLE FOR HOME OPERATION

The computer has created numerous opportunities for entrepreneurs seeking home-based business careers. The major ones are listed below.

Desktop Publishing / Graphic Design Services

Word Processing / Secretarial and Office Support Services

Programming / Software Development

Résumé / Job-Search Services

Typesetting

Transcription Services (legal, medical, meetings)

Technical Writing

Bookkeeping Services

Payroll Services

Income Tax Preparation

Data Entry

Mailing-List Services

Telemarketing

Medical Billing

Medical Forms Processing

Newsletter Publishing

Information Brokering

Computer Training

TELECOMMUTING

Telecommuting is an arrangement made with a company by an individual to work at home in some computer-related activity. While this is not, strictly speaking, a home business since it involves an employee-employer relationship, it does have some of the same advantages—flexible work hours, no commuting—and is briefly covered in this book.

Telecommuting growth has come about as a result of technological developments that make computer-related work at home a practical alternative to on-site employment. It involves a modest investment—generally under $7,000. Usually what's needed is an IBM or IBM-compatible personal computer, a modem for transmission and receipt of data, and a dedicated phone line. In some jobs facsimile, telephone-answering, and copying machines may also be required.

An estimated 8 million people now telecommute part- or full-time. Some states, like California, offer firms up to $2,000 in tax credits for each telecommuter. Many major firms have policies encouraging employees to work from home. JCPenney uses telecommuters to handle catalog sales. Merrill Lynch and AT&T have significant numbers of telecommuters. Telecommuting openings are rarely advertised. It's best to approach firms with a willingness to work at least six months a year as an on-site employee so a relationship can be developed.

Working at home in a telecommuting position isn't for everyone. Self-motivation is a must, as is the ability to work in relative isolation. You're out of the loop. E-mail can't substitute for human contact. Then there's the loss of definition between work and home life. The temptation to "clean up a few things" is always present. Consequently, the self-discipline of abiding by a structured work day, is also a requirement. Building a work day around nursery school and naps has its drawbacks. For married couples, too much contact can be a challenge. Wives have been heard to say— "I married you for better or worse, but not for lunch." Reduced office visibility can limit the chances of advancement and telecommuters rarely receive all the benefits of on-site employees.

Most opportunities tend to be localized since they almost always involve some training, and frequently the pickup and delivery of materials. The following types of companies have been known to regularly use telecommuters:

TYPE OF COMPANY	TELECOMMUTING JOB RESPONSIBILITIES
Department Stores	Customer service (order taking)
	Sales promotions (telemarketing)
Hotel/Motel Chains	Reservation taking (telephone)

(Continues)

TYPE OF COMPANY	TELECOMMUTING JOB RESPONSIBILITIES
Computer Services	Data entry Software development
Telemarketing	Telephone sales Telephone surveys
Insurance (health, casualty, etc.)	Data entry Claims processing
Market research	Telephone surveys
Publishers	Indexing Word Processing
Printers	Typesetting
Health care providers	Medical transcriptions
	Round-the-clock services (e.g. health care aides) Coordinating service fulfillment from phoned-in-requests

PART THREE

Home Business Descriptions

CASH FOR CRAFTS
Craft- and Hobby-Related Businesses

14

People are always drawn to individually designed, unique products not found in local stores, and individuals with creative imaginations may be able to develop their crafts and hobbies into thriving home businesses.

Craft and hobby products generally fall into two categories—handicrafts and artisan crafts. Handicrafts—stuffed animals, costume jewelry, ornaments, and so forth—require modest creative skills, sell for up to fifty dollars or so, and are likely to be produced in similar-in-design quantities. Artisan crafts are more original works, sometimes approaching museum quality, and can retail for hundreds, sometimes thousands of dollars each. While most people have or are able to develop handicraft skills, not everyone possesses the natural talents needed to become a craftsman.

In getting started it's obviously best to go with products with which you have some familiarity. However, if you want to learn a new craft or just brush up on an old one, there are many places to turn. Begin by going to arts and craft fairs, galleries, and gift shops to see what items are being shown and selling. Then search out workshops and courses offered by craft supply stores, local artisans, and schools that can provide the technical skills needed to produce the items.

Product demand varies by area but jewelry, porcelain pottery, art glass, handwoven clothing, quilts, leather items, wood sculptures, and toys, especially folk toys, appear to be popular just about everywhere.

GALLERY 10 LTD., *1519 Connecticut Ave., N.W. Washington 20036 (202) 232-3326.* This prestigious gallery is located in the shadow of the White House. Usually thought of first in terms of fine art, Gallery 10 does handle contemporary crafts as indicated by a recent show including the handmade paper of Bella Schwartz. We suggest that you query the gallery and include photographs or slides with your presentation.

Sales prices extend from $50. to $1,000. Purchase is on consignment (60% to craftsperson.)

Galleries are always seeking quality artisan crafts, usually on consignment.

CRAFT JEWELRY

Typical of an artisan craft business is handcrafted personal adornments—necklaces, pins, and earrings—crafted from nontraditional materials, not factory-made components. Flattened nails, tree bark, old photographs, marbleized heads made of overbaked plastic, or brass safety pins are artistically assembled into one-of-a-kind items or limited editions of twenty-five items and sold or consigned to galleries, which retail the creations for up to several thousand dollars.

MEGASUCCESS—CRAFTS: ANNIE'S ATTIC

Not many people have heard of Big Sandy, Texas, but that's the headquarters of Annie's Attic, the biggest publisher of crochet patterns in the country. How the company came to be is truly a rags-to-riches saga.

In 1975, "having to make a living," Annie Potter started a home-based mail-order business with two crochet patterns she designed. They were named Overall Sam and Sunbonnet Sue. She believed other craftspeople might be interested in copying them and made a $200 investment in a mailing list. The unexpectedly large response was processed on her kitchen table, with shoeboxes serving as the filing system.

Over the years more designs were added, some created by Annie, others purchased from craftspeople, and the customer list grew to over one million. Annie's Attic, of course, has outgrown Annie Potter's home. But she stayed close to her Big Sandy roots and expanded by purchasing adjacent homes and other nearby buildings, creating a campuslike setting that attracts tens of thousands of visitors. The firm is still privately owned, and its sales are in the multimillions—quite an accomplishment for a hobbyist who started with no business experience.

Holiday-related products such as Christmas ornaments are also good sellers but, of course, are limited to certain times of the year. Craft designs need not necessarily be new. More often than not they are variations of other products or copies of uncopyrighted designs of others.

Handicrafts and artisan crafts are sold to the consumer through various distribution channels. Indoor and outdoor craft fairs, mall exhibits, flea markets, gift stores, home parties, craft cooperatives, and fund-raising bazaars are successful outlets for the less expensive handicrafts. A few popular items such as quilts and wooden toys can also be sold by mail order. Higher-priced artisan crafts retail more successfully from the artist or craftsman's home, galleries, selective craft shows, and museum shops. Some of the better department stores will handle especially distinctive artisan craft items.

Exhibiting at several craft shows during the year is a must. While time consuming, it allows the craftsperson to directly see public reaction to products. The shows also enable the entrepreneur to view other exhibits and talk to other craftsmen, both of which help to generate new ideas. In most instances the shows are a pay-back situation, since most merchandise can be sold at full or close to full markups to the consumer. This is not the case when selling is done through middlemen. Picking the right shows to exhibit at is important and information supplied by other craft entrepreneurs can be helpful here. After a year or two a craftsman will develop a feeling for what shows are likely to produce good results.

Show availability is advertised in craft newsletters and newspapers. Booth rental ranges from twenty dollars for flea market space to several hundred dollars for prestigious shows like those put on by American Craft Enterprises. Some shows have no advance fees but take a percentage—from 5 percent to 30 percent of what is sold. The more professional shows require color slide prescreening by juries as well as entrance fees in the hundreds of dollars.

A recent development in craft selling has been the renting of space in shopping malls on a regular basis. Frequently the mall will supply the display in the form of an attractive cart or kiosk. Rentals vary but an active mall will charge about $150 a week, plus 10 percent of gross sales. Not all

HOLIDAY CRAFTS

Craft sales increase in the weeks preceding Christmas, Easter, Valentine's Day, Thanksgiving, and special religious and ethnic holidays. Popular craft items include: tree decorations, stockings, ornaments, wreaths, centerpieces, gingerbread houses, paper tree trims, dried-flower arrangements, sachet, decorated stationery, decoupage-decorated jewelry boxes, "personalized" letters to children from Santa Claus and the Easter Bunny, decorated eggs, giant Christmas coloring cards, balloon animals, wooden toys, and computer-printed Valentine's Day messages.

MEGASUCCESS—CRAFTS: THE VANESSA ANN COLLECTION

The Vanessa Ann Collection of Ogden, Utah, was a two-person venture that became a multimillion-dollar publishing operation in just three years.

Jo Packham and Terrece Woodruff, both cross-stitch hobbyists as well as professionally talented, decided there was a growing market for books that contained pictures of original needlework designs with unique finishing ideas and step-by-step instructions. Working from home, sometimes sixteen hours a day, they would conceive the ideas for the craftworks, draw them up, stitch or sew samples, write the instructions, and photograph the creations. Their initial effort in 1979 produced four cross-stitch books, which they published themselves and sold to stores. Orders totaled $10,000 and the Vanessa Ann Collection was born.

The company has grown over the years by staying on top of trends. Jo and Terrece regularly visit craft shows across the nation as well as attend trade fairs, so they can preview market shifts and gauge the success of new products. They have expanded their publishing spectrum to serve several segments of the craft industry— sewing, needlework, hardcore crafts, quiltmaking, and dolls. Major publishing firms such as Time, Inc., and Better Homes and Gardens commission the firm to write, design, and produce camera-ready art for craft books, which are mostly sold by direct mail and through book clubs. The Vanessa Ann Collection now employs a full-time staff of twenty, plus another forty to sixty people who work on a contract basis. About 125 books have been produced, with some selling as many as 200,000 copies.

malls rent on a regular basis, but even those that don't have occasional weekend or week-long promotional events with space charges of $100 to $150 for four or five days.

Retailing products through middlemen—gift stores, galleries, museum shops, craft cooperatives, or distributors—saves time but also means surrendering a hefty chunk of the selling price. Retailers who buy items outright will take 50 percent of what the consumer pays, while retailers who will only accept merchandise on a consignment arrangement receive 30 percent to 40 percent. Some craft stores will buy merchandise only from distributors, who usually receive a 10 percent commission. This means only 40 percent of the retail price will be left for the craftsman. Run-of-the-mill crafts can't be priced at high enough profit margins to be marketed through middlemen, and direct selling is frequently the only realistic alternative for an entrepreneur.

In addition to craft shows, mall exhibits, and flea markets, a craftsman's home can be a productive retail outlet in a properly zoned area. A

ILLUSTRATION: SIMPLE CONSIGNMENT AGREEMENT

The merchandise listed in section B was consigned to me by consignor *Peggy Brand Crafts* for the purpose of resale.

A. I agree to:
   1. Attractively display the items in my retail store.
   2. Forward a check for the listed retail price minus a 30 percent discount for all items sold. This payment will be made in the first week of the month following the sale.
   3. Be responsible for any merchandise breakage, fire, and theft, and to pay for all items not returned to returned damaged.
   4. Return all items on request. All merchandise remains the property of the consignor.

B. Merchandise consigned is:
   (describe each item, quantity, and list retail price)

_____   _____
                Consignee   Consignor

_____
                Date

Arts and Crafts Bonanza

Wednesday through Sunday, March 25 through 29, Sunrise Mall will host a Spring Arts and Crafts bonanza. Both upper and lower levels of the mall will be filled with original works of fine art and handmade crafts.

The lower level will include fine art creations in a variety of mediums including oil, water colors, and sculptures in wood and pewter. Artists on the lower level will also display graphics, photography and portraiture.

Handmade crafts will fill the upper level of the mall. Artisans will show original crafts in wood, fiber, quilting and silk, just to name a few.

Over fifty local and East Coast artists will be on hand to show their pieces. Some of the local Long Island artisans include Marv Herbert whose works are done in oils, featuring nostalgic New York landscapes and storefronts; Harry Glaubach, a popular native New Yorker whose works are a combination of wood sculpture and oil paintings, highlighting bygone eras in sports (i.e. New York Yankees and New York Mets); and Elsa Brickman, a craftsman featuring handmade and custom-made dolls.

The Sunrise Mall Spring Art Show is Wednesday, March 25, through Sunday, March 29, throughout the mall. Mall shopping hours are Monday through Saturday, 10 a.m. - 9:30 p.m. and Sunday, 10 a.m. - 6 p.m. Sunrise Mall is located on Sunrise Highway in Massapequa. For more information, call 795-3220.

Malls are becoming increasingly popular for arts and craft fairs. Some malls make space available on a monthly basis.

sign and, if possible, the craft items themselves, if placed in front of a house located on a well-traveled road, will attract drive-by customers. To add to revenues some craft entrepreneurs also sell consigned products of other craftsmen. Exhibiting items in community buildings, libraries, and office lobbies is another way of making the public aware of the crafts' availability. Sometimes groups of sideline craft entrepreneurs get together to produce holiday boutiques, which are one- and two-day events organized to sell merchandise from a private home. They are especially popular for seasonal craft items and it is reported that some home sales generate as much as $10,000 over a two-day period. Legally the one- or two-day sales are looked upon as garage or tag sales and are allowed under most town ordinances. Consumers are solicited by local media advertising, display posters, and invitations to friends, relatives, coworkers, and previous buyers. The events are considered newsworthy and community newspa-

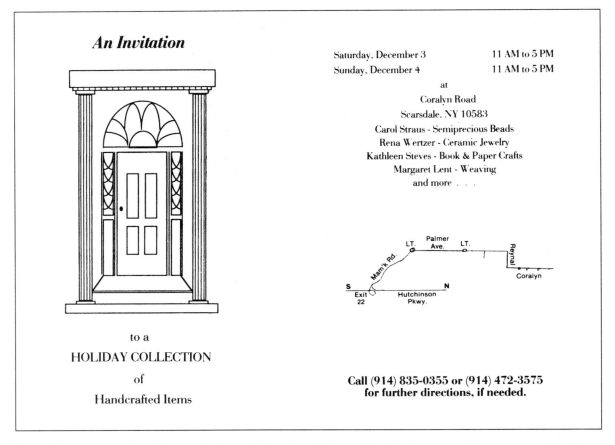

An Invitation

Saturday, December 3   11 AM to 5 PM
Sunday, December 4   11 AM to 5 PM

at

Coralyn Road
Scarsdale, NY 10583

Carol Straus - Semiprecious Beads
Rena Wertzer - Ceramic Jewelry
Kathleen Steves - Book & Paper Crafts
Margaret Lent - Weaving
and more . . .

to a

HOLIDAY COLLECTION

of

Handcrafted Items

**Call (914) 835-0355 or (914) 472-3575
for further directions, if needed.**

Some artisans group together and promote their own mixed-media craft shows. Other than the expense of the announcement mailing and refreshments, it costs little, and attendance is multiplied by the number of artists participating.

pers will frequently provide free publicity by publishing submitted news releases.

What products sell best? Experienced craftspeople say anything functional that is unique to some degree, would make a nice gift, and is priced under twenty-five dollars. There are no universal rules for pricing crafts other than that an item should at least recover materials and overhead costs as well as allowing a respectable return for the craftsperson's labor. Most experienced craft entrepreneurs price backward, that is, set a price they think customers will pay and then figure out if the amount will cover cost and profit. If it can't, they don't bother producing the item. A typical pricing pattern is first to establish a basic full retail price and then discount these prices for selling to retailers and distributors. Consignment selling requires a separate price schedule. Craftspeople sometimes also set a home price, which may be 80 percent of the price charged at shows. They feel the lower cost justifies this.

Entrepreneurs can add to income by creating kits for sale to craft and hobby stores, to catalog houses, and by mail order directly to consumers. Components for kits plus instructions—they may be patterns and accessories for needlecraft items or beads for jewelry—are usually packaged in standard plastic bags with an illustrated header card attached. As a general rule, kits retail for about four times the cost of the material.

Conducting workshops during slow periods is another source of supplemental income for well-organized individuals with the capacity to explain and demonstrate the tasks needed to produce a craft. Classes can be held at home or at local schools and community centers. Extra dollars are also sometimes derived from selling craft supplies to students taking the course. Other craft-related revenues can come from writing how-to books, publishing newsletters, or providing supplies via mail order.

A craft and hobby business can be ideal for those who can't or won't commit themselves to specific work hours or who reside in rural communities where other home business options may be limited. A combination of idea creativity, talent, and marketing know-how can be synergistic in effect and turn a sideline venture into a very profitable business.

MAIL-ORDER CRAFT AND HOBBY PRODUCTS

Some craft and hobby activities can also generate revenues through mail-order sales. A sampling of several craft and hobby magazines published a year apart had a number of repeat ads, meaning that the first ad probably drew a satisfactory response. The mail-order items advertised were either instructional material or catalogs containing supplies. Listed here are the repeat ad subject categories.

- ◆ Instructions: boat plans, stained glass, kid crafts, flower arranging, furniture, bird painting, dollmaking.
- ◆ Catalogs: wooden toys, clocks, plastic molds, needlecrafts, silk flowers, craft supplies, woodcraft patterns, earring parts.

Publications in specific crafts will be found in *Books in Print* and articles in *Reader's Guide to Periodical Literature*. Both references are available in most libraries. The best resource for professional craftsmen is the American Crafts Council (40 West 53rd Street, New York, NY 10019). The organization publishes *Craft Horizons* and *Contemporary Crafts Marketplace*, which is a compilation of information on how and where to sell crafts. Also check out *The Crafts Report* (P.O. Box 1992, Wilmington, DE 19899), a trade newsletter.

PRODUCT IDEAS FOR THE FORTY MOST POPULAR CRAFTS

Batik and tie-dyeing: wearing apparel; scarves.

Beads: jewelry; handbags; belts; ornaments; wall hangings.

Candle making: decorative candles (scented, colored, unique designs); figurines.

Ceramics: figurines; tiles; bowls; vases; cups; napkin holders.

Collage (gluing various materials to a surface): art forms.

Decoupage (decorating wood, glass, and ceramic surfaces with paper cutouts): jewelry boxes, lunchboxes; mounted mementos; tabletops; trays; wastebaskets; art forms.

Dolls: cloth dolls; patterns for cloth dolls; clothing for antique dolls; rag dolls.

Early American: reproductions of antique toys; implements; furniture.

Enameling (decorating or painting produced by fusion of glass and metal): jewelry.

Fiber hand weaving: clothing.

Flowers (using dried or silk): centerpieces; decorations for special events; bouquets, hospital pieces.

Glass blowing: goblets; glasses; pitchers; glass-art forms.

Indian: jewelry; leather products; rugs.

Jewelry: earrings; pendants; pins; bracelets; necklaces.

Kites: kites.

Lamps: lamps made from wine jugs, seashells, driftwood, cork, stained glass.

Lapidary (cutting, shaping, and polishing gemstones): decorative tabletop items.

Leather: handbags; belts; coin purses; wallets; vests; jackets; hats; plaques; art forms.

Macramé: wall hangings; flower-pot holders.

Metalworking: handwrought sterling silver flatware and serving pieces; hand-tooled copper trays and pictures.

Mobiles: unique designs made of wood, plastic, metal, glass.

Mosaics: tabletops; serving trays; pictures.

Nature (cones, pods, nuts, seeds, flowers, rocks, leaves, gourds): ornaments; wreaths; candle holders; jewelry; wind chimes; mobiles; centerpieces.

Nautical: bottle boats; driftwood lamps; driftwood abstracts (weathered wood can also be used).

Needlecrafts: clothing; placemats and napkins; pillows; pictures.

Origami (paper folding): art forms.

Paper quilling (the rolling of paper to create decorative designs): art forms.

Paperweights: tabletop art objects.

Papier-mâché: boxes

Plants: indoor plant propagation; flower drying; preservation and arranging; artificial flower creations; terrariums; bonsai plants and trees.

Pottery: earthen and stoneware decorative plates, pots, vases, teapots, dishes, planters, figures.

Quilting: quilts; wall hangings.

Rug making: braided, rag, hooked, or woven rags.

Scrimshaw: jewelry and belt buckles.

Shells: jewelry; flower arrangements; wind chimes; picture and mirror frames; lamps; mounted shellfish.

Soft sculpture: dolls; animals; wall hangings.

Stained glass: windows; lamps; art forms.

Toys: hand-painted toy soldiers; soft stuffed animals; teddy bears.

Wicker: baskets; decorative pieces; planters; tables; chairs; special furniture.

Wood: toys; marionettes; puppets; clocks; candle holders; weather vanes; lamps; wooden Indians; smoking pipes; birdhouses; bird feeders; carved birds; duck decoys; plaques; gun stocks; picture frames; napkin holders; nutcrackers; racks (spice, towel, key, magazine); boomerangs; breadboards; bookends; snuff boxes; silhouettes; lawn decorations; sculptured art forms; furniture (outdoor, plant stands, chests); dollhouses; miniature furniture; doll cradles.

COOKING UP A PROFIT

Food Products and Services from Home Kitchens

15

Americans have an infatuation with good food, especially the homemade variety, and qualified cooks willing to devote the considerable time and effort required for kitchen activities should be able to develop a home business capable of producing excellent earnings.

First, a word of caution. Before starting a food-product business of any significance, check with all appropriate government agencies. To protect the public, health and safety regulations clearly spell out the conditions under which food may be prepared. Licenses are always required, and there are usually on-site inspections of the premises before issuance as well as periodic checkups. Product liability insurance is recommended. As an added protection, incorporating the business will shield personal assets in the event someone claims injury from your product and sues.

There are four food-related categories that seem to achieve a high degree of home-business success: catering; preparing, and selling specialty food products; gift baskets; and cooking instruction. Less frequently mentioned but still worth considering in resort communities is a restaurant operation, especially from a place that has particular appeal, such as a Victorian-style home.

MEGASUCCESS—FOOD PRODUCTS: THE LITTLE PIE COMPANY

In 1983, it was likely the best apple pies being made in New York City were not coming from the kitchens of high-priced restaurants, but from an apartment on the forty-third floor of a high-rise building near the Broadway theater district. The bakers—Arnold Wilkerson, an actor, and Michael Deraney, a graphics designer—had only one customer at that time, a restaurant located at street level in the same building.

Two years later the firm, now named The Little Pie Company, was able to obtain a bank loan, and the bakery moved to a business location in the same building. Word of the superior products—sour cream walnut apple and other apple pie variations—got around and business multiplied. The repertory was enlarged to include other pie flavors, cheesecake, and poundcake, and the firm started to sell to better restaurants and gourmet shops, such as Bloomingdale's, which in turn retailed the products at ultrapremium prices.

In 1988, the bakery moved again to a much larger space in the same building, adding an outdoor cafe and counter food service. Over 1,000 pies a week are now sold, but the company hasn't forgotten its roots. It still makes everything on the premises by hand from fresh, natural ingredients.

SPECIAL EVENT CATERING

Catering can be done on any scale and can range from preparing meals for customer pickup to on-site cooking, serving, and cleanup. For this business cooking skill is less important than knowing how to handle gatherings of people.

What events can be catered? Everything you can think of—wedding receptions, engagement parties, anniversaries, bridal showers, graduations, confirmations. And then there are theme parties and home socials. For the business community there are business meetings and office parties for such occasions as holidays and employee retirements. Community organizations—women's clubs, political parties, social groups such as Kiwanis, and so forth—also require food service for their regular meetings and benefits.

Instead of full-service catering, you may choose to specialize:

♦ Limited-menu catering. Just provide hors d'oeuvres and finger sandwiches for cocktail parties.
♦ Preparing basket lunches for company and organizational affairs.
♦ Picnic and barbecue catering for business firms, social groups, and religious organizations.
♦ Preparing and selling box lunches to factory and office workers if you're near an area where eateries are limited.
♦ Special needs catering—diet, health, low-cholesterol, low-sodium, religious restrictive (e.g., Kosher), or complete meals for the elderly or disabled.
♦ Children's party catering—pizza, hot dogs, hamburgers, candy, plus decorations, games, entertainment, and other keep-busy activities.

Catering services are priced on a per-head basis, depending on the type of food the customer orders. Typically the charges are two to three times the cost of the food and paper products. An advance deposit, usually one-third of the total, is a must, since this is the money that will fund the purchase of the food ingredients.

Catering does require an investment in a large freezer and refrigerator, as well as food preparation utensils. In addition, if formal and business affairs are to be catered, tableware and linens will be needed.

SPECIALTY FOOD PRODUCTS

Getting into the specialty-food business can often be done with a minimum capital outlay—home stove or oven plus inexpensive pots, pans, and utensils. Startup can be more expensive if health regulations specify a cooking area apart from the family kitchen. Food ingredients can be purchased wholesale from product dealers and restaurant suppliers. Some retailers will give volume discounts.

Specialty-food products sold to gourmet shops, delicatessens, groceries, restaurants, and caterers have repeat-order advantages, which keeps sales development costs to a minimum. Once an outlet is established and customers get hooked on the products, it is simply a matter of preparation and periodic distribution.

Prices for specialty-food items are set by the market, that is, by what the customer is willing to pay. Unique products can command higher prices. Chokecherry jams, for example, are not available everywhere and can be priced higher than conventional fruit preserves. Someone who can skillfully decorate a cake with a company logo can get a premium. Extra services also command more. One entrepreneur delivers his cakes to the party in a tuxedo.

The most popular specialty-food products are:

◆ Made-to-order decorated cakes
◆ Homemade cakes, pies, pastries, and cookies
◆ Hors d'oeuvres
◆ Ethnic foods
◆ Health foods (e.g., low-calorie, cardiac-care diet, vegetarian, natural)
◆ Jams and jelly preserves, candy, and confections
◆ Gourmet foods (e.g., homemade bread, wild game, quiches, soups, soufflés)
◆ Holiday foods (e.g., fruitcakes, pumpkin pie, gingerbread houses, candies)
◆ Miscellaneous products (e.g., spicy relishes, salad dressings, barbecue sauces, such regional specialties as maple syrup)

In addition to selling food products to quality restaurants and food retailers, some items, such as jams and candy, may be suitable for mail order and gift stores. Holiday foods do well at bazaars and flea markets.

GIFT BASKETS

If you have no culinary talents whatsoever, try preparing and selling gift baskets. These are usually just creatively assembled fruits, jams, candy, wine, and specialties that are purchased for various occasions—get-well, baby, condolence, birthday, and so forth. And if you're near a college community, there is always a market for college survival kits—snacks, energy foods, study aids, and so forth—delivered to students at exam time. Acquire the students' home addresses and solicit orders from parents by mail.

COOKING INSTRUCTION

Entrepreneurs with teaching talents can earn income providing food classes for the kitchen hobbyist. Courses range from kitchen basics to gourmet cuisine preparation, with cake baking and decorating, ethnic foods (especially French and Chinese), party cooking (hors d'oeuvres, desserts), pasta, crêpes, and bread being the favorites.

It is best to attend some classes at an existing cooking school to see how they are conducted. Classes will vary with kitchen size but usually consist of eight to twelve people who pay fifteen to thirty dollars for a three-hour class. Many instructors use an angled mirror over the food preparation area to improve large group visibility. Extra money can be made selling utensils used in the course. Some cooks compile their specialty foods into recipe books, which they sell by mail order.

16 BUCKS FROM HELPING CONSUMERS

Personal Service Types of Home Businesses

S ervices to consumers offer an almost infinite range of home business choices, and it would be difficult for someone not to find something in this category that they are capable of doing. Opportunities will vary by community and type of population, so a knowledge of the market is essential. For example, an area with transient singles might need laundry services. Day-care businesses should do well in a community populated by young families. Tourist information services and guest houses are likely to do well in resort areas. Tax preparation and pet services do well just about anywhere.

CHILD DAY CARE

The number of working mothers today has greatly increased the demand for caretaker services. Entrepreneurs with the patience to work with children and with extra rooms that can be turned into play areas can earn extra money.

Sideline businesses can range from crib baby-sitting to licensed nurseries with structured programs. Most home entrepreneurs only provide a full day of activities—fun and games—for up to half a dozen preschool children. The investment in toys, play equipment, cots and so forth is easily justified by the income return.

MEGASUCCESS—FRANCHISED CHILD DAY-CARE:
MONDAY MORNING MOMS

Suzanne Schmidt began her home-based business in 1970 by caring for children in her Illinois home. The activity gave her younger child playmates and earned Suzanne some extra money. That, plus a background in early childhood development, provided her with the knowledge to care for children. She used that know-how to set up a family day-care management service in New Jersey in 1981. She named it Monday Morning.

Monday Morning targeted people who preferred family-type home day care over the care provided by centers. The firm advertises for providers, screens the applicants, requires written references, medical clearance, and inspects the home. Once approved, the management directs parents to them.

For nine years, Monday Morning operated only in New Jersey, providing services through about 125 "moms," and grossed $800,000 in 1988. In 1989, the company added "Moms" to the name and began franchising for a fee of $9,000 and royalties of 6 percent. Monday Morning Moms franchisees are provided with management and marketing training plus a customized computer software package. Annual revenues are about $2 million and corporate headquarters are still Suzanne's home.

For those who don't want to commit themselves to a full day's service there are other options. Some day-care services take children half a day, usually after kindergarten, or on weekends or weeks parents go on vacation. Some entrepreneurs provide only a Saturday service for parents who want to go shopping (or just out), or care for children from 3:00 P.M. when they come from school until 6:00 P.M. when the parents return from work. Child care is almost a sure success, but an entrepreneur had better know how to deal with preschoolers.

Licensing or certification requirements vary by state and can range from safety basics, such as ample exits, fire extinguishers, and smoke alarms to much more—outside playgrounds, for example. Fees charged for full-time care with meals are usually fifty-five to seventy-five dollars a week per child. Certified agencies may be eligible for some reimbursement from the federal childcare food program.

SEWING AND ALTERATION SERVICES

Almost everywhere there seems to be a demand for home tailoring—mending, alterations, zipper replacement, and so forth. This service can be

MEGASUCCESS—PERSONAL SERVICES: GEORGETTE KLINGER

In 1939, a refugee from Hitler's European rampage, Georgette Klinger, began giving skin-care treatments from her Manhattan apartment.

Georgette became interested in skin while trying to improve her own complexion. After studying with a number of dermatologists, she opened a salon in Brno, Czechoslovakia. Moving to America when war broke out, she operated out of her home for a year and then relocated to Madison Avenue to serve an upscale clientele. Business was good but not sensational until she treated the wife of a famous publisher, who suffered from particularly bad acne. The amazing result was written about, and Georgette Klinger became almost overnight the last word in skin care.

The Klinger concept stresses one-on-one consultation with a trained facial specialist. The firm also produces and sells its own products, thereby giving it total control over the skin-care process.

In the early 1970s Georgette's daughter, Kathryn (now president), joined the company and introduced more aggressive marketing and multicity expansion. About 30 percent of Georgette Klinger's business now comes from men. The firm grosses about $20 million a year. Georgette is still active as chairperson of the board and in all phases of her business.

provided directly to the general public and to area dry-cleaners and clothing stores. Items requiring alterations are picked up and delivered by the entrepreneur, who pays about a 25 percent commission to the retailer.

Supplementary income for tailors or seamstresses can come from creating and producing made-to-measure items. These could be high-quality women's clothing from purchased pattern designs or your own creations, customized products such as uniforms, wedding gowns, maternity clothes, costumes, slip covers and draperies, aprons for restaurants, or clothing for hard-to-fit people.

Entrepreneurs can also provide sewing services. Some jobs are not within everyone's skill level and are contracted out. Decorative hand stitching such as crewel and back stitching, blocking and sewing knitted pieces are examples. Services for stores—sewing names, emblems, letters, or numbers onto school jackets and uniforms—are also extra income options, as is personalizing clothing through monogramming.

Skills for needlework business can be polished by taking training courses with others, at fashion schools, and at stores that sell sewing machines and fabric. The businesses themselves can usually be started for under $1,000 for a sewing machine and the appropriate accessories—cutting table, mannequins, pattern tracing wheel, scissors, and supplies.

BED-AND-BREAKFAST ESTABLISHMENTS

Growing in popularity, especially in vacation areas and around college towns with sporting events, are bed-and-breakfast establishments. This is a great way to augment income without too much effort. Zoning, of course, is a major consideration, and the number of guests should be limited to avoid your being classified a hotel and coming under more stringent regulations. Insurance policies also must be reviewed to make certain you have adequate coverage.

Entrepreneurs start this type of business by getting listed in B&B guides and contacting the local tourist office for referrals.

Other rented-space home businesses worth considering are operating a guest house where rooms are rented but no food is provided, renting rooms by the month, and renting storage space in spare garages or barns.

CALLIGRAPHY SERVICES

The art of decorative lettering is frequently self-taught, and it is a service in constant demand. The most popular jobs are customized invitations and stationery, certificates, diplomas, awards, greeting cards, place cards, announcements, and menus. These items can be done directly for the consumer as well as for print shops and those handling parties of all types. Some calligrapher entrepreneurs add to their income by creating their own products, such as quotations and poems on wall plaques and parchment.

PET SERVICES

People love pets and that opens up a number of entrepreneurial business opportunities. Pet boarding is very popular. While large kennel operations require proper zoning, animal sitting for one or two pets—dogs, cats, birds, and other small creatures—is not restricted.

DID YOU KNOW. . .

. . . the birthplace of "Silicon Valley" was actually a Palo Alto garage. That's where, in 1938, two Stanford University graduates, William Hewlett and David Packard, crafted their first electronic product: an audio oscillator, used in the soundtrack of Disney's *Fantasia*. Later on, the Hewlett-Packard firm led in the development of hand-held calculators, general-purpose computers and laser and ink-jet printers.

Grooming—bathing and clipping—also can be profitable. Some entrepreneurs run private obedience training schools for dogs and their owners. Pet breeding—dogs, cats, birds, gerbils, hamsters, and tropical fish—is another possibility.

TAX PREPARATION SERVICES

This is a big business three and a half months a year, and it does not take a superbrain to learn how to prepare the basic tax forms filed by the majority of the general public. There are a number of correspondence schools where someone can learn the ropes, and H&R Block offers a training course.

During the months between tax seasons an entrepreneur might assist people with medical forms, do bookkeeping for small businesses, prepare résumés, and provide general clerical services for local firms.

HAIRDRESSER SERVICES

An entrepreneur with an extra room who is qualified to acquire a license from the Board of Cosmetology (he or she will need a diploma from an accredited school) can make good money operating a beauty parlor. Services include haircutting, washing, styling, conditioning, coloring, and giving manicures and pedicures. Personal as well as technical skills and the ability to satisfy the personal needs of clients are required by entrepreneurs in this business.

LAUNDRY SERVICES

In locations where there are singles, college students, and others who don't have the time or want to bother with laundry, an entrepreneur with limited skills can provide clothes washing, drying, and simple mending services. It is best to line up a regular clientele who drop off the items on their way to work or school.

CAR DETAILING

Car cleaning is a low-investment home business for individuals without special skills or formal training. Basic services would include washing and interior vacuuming, with waxing, upholstery cleaning, and rug shampooing offered as extras. Pickup and delivery can also be an extra service, which justifies an additional charge.

MEDICAL FORMS PROCESSING

The filing of Medicare and other medical insurance forms can be confusing to the layman and especially complicated for senior citizens. Many people are willing to pay to have someone take care of the paperwork necessary to get the maximum benefits. Fees are about twenty-five dollars an hour.

JOB RÉSUMÉ AND SEARCH SERVICES

There probably never has been a time when some people were not unemployed. If they seek positions above a factory or clerical level, a résumé is usually required, and many people don't know how to write a good one.

Operating a job résumé and search service requires good but not necessarily exceptional writing skills. Information relating to work history and job accomplishments must be drawn out of the customer and this can only be done by someone with good communication ability. Résumé preparation charges range from twenty-five dollars for a simple, one-page data listing to several hundred dollars for customized executive résumés.

Additional revenue can come from other services, which may include:

♦ Preparing the personalized form letter that accompanies the résumé.
♦ Advising the job seeker how to best search out a position and providing appropriate names and addresses of company executives for a mailing. These can come from purchased or library-available directories.
♦ Providing the clerical aspects of job search—résumé typing and duplicating, preparing personalized letters on a word processor, addressing envelopes, collating material, and mailing.

MATCHING SERVICES

Find a reason for bringing together providers of products or services with users for a fee and you have a business. Matching services are essentially agent or broker operations that are intended to quickly satisfy a demand. The basic startup elements are gathering the names of those willing and able to provide the service, and, through advertising and promotion, letting people know how convenient it is to use your firm rather than doing it themselves. Fees are charged to provider or user, and sometimes both, depending on the type of business.

Here is a list of the most common matching services suitable for home operation.

- ◆ Apartment-finding services
- ◆ Roommate-matching services
- ◆ Domestic and temporary-help personnel agencies
- ◆ Summer camp matching services
- ◆ College guidance and financial-aid services
- ◆ Tourist information services (for hotels, motels, and bed-and-breakfast establishments)
- ◆ Dating-matching services
- ◆ Entertainment talent brokers or agencies
- ◆ Child-sitting services (short-term, nannies)
- ◆ House-sitting services (pet and plant care)
- ◆ Tradesmen (plumbers, electricians, and so forth) matching services

EVENT PLANNING

Not everyone has the time or ability to plan all the details of throwing a party, and some people would prefer to use a one-stop service that handles all the planning for the affair. A well-organized entrepreneur should be able to do well in this type of business.

Opportunities are many. Birthdays, anniversaries, communions, Bar/Bas Mitzvahs, sweet sixteens, graduations, engagements, and holidays are all reasons for having affairs. For business there are private functions, sales promotional events, retirement parties, company picnics, and Christmas parties. Such organizations as political parties and community and religious groups also use party services for major events. School alumni use event planners for class reunions.

The services provided can be of a consulting nature only or personally taking care of all the arrangements, many of which can be made by phone. Details include site selection if not in a client's home or office; choosing a caterer; supplying music and appropriate entertainment; providing bartenders, waiters, waitresses, and cleanup personnel; preparing and sending out invitations; seeing to flowers, centerpieces, decorations, party favors, and imprinted gifts; supplying all serving items (chairs, tables, linens, glasses and dishes, silverware, and paper and plastic products); planning party games and other related activities; making arrangements for photographs, video, and press coverage; ordering tents, stages, lighting, sound systems, and gambling equipment if appropriate; and arranging for limousines and transportation and lodging for out-of-town guests.

Starting a party-planning business begins with lining up reliable suppliers. Sales are generated from telephone-directory listings and direct mailings to businesses and various organizations. When a potential client calls, an entrepreneur has to find out the number of people to be invited, when the party will be held, and the party budget. A typical contract will stipulate one-third of the total payment on signing, one-third just before the affair, and the final third just after the party on the same day. Party-plan fees usually are 10 percent to 15 percent of the total cost.

17 EARN STEADY INCOME ASSISTING OTHER BUSINESSES

Business Services That Can Be Home-Operated

S mall- to medium-size companies frequently operate with lean staffs and almost always have periodic and sometimes regular needs for outside assistance. Business-related services offer several advantages over most other home businesses and therefore have a better success rate. First, certain types of work are traditionally jobbed out, which makes the selling of home-based services not too difficult. Second, business-related services are relatively easy to market. The names and addresses of potential commercial customers can be found in business, telephone, and industrial directories available in many libraries. Companies can also be targeted by the home business through advertising. Inexpensive classified and small display ads run in the "Business Services" section will, almost always, generate some inquiries.

Sales solicitations are also relatively simple. Direct mail, telephone marketing, and personally canvassing prospects—dropping off business cards and other promotional material—all are effective and low in cost. Another advantage is that business-related enterprises can develop regular customers, permitting entrepreneurs to spend more time working on billable services and less time selling the services.

SECRETARIAL, WORD PROCESSING, AND TYPING SERVICES

One of the most consistent winners in home-operated businesses is providing secretarial and typing services—and for good reason. Almost everyone —businessmen, students, writers, doctors, lawyers, accountants—frequently has overflow work that can't be handled in the time available.

These services' home popularity is also a result of the ease with which people can get into business. Many already have typing skills or can get it at local schools. In addition, startup requires only modest investment and just about any corner of the home will do to work in. Getting a license to operate usually is not difficult.

Generally anyone who can type a double-spaced page in ten minutes can earn enough to support a sideline venture. Speed is less important than accuracy. Error-free work, the ability to follow a customer's format, and knowledge of grammar, spelling, and punctuation are essential.

A typical secretarial service includes the typing of correspondence, reports, statistical and financial data, manuscripts, dissertations, technical and professional reports, and résumés. Additional services might include doing transcription tapes, proofreading, and writing résumés.

Pricing usually is on a per-page basis (about $1.50 per page for straight typing) with a minimum. Unique formats are billed by individual job requirements. Basic equipment includes a personal computer, fax machine, and copier, which can be purchased or leased.

Customers are acquired through Yellow Page listings, ads in the business section of newspapers, and direct-mail promotions. If you are near a college or university, putting up display posters around campus will also bring inquiries.

TELEPHONE SERVICES

In recent years the telephone has become a very useful business tool and related services are ideal home ventures for shut-ins—housewives with young children, senior citizens, and the physically handicapped. While easy and inexpensive to start, the telephone service business does require entrepreneurs to be articulate, pleasant-voiced, persuasive, and aggressive enough to quickly overcome the resistance of people who resent telephone intrusions.

A quiet place to work is essential, as is a separate telephone line if family personal calls will interfere with the business operation. Successful telephone services run from the home include telephone surveys, answering services, sales lead solicitations, telephone sales, fund-raising, collection of overdue bills, and order taking.

◆ ◆ ◆

Telephone surveys. This business involves gathering information for market-research firms using their prepared questions and recording the answers. Payment generally is by the hour or by a fee per interview completed. The best way to get started is to notify research firms listed in the Yellow Pages and other directories of your availability.

Answering services. While the investment requirement of a major message service may be out of the reach of most small business entrepreneurs, a limited answering service is possible for professionals and tradespeople using call forwarding. This phone feature allows calls to one number to be automatically forwarded to another phone. Electricians going out on a job, for example, would have all incoming calls forwarded to the message service during their absence. They also could advise the service where they could be reached for emergencies.

Sales lead solicitations. Many businesses—carpet cleaners, insurance agents, home-improvement firms, lawn services, and so forth—use telephone prescreening to line up prospects for sales calls. Charges are by the hour with bonuses sometimes paid for confirmed appointments.

Telephone sales. Products such as office supplies, classified ads, and magazine and newspaper subscriptions are successfully sold by phone.

Fund-raising. Charitable organizations use telephone marketing to request contributions or to sell tickets to some fund-raising events.

Collection services. Some businesses, such as professionals and tradespeople, use the telephone to remind customers of past due bills.

Order takers. Occasionally local firms will need a service to handle abnormal volumes of call-in orders.

◆ ◆ ◆

In addition to conventional telephone services, special opportunities sometimes arise. One business finds available nurses on an emergency basis for hospital and home-care needs. Another individual provides a similar call-up service for schools seeking substitute teachers on short notice.

BOOKKEEPING AND TAX PREPARATION SERVICES

Many professionals don't like to do such essential business chores as record-keeping, bill paying, collections, and payroll. Small businesses frequently need similar help on a steady but part-time basis. These situations open opportunities for home entrepreneurs capable of providing such services.

While manual systems are not yet out of fashion and can be used in bookkeeping services, home entrepreneurs can do much more by using personal computers. Inexpensive off-the-shelf software is available for doing a small firm's payroll, accounting, taxes, invoicing, mailing-list maintenance, and so forth. Full-service capability maximizes earnings. Additional revenues can come from doing tax preparation for consumers during the January to April tax season.

GENERAL CLERICAL SERVICES

For those who don't possess the speed and quality needed for a secretarial typing service, there are various other clerical services used regularly by businesses that operate lean.

While large mailings are usually machine-handled by mailing services, smaller quantities or odd-size correspondence requires companies to use envelope stuffers. The work can entail typing the names and addresses or peeling off computer-generated labels and applying them on envelopes, inserting printed material, sealing, and zip code–sorting for bulk mailings, or putting on stamps for first-class material.

Another clerical service is maintaining mailing lists and providing addressing services for small businesses and nonprofit organizations. An inexpensive stencil system or computer can be used.

Some individuals prefer not to use their home address and choose instead the services of a private postal drop. This would require an entrepreneur to receive mail, holding or forwarding it. Additional services can be telephone answering and providing package-shipping services through the Postal Service or private courier services. Pricing is usually based on a monthly user charge plus a fee for each service.

Other clerical services that can be offered by home entrepreneurs are translation services, preparation of special reports, collating manuals, hand-addressing greeting cards, notary public services, and myriad other routine and nonroutine tasks that pop up periodically in just about every business, big or small. If a spare room is available, an entrepreneur might consider renting it to a businessperson along with his or her own "Gal Friday" services—correspondence, typing, filing, phone answering, and so forth.

Selecting a business for a general clerical service involves little more than mailing fliers to the president or director of purchasing of companies, professional businesses, associations, and retailers within twenty minutes' drive of home.

GRAPHIC ARTS SERVICES

While very competitive and not a low-investment business, a small-volume print shop can be operated from a basement or garage. A properly zoned location in a high-traffic area would produce walk-in customers, but most home enterprises deal with businesses and "the trade" (other printers) through pick-up and delivery services. The types of service that can be offered will depend on the market. It can be a full range—typesetting, pasteup, printing, collating, binding, and mailing services—or it can be only typesetting for printers and advertising agencies, or printing for commercial printers who prefer to job out low-priced, short-run jobs that they have to do for their big customers. Typical jobs will be letterheads and envelopes, form letters, price lists, menus, fliers, brochures, customized cards and invitations of all types, and personalized stationery. The investment—$10,000 to $15,000—can be financed through outright purchase or on a lease with monthly payments. Buying used equipment is also a way to bring down the initial cash outlay.

COOPERATIVE ADVERTISING SERVICES

To save money retailers and professionals often use cooperative advertising services—a bulk mailing of promotional material for a number of advertisers that goes out in the same envelope to area residents. It is a good home-business opportunity for entrepreneurs who can package the service and sell it to advertisers.

The mailing insert can be material prepared by the advertiser and just inserted in the envelope by the entrepreneur, or the entrepreneur can provide the whole service—ad design, typesetting, graphics, printing—as well as the cooperative mailing. The material has to be zip code sorted to benefit from the discounted bulk rates. Addresses, usually a minimum of 10,000, are obtainable from mailing-list brokers. Cooperative mailings also have a market for special-interest advertisers, such as craft enterprises.

Entrepreneurs going into this business should be sales-oriented and, if providing the full advertising service, also be knowledgeable in writing copy and the mechanics of preparing advertising.

REFERRAL SERVICES

Businesses often need personnel to do short-term project assignments and depend upon outside agencies to supply them. There are home opportunities in creating a pool of people with specialized talents and becoming a prime source for companies seeking such personnel. Here are some examples:

- ◆ A home-based entrepreneur in Illinois supplied food companies with product demonstrators for supermarkets.
- ◆ A work-at-home individual pulled together cleanup crews for builders readying houses for occupancy.
- ◆ A former nurse established a specialized personnel recruitment agency to locate health professionals for medical facilities.

DESKTOP PUBLISHING

Desktop publishing is a combination of hardware and software that permits type, photographs and illustrations to be assembled and manipulated electronically. Anyone with reasonable skills in word processing and some creative talents in graphic design can produce professional-looking newsletters, brochures, catalogs, pamphlets, and fliers for the business community. What's needed is a reasonably up-to-date computer system, with backup, both laser and color printers, and scanner. The cost would be $5,000 to $7,000. The most popular noncommercial software are *Microsoft Publisher*, *Adobe Home Publisher*, and *Presswriter from Broderbund*.

18 GETTING RICH THROUGH THE MAIL

Home-Run Mail-Order Businesses

M ail order is the offering of merchandise for sale through various forms of advertising. Since it can be worked around individual time schedules from just about anywhere geographically, and the mechanics—buying or creating products, selecting ways to reach markets, advertising, receiving, keeping track of and filling orders, and handling money—aren't all that difficult to master, mail order is considered the ideal home business. But putting everything together creatively enough to persuade sufficient numbers of people to stuff money into envelopes or phone in orders simply isn't as easy as some of the get-rich-through-mail-order books would like you to believe. The vast majority of entrepreneurs starting mail-order ventures perish rather quickly.

Mail order, or direct-response marketing as it is now called, is selling directly to the consumer without personal contact. Solicitation is done through media advertising, direct mail, and catalogs. Choosing the right product, of course, is important, but it's difficult to predict what the public will buy. Even the big boys with all their business acumen occasionally fall on their faces. In Cecil Hoge's book, *Mail Order Know-How*, he describes how Westinghouse lost $10 million when it closed down Longines-Wittenauer and the Capitol Record Club. General Foods set up a division

MEGASUCCESS—MAIL ORDER: BALLARD DESIGNS

Helen Ballard Weeks entered her condo in a *Metropolitan Home* magazine contest. The eclectic mélange of furniture was selected as a regional winner and featured in a 1983 issue. When several hundred requests were forwarded by the magazine, inquiring where the items shown could be purchased, Helen recognized the possibility of a profitable apartment-based mail-order business.

Ballard Designs' first "catalog" consisted of a two-page, eight-item black-and-white flier, which was sent to those answering ads running in several home magazines. Helen says, "The response was amazing—nine out of ten people bought." It was quickly apparent that Helen had found a unique niche in the very competitive furniture marketplace.

Ballard Designs specializes in classical Greek and Roman columns and statues that serve as table bases, lamps, and bookends, plus other decorative pieces for design-conscious consumers. The company that was started with $14,000 now distributes a 325-item, thirty-six-page color catalog to 4 million consumers. Annual sales are about $7 million

WHAT SELLS IN MAIL ORDER

- ◆ Craft- and hobby-related items: kits, plans, tools, supplies, newsletters.
- ◆ Special books and instruction: how-to, correspondence courses, food preparation, self-help.
- ◆ Personalized products: standard store-type merchandise but with a personal touch.
- ◆ Handcrafted items: toys, clothing, quilts, relics—anything distinctive, especially if it has regional appeal (e.g., Early American from New England, American Indian items from the Southwest, backwoods country crafts from Appalachia).
- ◆ Ready-to-wear clothing: imported, Western, outdoor, offbeat, special sizes.
- ◆ Novelties and gifts: purchased in bulk and sold individually. Imported items sell very well.

selling creative stitchery mail order and failed with it. Even mighty Sears could not achieve success with gourmet foods even though their research indicated a market existed.

Successful mail-order entrepreneurs are guided by what has worked in the past. They know the product itself must fit certain mail-order criteria. Books, for example, sell well; store-available merchandise does not. Most important, the professionals never invest extensively in advertising until the products prove salable through testing. Many a winning mail-order item originated with a small classified ad run in a specialized publication. Advertising creativity is also very important in mail order. Entrepreneurs must know how to put the right words together. For example, the words "buy one, get one free" usually get a better response than "half price" or "50 percent off" even though, in reality, the offer is the same. There's money to be made in mail order but only for those who are willing to take the time to learn.

The subject of mail order is too extensive to be covered in the few pages that can be allotted to it in this book. This section is limited to helping novice entrepreneurs avoid the pitfalls so common to startups by providing six guidelines used by experienced mail-order specialists.

"Can he really play?" a girl whispered. "Heavens no!" Arthur exclaimed. "He never played a note in his life."

They Laughed When I Sat Down At the Piano But When I Started to Play!—

ARTHUR had just played "The Rosary." The room rang with applause. I decided that this would be a dramatic moment for me to make my debut. To the amazement of all my friends, I strode confidently over to the piano and sat down.

"Jack is up to his old tricks," somebody chuckled. The crowd laughed. They were all certain that I couldn't play a single note.

"Can he really play?" I heard a girl whisper to Arthur.

"Heavens, no!" Arthur exclaimed. "He never played a note in all his life. . . . But just you watch him. This is going to be good."

I decided to make the most of the situation. With mock dignity I drew out a silk handkerchief and lightly dusted off the piano keys. Then I rose and gave the revolving piano stool a quarter of a turn, just as I had seen an imitator of Paderewski do in a vaudeville sketch.

"What do you think of his execution?" called a voice from the rear.

"We're in favor of it!" came back the answer, and the crowd rocked with laughter.

Then I Started to Play

Instantly a tense silence fell on the guests. The laughter died on their lips as if by magic. I played through the first few bars of Beethoven's immortal Moonlight Sonata. I heard gasps of amazement. My friends sat breathless — spellbound!

I played on and as I played I forgot the people around me. I forgot the hour, the place, the breathless listeners. The little world I lived in seemed to fade — seemed to grow dim — unreal. Only the music was real. Only the music and visions it brought me. Visions as beautiful and as changing as the wind blown clouds and drifting moonlight that long ago inspired the master composer. It seemed as if the master

musician himself were speaking to me—speaking through the medium of music—not in words but in chords. Not in sentences but in exquisite melodies!

A Complete Triumph!

As the last notes of the Moonlight Sonata died away, the room resounded with a sudden roar of applause. I found myself surrounded by excited faces. How my friends carried on! Men shook my hand — wildly congratulated me—pounded me on the back in their enthusiasm! Everybody was exclaiming with delight—plying me with rapid questions. . . . "Jack! Why didn't you tell us you could play like that?". . . "Where did you learn?"—"How long have you studied?"—"Who was your teacher?"

"I have never even *seen* my teacher," I replied. "And just a short while ago I couldn't play a note."

". . . Quit your kidding," laughed Arthur, himself an accomplished pianist. "You've been studying for years. I can tell."

"I have been studying only a short while," I insisted. "I decided to keep it a secret so that I could surprise all you folks."

Then I told them the whole story.

"Have you ever heard of the U. S. School of Music?" I asked.

A few of my friends nodded. "That's a correspondence school, isn't it?" they exclaimed.

"Exactly," I replied. "They have a new simplified method that can teach you to play any instrument by mail in just a few months."

How I Learned to Play Without a Teacher

And then I explained how for years I had longed to play the piano.

"A few months ago," I continued, "I saw an interesting ad for the U. S. School of Music—a new method of learning to play which only cost a few cents a day! The ad told how a woman had mastered the piano in her spare time at home—and *without a teacher!* Best of all, the wonderful new method she used, required no laborious scales — no heartless exercises — no tiresome practising. It sounded so convincing that I filled out the coupon requesting the Free Demonstration Lesson.

"The free book arrived promptly and I started in that very night to study the Demonstration Lesson. I was amazed to see how easy it was to play this new way. Then I sent for the course.

"When the course arrived I found it was just as the ad said — as easy as A.B.C! And, as

the lessons continued they got easier and easier. Before I knew it I was playing all the pieces I liked best. Nothing stopped me. I could play ballads or classical numbers or jazz, all with equal ease! And I never did have any special talent for music!"

• • • •

Play Any Instrument

You too, can now *teach yourself* to be an accomplished musician—right at home—in half the usual time. You can't go wrong with this simple new method which has already shown 350,000 people how to play their favorite instruments. Forget that old-fashioned idea that you need special "talent." Just read the list of instruments in the panel, decide which one you want to play and the U. S. School will do the rest. And bear in mind no matter which instrument you choose, the cost in each case will be the same—just a few cents a day. No matter whether you are a mere beginner or already a good performer, you will be interested in learning about this new and wonderful method.

Send for Our Free Booklet and Demonstration Lesson

Thousands of successful students never dreamed they possessed musical ability until it was revealed to them by a remarkable "Musical Ability Test" which we send entirely without cost with our interesting free booklet.

If you are in earnest about wanting to play your favorite instrument—if you really want to gain happiness and increase your popularity—send at once for the free booklet and Demonstration Lesson. No cost — no obligation. Right now we are making a Special offer for a limited number of new students. Sign and send the convenient coupon now—before it's too late to gain the benefits of this offer. Instruments supplied when needed, cash or credit. U. S. School of Music, 1631 Brunswick Bldg., New York City.

U. S. School of Music,
1631 Brunswick Bldg., New York City.

Please send me your free book, "Music Lessons in Your Own Home," with introduction by Dr. Frank Crane, Demonstration Lesson and particulars of your Special Offer. I am interested in the following course:

....

....

Have you above instrument?...................

Name...
(Please write plainly)

Address..

City..........................State.............

Pick Your Instrument

Piano	'Cello
Organ	Harmony and
Violin	Composition
Drums and	Sight Singing
Traps	Ukulele
Banjo	Guitar
Tenor	Hawaiian
Banjo	Steel Guitar
Mandolin	Harp
Clarinet	Cornet
Flute	Piccolo
Saxophone	Trombone
	Voice and Speech Culture
	Automatic Finger Control
	Piano Accordion

The best mail-order advertisement ever: This ad for music lessons is considered by many to be one of, if not the best, mail-order advertisement ever written and brought in an overwhelming response. It was written in 1925 by John Caples, who later went on to become a recognized authority on copywriting. It's a textbook example of what makes a good ad—attention-grabbing headline, clear, interesting copy in the form of a personal testimonial, a limited time-offer call to action, free information with no obligation, and an easy-response coupon.

- *Guideline one: Choose a product or service category that traditionally sells well through mail order.*

Not everything does. Common sense tells us that people are not going to wait weeks for delivery and pay shipping charges for items available in local stores. Sometimes the products are good value but can't be adequately described in affordable advertising space to be sold mail order. There are various other reasons, but from experience we know year after year certain product and service categories seem to be repeated in mail-order advertising while other categories quickly disappear.

- *Guideline two: Plan your mail-order program so initial orders result in multiple sales.*

Except for "hot" fad items and high-priced merchandise, rarely can mail-order firms make it with one-shot products. Repeat sales come naturally to self-depleting items, such as cosmetics or stationery, but for other products tie-in promotions for the sale of related items must be included with the initial order response. This could be in the form of a catalog or circular. "Bounce-back" circulars can produce additional sales, and this frequently makes the difference between success and failure for a mail-order firm.

- *Guideline three: Don't overestimate the market appeal of the product or service.*

Too many idea originators tend to think customers will be waiting in line to buy their product or service once they know it's available. More than likely, however, the percentage response will be no better than what other typical mail-order promotions bring. For direct mail this is seven to fifty orders per thousand solicitations. Full-page advertising pulls one-half to two responses per thousand circulation. Consequently, if you run a small ad, don't expect more than a few hundred replies from a million circulation publication. What's important here is that entrepreneurs make certain their costs—product, overhead, advertising—will be covered at those sales levels.

SHOPPER'S GALLERY

RECIPES & COOKBOOKS

THE LITTLE CLASSIC GOURMET COOKBOOK OF INTERNATIONAL SPECIALTIES. From Peasant food to Desserts, a remarkable collection of culinary delights, made simple and mistake-free, that are sure to become "conversation pieces." To receive your "Specialties" Collection Cookbook and a Brochure of our other Little Classic Gourmet Cookbooks, send $7.95 to: CLASSIC GOURMET, PO Box 368, Vails Gate, NY 12584-0368

FREE-FAST ECONOMICAL want something easy, different & unusual, CALL today for your assortment of FREE recipes. Call 1-900-535-9898 Ext. 175. $2.00 per minute per call.

FREE-SWEETS RECIPES Call now to receive your assortment of candy, cakes & cookie recipes. Some unusual & fun to make. Call 1-900-535-9898 Ext. 176. $2.00 per minute per call.

UNIQUE HOT DOG COOKBOOK. Hundreds of tasty ideas. Send $7.00 to: UHDC, 608 W. Vine, Kiss., FL 32741

BAKED ORANGES & STUFFED ORANGES. Vitamin C Delight. Send $3 & SASE to: CHIC, P.O. Box 4308, Boca Raton, Fla. 33429-4308

MAKE HOMEMADE RAVIOLI the easy way! Solid brass, chrome plated device, recipe included. Send $11.95 to: R.D.R. IMPORTING, P.O. Box 4874, Waterbury, CT 06704

DELICIOUS SALT WATER TAFFY Made In Minutes. Send $2.75 & SASE to: EMD, PO Box 836, Troy, Ohio 45373

EASY WINDOW CLEANER & DEGREASER, plus simple wood waterproofing. $3/SASE: WENDY, 974 Lamberton St., Trenton, NJ 08611

BETTY'S BAKLAVAH MELTS in your mouth. Snowball cookies, everyone's favorite. Low cholesterol quiches, delicious. Trade secrets. $4.50, SASE. COUNTRY QUICHE, P.O. Box 2633, Bala Cyn Wyd, PA 19004

TRY WHIMPEY'S FRUITTREATS! Families will love them! Sauces, Dips, and Serving Ideas. Send $3.00 & SASE to: FRUITTREATS, P.O. Box 604, Morgan, Utah 84050

BAVARIAN CAKE BOOK. $5 to: FRAU HARTERT'S BAVARIAN CAKE WORKS (BCW), 2464 Entrada Dr., Virginia Beach, VA 23456

OLD-FASHIONED VERMONT CAKES—Two simple, scrumptious recipes. $3 SASE to: W. MARTIN, Box 5, Grafton, VT 05146

MILK/EGG ALLERGIES? Watching your cholesterol? Try these 2 recipes: Pancakes—Chocolate Chip Cookies. Send SASE, $1.00: STB, Box 683, Colstrip, Montana 59323

ABSOLUTELY TO DIE FOR double Chocolate Raspberry Truffle Cheesecake, it's heavenly. Recipe $4.00/SASE: R.W. YERZYK, P.O. Box 5172-FC, Westhills, CA 91308-5172

DELICIOUS! EASY! DINNER ROLLS, Cinnamon Rolls, Sticky Buns, More. $4—to: STUDINGER'S, 1501 E-Grand # 2208, Escondido, CA 92027

ITALIAN MOTHER'S OWN SPECIALTIES—Recipe Booklet—"Outstanding"—S.A.S.E. with $5—E. GRECO, 1802 Hulseman St., Philadelphia, PA 19145

CHERRY CHEESECAKE PIE fast and delicious. Send $2.00 & LSASE To: ELIZABETH, PO Box 123, Waterford, New York 12188

AWARD-WINNING RECIPE! Out of this world apple salad dessert. $3.00, SASE, Ol' COUNTRY HOME, POB 18945FC, Greensboro, NC 27419

NO COOK RECIPES Bread & Butter Pickles, 10 minute Jello, Chocolate Clouds, $2/EA, 2/$3, SASE: BJC, PO Box 282, Caledonia, WI 53108

FANTASTIC HOMEMADE SOUPS. Send $5.00 SASE for 5 recipes. MRS. B, 211 Newbury St., Boston, Mass. 02116

PAPA'S PANCAKES light quick easy! $2.00 SASE to: PAPA, 22 North Main Street, Suite 445, New City, NY 10956

SOUTHERN STYLE Barbecue Sauce and Brunswick Stew. Old family recipes. Delicious! $3.00/S.A.S.E. PIP'S, 2469 McGarity Rd., McDonough, GA 30253

PARTY PUNCHES. Luscious, lovely, lively drinks for showers, parties, receptions. $3.00/S.A.S.E. PIP'S, 2469 McGarity Rd., McDonough, GA 30253

GRANDMA'S BUTTER POUND CAKE WITH STRAWBERRIES. Send $3.00 + S.A.S.E. To: P.A.L., P.O. Box 864, Island Lake, IL 60042

COOKING WITH KIDS: a 70 page treasury creating golden moments with kids around the kitchen. $9.98: PROSPECT PUBLISHING, 1285 Baring Blvd., Suite 476, Sparks, NV 89434

FRIENDS WILL BRAG ENDLESSLY ON YOUR BAKING & LOVE this mouth-watering cookie recipe. $1.00 + S.A.S.E., DANA, 410 Rainbow, Whitehouse, TX 75791

SPEARMINT/PEPPERMINT LIQUEUR RECIPES Makes Half Gallon. $5.00 SASE: DEAMONDO, PO Box 1572, Belleville, IL 62223

GRANDMA'S OLD FASHIONED CHESS PIE. 5 other pies. Send SASE $3.00: F. LEONARD, 11627 Killian St., El Monte, CA 91732

A MUST FOR THE BUSY COOK! A fun, informative newsletter. Menus, recipes, short-cut hints. $3.00: COOKIN' GOOD, 236 S. Rainbow #292C, Las Vegas, NV 89128

AUTHENTIC ITALIAN DISHES: easy, delicious; Eggplant Parmesan, Homemade Manicotti & Zucchini over Linguine; $3 SASE, MarianaG, 48A Old Rt. 22, Pawling, NY 12564

FROM EATIE GOURMET'S KITCHEN. Ten Simple Cheese Appetizer Recipes $5.00 + SASE to: PO Box 2724, Hollywood, CA 90078

OAT, FRUIT & BRAN MUFFIN. First Offer. Original. SASE $3.00: JOANN, Box 271, Powell, WY 82435

SCRUMPTIOUS CHOCOLATE CARMEL BARS. $3.00 SASE to: FSTN—T DAVIS, 361 Frontage Road, Suite 102, Burr Ridge, IL 60521

HOMEMADE BABYFOOD RECIPES—Fun, Easy and Economical. Send $3.95/LSASE to: KERRY MAHATCEK, P.O. Box 1206, Inverness, FL 32651

POTATO CANDY. Ideal for the sweet tooth. Send $3.00 SASE to: JACKIE, P.O. Box 4, Scranton, PA 18504

NEED HELP WITH DINNER? Easy directions/familiar ingredients. 49 recipes only $4.00. CRYSTALWOOD, 3418 Hamilton Blvd., Allentown, PA 18103

ORIGINAL SECRET RECIPE NEVER PUBLISHED; Special spiced honey glazed BBQ ribs. SASE + $3.00, MINNIE, Box 4853, Boise, ID 83711

COUPONS & REFUNDS

CASH FOR BOXTOPS, LABELS. For information send a long, self-addressed, stamped envelope: CONTINENTAL, Box 11616, Philadelphia, PA 19116

REAL ESTATE

GOVERNMENT HOMES from $1 (U repair). Delinquent tax property. Repossessions. Your area 1-805-962-8000 Ext. GH-20091 for current repo list. Fee for dir. (Refundable).

AUTOS FOR SALE

GOVERNMENT SEIZED Vehicles from $100. Fords. Mercedes. Corvettes. Chevys. Surplus. Your area. 1-805-962-8000 Ext. S-20091. Fee for dir. (Refundable).

THRIFTY SHOPPER

CARPET SPECIALS Major Brands. Price Quotes/FREE Samples: 1-800-749-5013 GA. 404-277-3374. SOUTHERN COMFORT CPT., 3028 N. Dug Gap Rd., Dalton, GA 30720

CLOSEOUT JEWELRY. 55¢ Dozen. Also closeout craft supplies. Catalog 50¢. ROUSSELS, 107-610 Dow, Arlington, MA 02174-7199

CARPET SAVINGS Major Brands. Price quotes and information: 1-800-526-2229, or 404-226-2229. WAREHOUSE CARPETS, INC., Box 3233, Dalton, GA 30721

VACUUM CLEANERS "Discount Prices" New Rainbow $699.95, Kirby, Filter Queen, Tri-Star, Panasonic, Royal, Oreck. Details: ABC VACUUM WAREHOUSE, 6720 Burnet-FC, Austin, Texas 78757, (512) 459-7643.

ADVERTISING INFO

DEAR ENTREPRENEUR: *Looking for an affordable advertising vehicle? Try Family Circle's* **Shopper's Gallery** *or* **Wholesale By Mail** *advertising sections. Next available issue is Oct. 15, 1991, on-sale September 24 and closing July 12, 1991.* Contact: **Susan Corradi,** FAMILY CIRCLE, 110 Fifth Avenue, NYC 10011. (212) 463-1535.

Better responses can be expected from media that have created successful marketplaces for mail-order advertisers.

♦ *Guideline four: Use tried and proven effective mail-order advertising media.*

Novice mail-order entrepreneurs often equate media numbers with potential mail-order sales. Not all publication readers, radio listeners, and television viewers are mail-order buyers. Some magazines, for example, develop circulation through heavily discounted subscription rates and may not be as well read as publications with lower numbers but higher newsstand sales. In addition, some media are better than others as mail-order marketplaces.

Don't just look at the promotional data but analyze the media products themselves. In the case of magazines, peruse a number of issues, old and new, and determine if mail-order ads are being repeated. That usually is pretty good proof the ads are "pulling," at least for those products advertised.

As far as when to run ads, January, February, September, October, and November are the best months, while June, July, August, and December tend to be less productive. Seasonal items, of course, have different response patterns.

♦ *Guideline five: Give top priority to developing and maintaining a mailing list from inquiries and orders.*

One sure way of going bust fast in mail order is to depend too much on purchased lists or those rented from list brokers. House lists produce the best results and don't have extra costs attached to the use of names and addresses. Classified ads have proven to be an effective way of building lists and also selling items priced at five dollars or less. Often both these things can be accomplished with the same ad.

♦ *Guideline six: Key all ads and closely monitor results.*

It sounds obvious but novices sometimes don't do it carefully enough. All ads lose impact after a period of time and should be replaced or restructured. Since magazines operate on three-month deadlines, response patterns have to be watched for warning signals in order to predict when ad pull will be below the profit level.

MAKING IT IN MAIL ORDER—A THREE-STEP PROCESS

Some products sold by mail order and priced at ten dollars or more can't be adequately described in affordable small display or classified ad space. Experienced mail-order specialists work around this using a three-step process.

1. A small classified ad is run in the appropriate medium offering information on the product. Leads are generated.

2. The leads are followed up with a package of promotional material. This can be a single mailing or a series of solicitations if the product price justifies it.

3. A percentage of these leads will be converted into sales. When fulfilling the orders, promotional material for related products or products likely to be of interest to the same audience are included with the order. This technique, known as bounce-back, usually has a return of 10 percent to 20 percent. Often it is the bounce-back revenue that makes the whole process profitable.

NEWSLETTER PUBLISHING

"Paper" is one of the more successful mail-order items because the cost of both product and advertising is low and the profit margins high. Plans, instructions, patterns, and so forth do exceptionally well, as do special-topic, limited-circulation newsletters. More than 8,000 newsletters are now published and many of these are created by home entrepreneurs on their own word processors or personal computers. Opportunities are increasing as desktop publishing allows home entrepreneurs to produce newsletters inexpensively.

There are three types of newsletters. Some provide information on specialized subjects. Others distill important items from other publications and condense them for busy readers. The last are advisory newsletters usually containing insider tips.

Most newsletters are started by entrepreneurs with knowledge of or an interest in a particular subject. Subscriptions are generated through ads in similar-interest magazines and by direct mail. Usually a year's subscription is sold, with the first month's issue free, and with the right of cancellation

MAIL-ORDER PUBLICATIONS

Media that are considered a mail-order marketplace historically produce a better-than-average response rate. Here is a list of the major nationally distributed publications appealing to general audiences with classified or mail-order sections or both. Only those with circulation of over a million are included.

◆ Monthly magazines: *Woman's Day, Family Circle, Ladies' Home Journal, Redbook, MacFadden's Women's Group of Romance Publications, Field & Stream, Popular Science, Popular Mechanics, Outdoor Life.*

◆ Weekly magazines: *National Enquirer, Star, National Examiner.*

◆ Newspaper-distributed magazines: *Parade, USA Weekend, New York Times, Los Angeles Times, Chicago Tribune, Washington Post.*

◆ National newspapers: *The Wall Street Journal, USA Today.*

Anyone interested in starting a mail-order business should write for information to the industry trade organization, Direct Marketing Association, 1120 Avenue of the Americas, New York, NY 10036.

Two publications on mail order are considered exceptional. They are Julian Simon's *How to Start and Operate a Mail Order Business* (McGraw-Hill) and *Building a Mail Order Business* by William Cohen (John Wiley & Sons).

> ## DROP-SHIP MAIL-ORDER FIRMS
>
> The mailing of another firm's stock catalog generally is not recommended. In most of these situations the catalog company sells a package of direct-mail materials—catalogs with the buyer's name imprinted, instruction booklets, and mailing lists. The buyer mails the catalogs, receives orders, and sends part of the money to the seller, who drop-ships the merchandise to the customer. Unfortunately the mailing lists provided rarely generate enough sales to cover costs.

if not satisfied. Many publishers use the negative option, that is, if the invoice is not returned marked "cancel," other issues are forwarded. Renewal incentives may be eighteen issues at a regular year's subscription rate. On the average 25 percent to 35 percent of the subscribers will renew.

Newsletters cover a wide range of subjects. Here is a sampling of the topics of publications started by home entrepreneurs.

- ◆ Home sewers newsletter, which includes paid-for discount coupon advertising.
- ◆ Contest newsletters (lists availability, how to enter, and the best ways to win).
- ◆ Travel newsletter (e.g., guide to French hotels and restaurants).
- ◆ Newsletter for parents with handicapped children.
- ◆ Cat lovers newsletters.
- ◆ Antique information newsletter covering regional area.
- ◆ Newsletter for quilters, knitters, and crocheters with product ideas and supply sources.
- ◆ Newsletter listing products available for sale or licensing.
- ◆ Stock photography newsletter (lists available photos and is distributed to magazines and advertising agencies).

19 INCOME FROM UNIQUE TALENTS

Freelance Professionals Working at Home

There is a potpourri of challenging work-at-home opportunities that require professional talents or technical skills. Those engaged in these activities are known as freelancers. Most work alone and are classified by the IRS as self-employed independent contractors.

Some freelance work depends on assignments from outside firms, while other freelancers, such as writers and artists, also have independent money-generating opportunities. Here we will describe the businesses that regularly use freelancers. Back-to-back assignments can lead to fairly steady income.

Publishing. The publishing industry, in general, depends upon a variety of freelancers—writers, editors, illustrators, graphic artists, cartoonists, photographers, and so forth—for a variety of creative assignments. These firms should also be checked for somewhat less technical work-at-home projects requiring good language skills, such as proofreading. Work inquires should be directed to the following trade directory and Yellow Page listings: Publishers (book, periodical, directory, guides), Newspapers, Newspaper Feature Syndicates.

Advertising, promotion, public relations. Opportunities for freelance writers, graphic artists, illustrators, and photographers exist for creative advertising, preparing brochures and corporate reports, writing publicity articles, developing instructions manuals, and so forth. Check the following lists in directories and Yellow Pages: Advertising Agencies and Counselors, Advertising—Direct Mail, Public Relations, Writers—Business, and Technical Manual Preparation. Also check agencies using graphic designers, artists, and commercial photographers.

Stationery and manufacturing. Photographers and artists of all types will find freelance work with firms in the stationery field. Greeting-card manufacturers, such as Hallmark and Abbey Press, are constantly on the lookout for writers, poets, and artists to design cards. Geographic location is not a limitation, but individuals should be prepared to offer solid evidence of artistic talent. Assignment inquiries should be directed to the following stationery items manufacturers in trade directories and Yellow Pages: Greeting Cards, Calendars, Postcards, Gift Wrap.

Calligraphy. Firms offering calligraphic services for invitations, announcements, and awards job out many assignments to freelance calligraphers. Printers also are a good source of contract calligraphy work. Most

---

MEGASUCCESS—COMPUTER PROGRAMMING: T/MAKER

Peter Roizen, working out of his Washington, D.C., home, devised a computer system to calculate tables of columns and numbers (an electronic spreadsheet), which he named T/Maker, a shortened version of "tablemaker." For several years the program was sold through a software publisher and distributor. By 1983, sales had fallen off and Peter was looking for a new way to promote new versions of T/Maker. Peter's sister, Heidi, an MBA student at Stanford, asked to take over distribution of the software. Peter agreed, a corporation was formed, and Heidi displayed the product at a West Coast trade show. T/Maker was off and running—out of Heidi's bedroom.

Within a short time T/Maker had to move to larger leased space, and the firm posted $600,000 in sales for the first year. When Apple developed the Macintosh computer it invited software houses to develop new applications. T/Maker came up with its first graphics-related program, called ClickArt. This was followed by WriteNow, T/Maker's award-winning word processor for the Macintosh, and other desktop publishing software. As the market grew, T/Maker grew with it.

Located in Mountain View, California, T/Maker now employs close to forty people and has sales in excess of $20 million. The products of the software development and publishing corporation are sold through distributors, retailers, and direct-to-consumer organizations.

FREELANCE OCCUPATIONS

- Creative writers: books, magazine articles, speeches, poetry
- Copywriters: advertising and promotion, public relations
- Technical writers: instruction manuals
- Copyeditors: books, articles
- Book reviewers
- Graphic and commercial artists and designers
- Artists, illustrators, and cartoonists
- Photographers: commercial
- Calligraphers
- Computer programmers
- Computer systems analysts
- Translators
- Counselors and consultants

MEGASUCCESS—ARTIST: SUZY'S ZOO

Suzy Spafford's entrepreneurial career began in the 1960s while she was a student at San Diego State University. An art major, she painted watercolors and sold them at an art mart in Balboa Park, earning $3,000 to $4,000 a year. Later she created colorful pastel cartoon characters—animated birds, frogs, and turtles—which sold for three dollars apiece.

In 1967 Suzy's work was seen by a businessman who was willing to put up $6,000 to print 80,000 greeting cards featuring Suzy's apartment-drawn characters, like Suzy Ducken and Corky Turtle. The cards were placed at local shops, and within a few months reorders began to come in and Suzy's Zoo was born.

West Coast greeting-card sales representatives picked up the line and in two years sales approached $200,000. Suzy incorporated in 1976, expanded the card line, began distributing nationally, and added paper goods. Thirteen years after Suzy created the cartoon characters, company sales reached $1 million.

Suzy's Zoo now has more than fifty employees and annual sales of $6 million. A diversity of licensing agreements—allowing others to reproduce the cartoon characters on balloons, T-shirts, and so forth—helped maintain growth and profits of the still privately owned firm.

firms seek out local talent. For work-at-home opportunities contact companies listed under Yellow Pages headings: Calligraphers, Invitational Announcements, Printers.

Computer industry. Software development firms often contract original program development, conversions, and documentation assignments. Contract opportunities may also exist for technical writers for manuals and documentation. For firms offering work-at-home opportunities, see trade directories and Yellow Page listings: Computer System Designers and Consultants, Technical Manual Preparation.

Translation. Translation service firms use people fluent in foreign languages for translation of literature, legal documents, business-meeting minutes, and technical and sales material into English and other languages. Geographic location is not a restriction, but homeworkers should have a modem tied to a personal computer for electronic transmission. Payment is by the word. For work-at-home opportunities check national directory listings under Translators. Also check with foreign-owned firms.

WRITING

In addition to freelance assignments, many other types of written media can be a source of revenue for those who can creatively string words together.

- Prepare articles for magazines and trade publications. How-to, personal experiences, and children's material are subjects that sell best. Payment runs anywhere from $250 to $800 for a 2,000-word article. Add pictures and you have a better chance of being published. It's essential you know the type of material publications seek before submission. Peruse the magazines and refer to *Literary Market Place* and *Writers Market*.
- Write filler—short items up to 300 words. Jokes, quotations, quips, anecdotes, puzzles, recipes, amazing facts, hints and tips, quizzes, and games all fall into this category and are good for $25 to $50 per submission.
- Write a regular column for newspapers and magazines. Special subjects—local history, antiques, crafts, gardening, photography, and so forth—are most in demand. Restaurant critiques and movie and local theater reviews are sought after by community newspapers.
- Write an advertising shopper's column. You've probably seen "Best Buy" columns in small daily newspapers and community weeklies. They are not editorial material but paid-for advertising. The space is purchased from the newspapers by the writer, who prepares the commercial promotional material and charges the merchant.

PUBLIC RELATIONS AND ADVERTISING

Public relations and advertising is one of the more interesting professional businesses, and it can easily be done from home. Home-based entrepreneurs do well serving small business firms and nonprofit agencies. Services include preparing news releases, press kits, newsletters, brochures, public service announcements, and house organs, and writing speeches. Some home entrepreneurs have also added limited advertising agency services and assist clients in creating ads and direct mail and in media selection.

ANN STRATFORD'S
Best Buys

P.O. Box 1172, Fair Lawn, NJ (201) 796-3331

I'm thankful I discovered **CARNEY'S DELI &
DESSERTS** before Thanksgiving! Much more than a
Deli, this shop at **74 Ramapo Valley Rd., Mahwah (529-
1209)** is a hostess' dream come true. First, meet the
CARNEY'S: Joanne is former pastry chef at Stony Hill
Inn, and Jim's credentials include head banquet chef at
Rockleigh Country Club. Quite a combination! No won-
der apple, pumpkin, chocolate pecan pies are in such
demand. Order now and celebrate Turkey Day with roast
turkey and trimmings a la **CARNEY'S DELI &
DESSERTS.**

• • • • •

I love coming to the rescue when readers need a special gift or something pretty and practical for their own
home. Off the beaten path is a **new factory outlet—
ACRILANA, 218 S. Van Brunt St., Englewood.** Their
showroom sparkles with lucite and plexiglass tables, TV
carts, shelves, frames, letter and napkin holders, cutting
boards, plus stunning accessories for bath and kitchen.
Among all these Best Buys (40-60% off dept. store
prices) is a Super Buy—modern table with 4 chairs — just
$299.50! Call **568-5360** for directions; 1/2 mi. off Rt. 4.

• • • • •

What's better than a store filled with children's books?
Answer: **WHALE OF A TALE!** I overheard a teacher
telling the owner, "You have the best selection of Early
Readers." The same is true for Middle Readers and
Young Adults. Sections are devoted to Science & Geog-
raphy, Classics, Poetry, Picture and Activity Books—
even Award Winners! Babies are intrigued with cloth,
touch and Beatrix Potter board books. Pre-schoolers like
Pop-Ups. Holiday books are now arriving at **WHALE OF
A TALE!, 16 N. Walnut St., Ridgewood (445-4845).**

• • • • •

This year, coats look exciting, elegant and expensive—but prices at **BURLINGTON** are amazingly low.
Calvin Klein, Bill Blass, J.G. Hook have created styles
short and shaped or long and draped. Swing coats and
cozy parkas brighten the landscape in clear, bold shades.
You'll love the affordable winter coat collections in the
Men's and Children's Depts. The scores of options here
have one strong message—Best Buys await at
**BURLINGTON COAT FACTORY WAREHOUSE, 651 Rt.
17 Paramus; Rt. 46, Pine Brook; 275 Hartz Way,
Secaucus; Willow Ave., Hoboken.**

• • • • •

From one pie-lover to another, have you ever tasted
the equal of **Grandma Tice's** luscious pies? I doubt it.
On Thanksgiving Day, much as I enjoy turkey, I can't wait
for dessert. Of course, if you want to bake your own,
you'll appreciate the huge variety of crisp apples and specially grown sweet milk pumpkins at **TICE FARMS,
Chestnut Ridge Rd. (GSP 171), Woodcliff Lake.**
Before the season ends, treat yourself to fabulous fres-
milled apple cider. Just as fresh as their delicious vegeta-
bles are flowers for your table--exceptional from **TICE.**

Anyone skilled at both selling advertising and putting words together can write an advertising
shopping column.

PHOTOGRAPHIC SERVICES

Several photography-related business options are available to professionals or talented hobbyists with extra rooms or basements that can be turned into studios or service areas.

- Take portrait, family, pet, and passport pictures.
- Provide a commercial photographic and custom processing service for the advertising and business community.
- Restore old photos and provide antique photo services. Retailers can serve as customer drop points.

COMPUTER PROGRAMMING/SOFTWARE DEVELOPMENT

Home-business opportunities for computer entrepreneurs have grown dramatically and that growth is not over yet. The introduction of the inexpensive personal computer makes it practical for professional programmers to work from home. It has also expanded the market for products and services to millions of computer hobbyists.

In addition to supplying specialized programs for companies on a freelance basis, there are other options for computer-knowledgeable entrepreneurs.

- Write programs that can be sold to consumers through retail stores and mail order.
- Educate others on computer programming. Companies will pay for employee training on the more business-oriented. Hobbyists are also a market for such courses as "Introduction to the Internet."

COUNSELING AND CONSULTING

Those with specialized knowledge can command respectable fees for giving advice to others. Counseling and consulting businesses require an appropriate setting, and a room in the house or apartment should be set aside for meeting clients. In addition to conventional advertising, public exposure is a big plus for developing business. Having articles published in newspapers and magazines, being a guest on radio and TV, and speaking before groups will help build a reputation.

◆ Investment counseling and financial planning: Showing people how to employ their assets so that the after-tax return is greater is advice that people will gladly pay for. Those starting such a business must be knowledgeable about funds, commodities, life insurance, real estate, and related tax laws.

◆ Marketing consulting: Develop new product ideas for firms and guide them through to marketing. Small companies are the best target for this type of service because they have limited staff to do the work themselves.

◆ Personal help counseling: Provide psychological assistance—marriage, divorce, and family counseling and mediation, group therapy, child guidance, and speech therapy. Licensing is required in most states.

◆ Career and vocational counseling: Help select the right career paths and appropriate colleges and schools.

ARTISTS

Not everyone has the talent to creatively express ideas in the form of salable art products and services, but those who can should be able to earn income operating from home. In addition to freelance assignments some of the best art-related opportunities are for:

◆ Oil and watercolor artists doing landscapes, still lifes, and portraits done from sittings or photographs (people, houses, pets). Restoring old paintings for museums, galleries, and the public can add to income, as will group instruction to hobbyists.

◆ Artists doing conventional and free-form sculpture in any material. Interior decorators and galleries are a market for this type of art.

◆ Art appraising, brokering, and art gallery operation.

TURN A SPARE ROOM INTO A MONEY-MAKING FACTORY

20

Manufacturing Your Own or Another Firm's Product

S pare rooms, basements, and garages can be used to fabricate products or assemble kits—either a creation of your own or items you do on a contract basis for another company.

HOME MANUFACTURING A PRODUCT

While a product of your own design manufactured in quantity offers the potential of greater financial rewards, it also means stepping into an operation that is fairly complex, requiring the entrepreneurial talent to run a "big" little business. Equipment must be purchased, credit established, materials and supplies acquired, inventories maintained, and working capital monitored. And, of course, the finished products still must be marketed. Since selling direct to consumers is not likely to move sufficient merchandise quantities, an entrepreneur also has to become familiar with wholesale channels of distribution—or mail order.

The government views home-manufacturing business as it does any business when it comes to employing labor. Income, unemployment, and disability taxes must be paid by the business or withheld from employee

INDEPENDENT CONTRACTOR

The IRS recognizes the tax advantages to an employer of classifying workers as independent contractors and not employees, so it has set up some guidelines. If you use independent contractors, make sure: (1) they are paid on a performance fee, not time basis; (2) there is no reimbursement for expenses; (3) they submit estimates on jobs, offer their services to others, and pay their own taxes. It may help to clarify everything in a written agreement.

MEGASUCCESS—HOME MANUFACTURING: CRAZY SHIRTS

When art major Rick Ralston decided to earn spending money by hand-painting beach towels, T-shirts, and sweatshirts at home, he never realized it would put him on an entrepreneurial career path that would make him into a millionaire.

It all started in 1960 when Rich was a freshman in a Los Angeles art school. He and his buddy would do the painting, sweatshirts at first, and sell them to bathers at Catalina Island. Two years later Rick moved to Hawaii where a major part of his market turned out to be sailors on shore leave. A T-shirt showing a sailor using a marine for a surfboard was the most popular.

In 1964, Rick opened a small store and started to screen-print the shirts. Business was greatly helped by the war in Southeast Asia that created a huge demand for T-shirts with political messages, such as "Draft Beer, Not Students" and "Fly the Friendly Skies of Cambodia." Over the years Crazy Shirts added stores and expanded to a larger factory and warehouse. Today the firm sells through twenty-five outlets in Hawaii, seventeen in Colorado and California, and by mail. Annual revenues of the still privately owned firm are approximately $40 million.

paychecks. Periodic reports are required and this could mean, for a small enterprise, having to retain the part-time services of an accountant. Adherence to all health and safety codes is also a must when outside workers are involved.

Entrepreneurs sometimes can avoid the problems related to employing workers by jobbing out to independent contractors—self-employed individuals who do the work on their premises. But an employee working at home for you can't just be called an independent contractor. Government guidelines are used in determining whether an individual is really an independent contractor and not an employee in disguise. Entrepreneurs interested in contracting out work should acquaint themselves with the pertinent federal Department of Labor and IRS regulations. Also, check with the Department of Labor in your state, since about eighteen states have restrictions on the types of products that can legally be manufactured at home. Some states also require homeworkers to obtain homeworker certificates so they can monitor wages and safety.

CONTRACT HOMEWORK

Cottage industries have long been important in rural communities, where commuting time makes it almost impossible for some people to hold regular jobs. More recently, however, the need for second incomes in families with children plus the shortage of qualified industry labor have given contract homework a boost in all areas of the country.

Needlework has always been the most popular activity for homeworkers, sometimes jobbed out legally, sometimes not. The lifting of the federal ban on certain sewn products should increase the number of firms contracting out work. The type of work varies widely—sewing trim and linings, machine and hand knitting, complete product fabrication, stitching and assembly of parts, and so forth. Almost all companies use a piece rate system of compensation and expect the homeworkers to provide any necessary equipment. Some contracting firms will also provide pickup

---

MEGASUCCESS—HOME MANUFACTURING:
I WAS FRAMED

In the early 1970s, the Stantons crafted ribbon-covered picture frames to give out as Christmas gifts. Steve, an architect, made the wooden frames while wife Jan, a former fashion-school student, did the fabric cutting and gluing. The reaction of friends prompted the Stantons to ask, Would people pay for their creations? Jan's mother took some samples to stores in Beverly Hills and the answer was yes. She made the first sales and I Was Framed was no longer a hobby but a business.

For three years the operation was home-based, the den serving as a manufacturing space and the garage used for shipping. Sales growth forced a move to a much larger production facility and the product line was enlarged to encompass all sorts of boxes—gift, makeup, jewelry, and storage chests, as well as photo albums and desk blotters. Success was attributed to merchandise that had a unique, antique look, setting it apart from most shelf items. Dealers liked the items because the price gave them a nice markup. A treasure chest, for example, sold for $150.

More recently I Was Framed has focused on the promotional and premium markets and makes specialty items for firms such as Estée Lauder and Victoria's Secret. Less dependency on seasonal gifts has helped to even out cash flow. The Gardena, California, company employs 200 and annual sales are over $12 million.

MAIL-ORDER CATALOG COMPANIES REGULARLY PURCHASING PRODUCTS FROM SMALL BUSINESSES

A home-based entrepreneur is not likely to sell products to Sears or JCPenney, but there are many other mail-order catalog houses that will deal with small businesses. It's an excellent way for firms without an established marketing network to build sales volume. A formal product submission procedure must be followed and the catalog companies will forward the forms on request. To save submission time and wasted effort entrepreneurs should first become familiar with the catalog's products and prices. Listed below are major catalog companies selling gift and variety merchandise. There are many other catalog houses selling specialty items such as country wares, hobby products, and sport-related items. A complete compilation of almost 6,000 mail-order companies, listed by category, can be found in *The Directory of Mail Order Catalogs*, published by Grey House Publishing, Inc., Pocket Knife Square, Lakeville, CT 06039. Another valuable catalog source is Mail Order Business Director, B. Klein Publications, P. O. Box 8503, Coral Springs, FL 33065.

◆ Abbey Press, State Road 545, St. Meinrad, IN 47577. (Generally handles gifts, Christmas decorations, and a large variety of other items in the lower price range. About 20 million catalogs are mailed each year.)

◆ Bruce Bolind, 5421 Western Ave., Boulder, CO 80302. (Mails six catalogs a year. Specializes in inexpensive gifts and labels.)

◆ Harriet Carter Gifts, Stump Rd., Montgomeryville, PA 18936. (Mails gift catalogs six times a year to 950,000 families.)

◆ Spencer Gifts, 590 Spencer Building, Atlantic City, NJ 08411. (Sends out ninety-six-page catalog with inexpensive variety merchandise and also markets through retail outlets.)

◆ Walter Drake & Sons, Drake Building, Colorado Springs, CO 80940. (Sends general gift catalog to mailing list of over 2 million addresses.)

◆ Taylor Gifts, 355 E. Conestoga Rd., Wayne, PA 19087. (Mails three gift catalogs a year to three-quarters of a million prospective customers.)

◆ Carol Wright Gifts, 70 Seaview Avenue, Stamford, CT 06905. (General gifts for the home with a mailing list of 1.2 million.)

◆ Lillian Vernon, 543 Main Street, New Rochelle, NY 10801. (Moderate-priced products primarily targeted for female audience.)

◆ Miles Kimball, 41 W. Eighth Ave., Oshkosh, WI 54960. (Markets low-cost home and novelty items.)

and delivery services. For needle-trade companies offering work-at-home opportunities see Yellow Page listings under: Embroidery, Knit Goods, Hairpieces, Women's Apparel Manufacturing, Men's Clothing Manufacturing, Leather Clothing Manufacturing, Shirt Manufacturing, Sweaters, Tie Manufacturing.

Certain types of manufacturing companies are likely to job out work requiring basic factory skills. Homeworker entrepreneurs interested in assignments of this nature should make inquiries to firms engaged in industries such as shoe manufacturing, electronics, electromechanical products, wire harnesses, packaging, giftware, jewelry, hobby and model manufacturing, and craft items. However, any industrial company might be a source of work and solicitation letters could be written to all manufacturing businesses within a reasonable driving time from the home. Most libraries have industrial directories that list firms by county and city. Since the number of homeworkers usually exceeds the demand for suppliers, prices quoted must be very competitive.

SAMPLE LETTER TO LOCAL FIRMS SOLICITING CONTRACT WORK

Attention: Purchasing Director

I am a responsible, hard-working housewife with small children, seeking contract work to do at home. My prior experience includes assembly and packaging work at several industrial firms. I would also be amenable to jobs involving office work, such as collating and envelope stuffing.

I can assure you of quality work with fast turnaround. If you wish to discuss this further with me, I'm available for an interview at your convenience.

◆ ◆ ◆

A brief letter, such as the one above, sent to local firms within twenty minutes' driving time may net several at-home work assignments.

STATE OF NEW JERSEY
DEPARTMENT OF LABOR

Industrial Homeworker's Certificate

Number   **C №**

Issued at Trenton, N. J., on ....

THIS CERTIFICATE is issued in accordance with the provisions of Chapter 308, Laws of 1941, and entitles —

Name of Homeworker ....

Address ....

To manufacture industrial homework for —

Name of Employer ....

Address of factory or ....
business from which industrial
homework is distributed ....

THIS CERTIFICATE is not valid for any other employer and is issued for the following kind of industrial homework; no other work being permitted:

THIS CERTIFICATE is valid only for use of homeworker whose name appears hereon and expires on .... unless sooner revoked. It is not transferable.

Inspected by: .... on ....

Application approved: ....
Assistant Director, Office of Wage and Hour Compliance

Issuance authorized:

Charles Serraino
Commissioner
N.J. Department of Labor

NOTE: POST IN A CONSPICUOUS PLACE in room where work is being done. Keep your home in a clean and sanitary condition at all times. Industrial homework can only be done at address given above by person whose name appears hereon and only for employer whose name is shown above.

Some states require those working from home to obtain homeworker certificates to assure compliance with the law.

REVENUE FROM SELLING

Retailing from Home

21

For individuals who are comfortable with people, have talents in communication, and are assertive, home retailing can be quite lucrative. It can take two forms. The first is using the home essentially as a store—displaying merchandise and soliciting walk-in or drive-by customers. The second, however, is by far the most popular—distributing products for one of the many direct-selling companies that merchandise nationally.

STORE-TYPE RETAILING

Starting a home-retailing operation—a business that involves selling purchased merchandise from a variety of sources—requires: (1) having a home in an appropriately zoned area accessible to traffic; (2) knowing where to find and the price to pay for merchandise; and (3) the desire and ability to deal with the public. It is similar to other forms of retailing and entrepreneurs must learn how to attractively display products, negotiate prices with their suppliers, use persuasive techniques on customers, and do routine tasks such as handling cash, checks, and credit cards.

There are three types of retail stores that tend to do well from a home base: specific kinds of merchandise, antique shops, and consignment stores.

MEGASUCCESS—DIRECT SELLING: MARY KAY COSMETICS

Mary Kay Ash received her basic training in direct selling as marketing representative for Stanley Home Products. Operating out of her home, she held product demonstrations at customers' homes. This later became the primary selling technique of her cosmetics company.

After some years as a training director for another direct-sales organization, in 1963 she and her son opened a small cosmetics shop in Dallas with $5,000 in life savings. The firm promoted a new skin-care line and began recruiting women who conducted in-home beauty shows. Each home hostess received gifts and attendees were given lessons on skin care and makeup. This marketing strategy was in contrast to that of Mary Kay's leading direct-selling competitor, Avon, whose sales representatives functioned mostly as catalog order takers. Within three years Mary Kay Cosmetics was doing $800,000 a year in sales.

The company, still Dallas-based, now markets up to 250 personal care products, employs 1,500, and has an independent sales force of more than 200,000 consultants worldwide. Annual wholesale sales are over one billion dollars.

Merchandise. Home location determines to some degree the choice of product to retail. An entrepreneur on a thoroughfare with heavy traffic can survive on one-time purchases. Out-of-the-way sites must rely on repeat business from steady customers. While theoretically anything that can be sold retail can also be sold from home, certain types of businesses appear to be more successful than others. They include hobby and craft supplies, religious articles, stamps and coins, framing shops, and discount fashions.

Antique Shops. Just drive down any country back road used by tourists and you're likely to pass a number of houses or barns used as home-based retail stores for selling antiques, collectibles, handicrafts, and other items. Genuine antiques should be at least 100 years old but most antique dealers will carry anything old that they think will sell, such as collectibles. Antique merchandise is acquired from house auctions, at garage and yard sales and flea markets, and from browsing through secondhand shops. Antique dealers also trade and buy from one another. But don't put out the open-for-business sign before becoming reasonably familiar with what to pay for antiques. It takes time, study, and visits to other shops to learn the business.

Consignment Stores. There is little risk in selling merchandise you don't have to pay for until the cash is in hand. The most successful consignment shops deal in locally produced arts and crafts, with the entrepreneur receiving 20 percent to 40 percent of the selling price. General merchandise and clothing are also often sold through consignment shops, with second-hand children's items being the best movers.

DIRECT SELLING PRODUCT DISTRIBUTOR

Direct selling to the consumer is an $8-billion business and provides part-time employment to about 5 million people. A significant portion of this business is carried out by home entrepreneurs who serve as independent agents and distributors for firms such as Mary Kay, Amway, and Shaklee.

Product distributorships have some decided advantages for those new to the business world. Many products are well established and have consumer acceptance. In some instances selling simply consists of order taking, which may suit less sales-oriented entrepreneurs just fine. Some products, however, require disseminating information. For example, Mary Kay's beauty consultants are also expected to teach skin care. Discovery Toys' representatives educate mothers in the suitability of the various types of educational toys and games for individual children. Direct-sales firms also provide comprehensive promotion packages consisting of sales training, demonstration kits, and promotional literature—again, ideal for a novice with little business experience. A third advantage is that only minimum cash outlays are required, since merchandise is shipped on an as-ordered basis.

Sales are made by telephone contact, door-to-door solicitation, and customer drop-ins, and in business locations. However, the most popular selling technique is through party plans. Here the distributor-entrepreneur asks someone to serve as a hostess and invite friends and acquaintances to attend the product demonstration. Usually this takes place at the residence of the hostess, but it also can be at the home of the distributor. The gathering includes light refreshments and socializing—hence the term "party." After the demonstration, product orders are taken and bookings for future parties are solicited from guests at the same time. Some product distributors have stock on hand, while others deliver at a later date. The hostesses can share in the party profits, but usually the compensation is in distributor merchandise or gifts.

Distributors earn eight dollars to fifteen dollars an hour from product selling but much more money comes from multilevel marketing. This is the recruiting of other distributors and receiving commissions on their orders. For repeat-sale products, such as cosmetics and food supplements, earnings can reach very high levels for those supervising a number of aggressive distributors. A first-level manager for Tupperware, for example, can average about $25,000 a year in earnings.

There are also negatives to product distribution. Competition can be severe, since the products themselves are rarely unique and selling territories are not exclusive. Nevertheless, direct selling can be very lucrative for entrepreneurs skilled in the art of persuasion and motivated to go after new customers and other sales agents. What products are best to sell? The way to check out a company and its products is by hosting your own party and seeing firsthand how well the merchandise moves. Do this for several products and then make a decision.

DIRECT SELLING COMPANIES
(MEMBERS OF DIRECT SELLING ASSOCIATION)

Achievers Unlimited, Inc.	West Tower, 9th Floor 777 S. Flagler Drive West Palm Beach, FL 33401 **Phone: (561) 835-3777**	**Person-To-Person** Nutritional Products
Act II Jewelry, Inc., **Lady Remington**	818 Thorndale Avenue Bensenville, IL 60106 **Phone: (800) 487-3323**	**Party Plan** Jewelry
AdvoCare International	11431-A Ferrell Avenue Dallas, TX 75244 **Phone: (214) 831-1033**	**Person-To-Person** Weight Management Products, Skincare
Alliance U.S.A., Inc.	1100 East Campbell Richardson, TX 75081 **Phone: (214) 783-4994**	**Person-To-Person** Nutritional Products
AMC Corporation	595 Summer Street Stanford, CT 06901 **Phone: (203) 363-0331**	**Party Plan** Cookware, Multi- Cooking Systems

American Coin Collectors, Inc. (Gold Marketing Associates)
3403 North Pine Hills Road
Orlando, FL 32808-2835
Phone: (407) 296-9457

Party Plan and Person-To-Person
Collectibles

American Communications Network, Inc. (ACN)
100 West Big Beaver Road
Suite 400
Troy, MI 48084
Phone: (810) 528-2500

Person-To-Person
Long Distance Service, Debit Calling Card, Pay Phones, Telecommunications Services

Amway Corporation
7575 Fulton Street East
Ada, MI 49355-0001
Phone: (616) 787-6000

Person-To-Person
Homecare Products, Home Technology Products, Nutritional Products, Personal Care Products, Commercial Products/Services

Applebrook Family Enrichment Network
PO Box 40
Fremont, MI 49412
Phone: (616) 924-7113

Party Plan and Person-To-Person
Parenting Products, Nutritional Products

Arts Finds International, Inc.
1810 S. Lynhurst Drive
Suite A
Indianapolis, IN 46241
Phone: (317) 248-2666

Party Plan
Art

Artistic Impressions, Inc.
240 Cortland Avenue
Lombard, IL 60148
Phone: (630) 916-0050

Party Plan
Art

Assured Nutrition Plus
4279 Crumrine Road
Greenville, OH 45331
Phone: (513) 548-7713

Party Plan and Person-To-Person
Nutritional Products, Weight Management Products

Avon Products, Inc.
Nine West 57th Street
New York, NY 10019
Phone: (800) FOR-AVON

Person-To-Person
Cosmetics, Decorative Accessories, Giftware, Jewelry, Skincare, Toys/Games, Nutritional Products

Body Wise International, Inc.
6350 Palomar Oaks Court
Carlsbad, CA 92009
Phone: (617) 438-8977

Person-To-Person
Nutritional Products

Book of Life	PO Box 6130 Grand Rapids, MI 49516 **Phone: (800) 829-5233**	**Person-To-Person** Bible Reading Program, Educational Materials
Brite International	3421 South 500 West PO Box 65688 Salt Lake City, UT 84115 **Phone: (801) 263-9191**	**Party Plan and** **Person-To-Person** Cassettes, Books, Videos, Educational Materials
The Bron-Shoe Company	1313 Alum Creek Drive Columbus, OH 43209 **Phone: (614) 252-0967**	**Person-To-Person** Baby Shoe Bronzing
Busy Woman	919 South Main Street Snowflake, AZ 85937 **Phone: (520) 536-7705**	**Party Plan** Time Management Programs
Chambre' International	PO Box 995 West Union, SC 29696 **Phone: (864) 718-9119**	**Party Plan and** **Person-To-Person** Skincare, Cosmetics, Nutritional Products, Homecare Products
Charmelle	101 Townsend Suite 303 San Francisco, CA 94107 **Phone: (415) 284-1684**	**Party Plan and** **Person-To-Person** Jewelry
Cleveland Institute of **Electronics, Inc.**	1776 East 17th Street Cleveland, OH 44114 **Phone: (216) 781-9400**	**Person-To-Person** Vocational Training
Colesce Couture, Inc.	9004 Ambassador Row Dallas, TX 75247 **Phone: (214) 631-4860**	**Party Plan** Lingerie/Sleepware
Color Me Beautiful	14000 Thunderbolt Place Suite E Chantilly, VA 22021 **Phone: (703) 471-6400**	**Party Plan and** **Person-To-Person** Cosmetics, Skincare
Conklin Company, Inc.	551 Valley Park Drive PO Box 155 Shakopee, MN 55379 **Phone: (612) 445-6010**	**Party Plan and** **Person-To-Person** Personal Care Products, Homecare Products
Cookin' the American Way **(Division of House of Lloyd)**	11901 Grandview Road Grandview, MO 64030 **Phone: (800) 733-2465**	**Party Plan** Cookware

Cooks Know How	69 Mid County Drive Orchard Park, NY 14127 **Phone: (716) 667-1543**	**Party Plan** Cookware
Country Neighbors, Inc.	304 East 37th Street Vancouver, WA 98663 **Phone: (800) 681-8148**	**Party Plan** Crystal/China, Decorative Accessories
The Country Peddlers & Company of America, Inc.	5625 W. 115th Street Alsip, IL 60482 **Phone: (708) 597-1085**	**Party Plan** Decorative Accessories
Creative Memories	2815 Clearwater Road PO Box 767 St. Cloud, MN 56302 **Phone: (800) 328-2344**	**Party Plan** Photo Albums, Photo Album Supplies
CUTCO/Vector Corporation	1116 East State Street PO Box 1228 Olean, NY 14760-1228 **Phone: (716) 372-3111**	**Person-To-Person** Cutlery
Designer Nutrition America	3535 Route 66 Bldg. 2 Neptune, NJ 07753 **Phone: (908) 922-0777**	**Party Plan and Person-To-Person** Nutritional Products, Personal Care Products
Discovery Toys, Inc.	6400 Brisca Street Livermore, CA 94550 **Phone: (800) 426-4777**	**Party Plan** Toys/Games, Books, Childcare Products, Educational Materials, Videos
DK Family Learning	7800 Southland Boulevard Suite 200 Orlando, FL 32809 **Phone: (407) 857-5463**	**Party Plan and Person-To-Person** Books, Videos
Doncaster	Oak Springs Road Box 1159 Rutherforton, NC 28139 **Phone: (800) 669-3662**	**Person-To-Person** Clothing, Fashion Accessories
DS-MAX U.S.A., Inc.	15 Chrysler Street Irvine, CA 92718 **Phone: (714) 587-9207**	**Person-To-Person** Books, Business Products, Plants/ Foliage, Toys/Games, Giftware, House and Kitchenwares

Dudley Products, Inc.	1080 Old Greensboro Road Kernersville, NC 27284-3222 **Phone: (910) 993-8800**	**Person-To-Person** Cosmetics, Fragrances, Skincare, Haircare
Eagle Distributing Company, Inc.	7635 Main Street PO Box 410 Fishees, NY 14453 **Phone: (716) 924-2150**	**Person-To-Person** Fire Alarms/ Extinguishers
Ekco Home Products Company	2488 Townsgate Road Suite A Westlake Village, CA 91361 **Phone: (805) 494-1711**	**Person-To-Person** Cookware, Cutlery, Water Treatment Systems
Electrolux Corporation	2300 Windy Ridge Parkway Suite 900 Atlanta, GA 30339 **Phone: (770) 933-1000**	**Person-To-Person** Vacuum Cleaners, Homecare Products
Encyclopaedia Britannica, Inc.	Britannica Centre 310 South Michigan Avenue Chicago, IL 60604 **Phone: (312) 347-7247**	**Person-To-Person** Encyclopedias, Educational Materials
Enrich International	748 North 1340 West Orem, UT 84057 **Phone: (801) 226-2600**	**Party Plan and Person-To-Person** Health/Fitness Products, Skincare
ENVION International	472 Amherst Street Nashua, NH 03063 **Phone: (603) 881-7873**	**Person-To-Person** Nutritional Products, Personal Care Products
Equinox International	1211 Town Center Drive Las Vegas, NV 89134 **Phone: (702) 877-2287**	**Person-To-Person** Water Treatment Systems, Air Filters, Nutritional Products, Skincare, Cosmetics, Haircare, Personal Care Products, Homecare Products, Weight Management Products
Excel Communications, Inc.	8750 North Central Expressway Suite 2000 Dallas, TX 75231 **Phone: (214) 863-8000**	**Person-To-Person** Long Distance Service

Finesse	668 Beale Street Memphis, TN 38103-3205 **Phone: (901) 526-1137**	**Party Plan** Jewelry
ForYou, Inc.	4235 Main Street PO Box 1216 Loris, SC 29569 **Phone: (803) 756-9000**	**Party Plan and** **Person-To-Person** Skincare, Self-improvement Programs
The Fuller Brush Company	One Fuller Way PO Box 729 Great Bend, KS 67530 **Phone: (800) 874-0016**	**Person-To-Person** Homecare Products, House and Kitchen- wares, Personal Care Products
Gold Marketing Associates	3403 North Pine Hills Road Orlando, FL 32808-2835 **Phone: (407) 296-9457**	**Party Plan and** **Person-To-Person** Collectibles, Jewelry
Golden Neo-Life Diamite International	3500 Gateway Blvd. Fremont, CA 94537-5012 **Phone: (510) 651-0405**	**Person-To-Person** Nutritional Products, Homecare Products, Skincare, Water Treatment Systems, Weight Management Products
Golden Pride/Rawleigh, Inc.	PO Box 21109 West Palm Beach, FL 33416-1109 **Phone: (561) 640-5700**	**Person-To-Person** Nutritional Products, Weight Management Products, Health/ Fitness Products, House and Kitchen- wares, Water Treat- ment Systems, Food/ Beverage Products, Skincare
Goldlinx USA, Inc.	6725 Millcreek Drive Suite 5 Mississauga, Ontario L5N 5V3 Canada **Phone: (905) 567-9449**	**Person-To-Person** Skincare, Cosmetics, Nutritional Products
Herbalife International	PO Box 80210 Los Angeles, CA 90080-0210 **Phone: (310) 410-9600**	**Person-To-Person** Weight Management Products, Nutritional Products, Personal Care Products, Fragrances

Highlights for Children, Inc.   2300 West Fifth Avenue   **Person-To-Person**
PO Box 269   Educational Materials
Columbus, OH 43216
Phone: (614) 486-0631

Home Interiors & Gifts, Inc.   4550 Spring Valley Road   **Party Plan**
Dallas, TX 75244-3705   Decorative
Phone: (972) 386-1000   Accessories, Giftware

The Homemakers Idea   1420 Thorndale   **Party Plan**
Company (Wicker World   Elk Grove Village, IL 60007   Decorative
Enterprises)   **Phone: (800) 800-5452**   Accessories

House of Lloyd, Inc.   11901 Grandview Road   **Party Plan**
Grandview, MO 64030   Christmas Decorations,
Phone: (800) 733-2465   Giftware, Decorative
Accessories,
Toys/Games

H.Q. International, Inc.   1985 Forest Lane   **Person-To-Person**
Garland, TX 75042   Nutritional Products,
Phone: (972) 272-9400   Skincare, Personal
Care Products,
Autocare Products

Hsin Ten Enterprise   100 Commercial Street   **Party Plan and**
USA, Inc.   Plainview, NY 11803   **Person-To-Person**
Phone: (516) 576-1616   Health/Fitness
Products

Hy Cite Corporation   333 Holzman Road   **Party Plan and**
Madison, WI 53713-2109   **Person-To-Person**
Phone: (608) 273-3373   Cookware, Crystal/
China, Water
Treatment Systems

Integrity International, Inc.   220 Reese Road   **Person-To-Person**
State College, PA 16801   Stop Smoking
Phone: (814) 237-9111   Products, Weight
Management
Products, Nutritional
Products, Long
Distance Service, Fire
Alarms/Extinguishers

Intelligent Nutrients   321 Lincoln Street, NE   **Person-To-Person**
Minneapolis, MN 55413   Weight Management
Phone: (612) 617-2000   Products, Nutritional
Products

Interior Design Nutritionals (Division of Nu Skin International)	75 West Center Street Provo, UT 84601 **Phone: (801) 345-9000**	**Person-To-Person** Nutritional Products, Weight Management Products
Interstate Engineering	522 E. Vermont Avenue Anaheim, CA 92805-5698 **Phone: (714) 758-5011**	**Person-To-Person** Vacuum Cleaners
Jafra Cosmetics International, Inc.	2451 Townsgate Road Westlake Village, CA 91361 **Phone: (800) 551-2345**	**Party Plan and Person-To-Person** Skincare, Cosmetics, Fragrances
Jeunesse Cosmetics, Inc.	342 Madison Avenue Suite 823 New York, NY 10173 **Phone: (212) 682-7282**	**Party Plan and Person-To-Person** Cosmetics, Skincare
Jeunique International, Inc.	19501 E. Walnut Drive PO Box 1950 City of Industry, CA 91749 **Phone: (909) 598-8598**	**Party Plan and Person-To-Person** Cosmetics, Lingerie/ Sleepwear, Nutritional Products, Skincare
JewelQuest	PO Box 749 Great Falls, VA 22066 **Phone: (800) 771-4566**	**Party Plan and Person-To-Person** Jewelry
KareMor International, Inc.	2401 S. 24th Street Phoenix, AZ 85034 **Phone: (602) 244-8976**	**Person-To-Person** Nutritional Products, Weight Management Products
Kids Only Clothing Club, Inc.	5775 11th Street, SE Calgary, Alberta T2H 1M7 Canada **Phone: (403) 252-9667**	**Party Plan** Clothing
The Kirby Company	1920 West 114th Street Cleveland, OH 44102-2391 **Phone: (216) 228-2400**	**Person-To-Person** Vacuum Cleaners
Kitchen Fair (Regal Ware, Inc.)	1090 Redmond Road PO Box 100 Jacksonville, AR 72076 **Phone: (501) 982-0555**	**Party Plan** Cookware, Decorative Accessories, House and Kitchenwares
Kizure Products Company, Inc.	1950 North Central Avenue Compton, CA 90222 **Phone: (310) 604-0032**	**Person-To-Person** Haircare

Lady Love Skin Care	PO Box 867687 Plano, TX 75086-7687 **Phone: (214) 596-5239**	**Party Plan and** **Person-To-Person** Skincare
Lancié, Inc.	800 3rd Avenue 36th Floor New York, NY 10022 **Phone: (212) 308-3383**	**Party Plan and** **Person-To-Person** Cosmetics, Skincare, Haircare, Personal Care Products, Fashion Accessories
LifeRich Limited Company	360 B Street PO Box 51980 Idaho Falls, ID 83405-1980 **Phone: (208) 525-7850**	**Person-To-Person** Nutritional Products, Personal Care Products
The Longaberger Company	95 Chestnut Street Dresden, OH 43821-9600 **Phone: (800) 966-0374**	**Party Plan** Decorative Accessories, House and Kitchenwares
Longevity Network, Ltd.	15 Cactus Garden Drive Henderson, NV 89014 **Phone: (702) 454-7000**	**Person-To-Person** Nutritional Products, Skincare, Haircare, Personal Care Products
Market America, Inc.	7605-A Business Park Drive Greensboro, NC 27409 **Phone: (910) 605-0040**	**Person-To-Person** Personal Care Products, Nutritional Products, Homecare Products, Autocare Products, Photography
Mary Kay, Inc.	16251 Dallas Parkway Dallas, TX 75248 **Phone: (800) MARY-KAY**	**Party Plan and** **Person-To-Person** Cosmetics, Skincare
Masterguard Corporation	155 Howell Street Dallas, TX 75207 **Phone: (214) 651-7300**	**Party Plan and** **Person-To-Person** Fire Alarms/ Extinguishers
Melaleuca, Inc.	3910 South Yellowstone Hwy. Idaho Falls, ID 83402 **Phone: (208) 522-0700**	**Person-To-Person** Nutritional Products, Personal Care Products, Homecare Products

Melissa Rice and Company	6937 Flintlock Houston, TX 77040 **Phone: (800) 345-1133**	**Party Plan and** **Person-To-Person** Clothing, Home Accessories
Multiples At Home	1431 Regal Row Dallas, TX 75247 **Phone: (800) 727-8875**	**Party Plan** Clothing
Muscle Dynamics Fitness Network, Inc.	20100 Hamilton Avenue Torrance, CA 90502 **Phone: (310) 715-8036**	**Person-To-Person** Health/Fitness Products, Nutritional Products, Weight Maintenance Products
National Telephone & Communications, Inc.	2801 Main Street Irvine, CA 92614 **Phone: (714) 251-8000**	**Person-To-Person** Long Distance Service
Natural World	7373 North Scottsdale Road Suite A-280 Scottsdale, AZ 85253 **Phone: (602) 905-1110**	**Person-To-Person** Haircare, Homecare Products, Nutritional Products, Skincare
Nature's Sunshine Products, Inc.	75 East 1700 South PO Box 19005 Provo, UT 84605-9005 **Phone: (801) 342-4300**	**Person-To-Person** Nutritional Products, Skincare, Water Treatment Systems, Cookware
Nest Entertainment, Inc.	6100 Colwell Blvd. Irving, TX 75039 **Phone: (214) 402-7100**	**Party Plan and** **Person-To-Person** Bible Video Tapes, Videos, Audio Tapes, Educational Materials
New Image International, Inc.	PO Box 1038 Georgetown, KY 40324 **Phone: (502) 867-1895**	**Person-To-Person** Weight Management Products, Nutritional Products
Newone Cosmetics Corporation	4525 Wilshire Blvd. Suite 140 Los Angeles, CA 90010 **Phone: (213) 930-1701**	**Party Plan and** **Person-To-Person** Skincare, Cosmetics, Nutritional Products
Nikken, Inc.	15363 Barranca Pkwy. Irvine, CA 92618 **Phone: (714) 789-2000**	**Party Plan and** **Person-To-Person** Bedding Products, Nutritional Products

Noevir USA, Inc.	1095 SE Main Street Irvine, CA 92714 **Phone: (800) USA-8888**	**Person-To-Person** Skincare, Cosmetics, Nutritional Products
NSA	4260 East Raines Road Memphis, TN 38118 **Phone: (901) 366-9288**	**Person-To-Person** Air Filters, Water Treatment Systems, Educational Materials, Nutritional Products
Nu Skin International, Inc.	75 W. Center Street Provo, UT 84601 **Phone: (801) 345-1000**	**Party Plan and** **Person-To-Person** Haircare, Nutritional Products, Skincare
Nutri-Metrics International (USA) Inc.	12723 166th Street Cerritos, CA 90703-2157 **Phone: (310) 802-0411**	**Party Plan and** **Person-To-Person** Skincare, Cosmetics, Nutritional Products, Homecare Products
Nutrix International, LLC	2001 North Clybourn Avenue Suite 403 Chicago, IL 60614 **Phone: (800) 468-8749**	**Party Plan and** **Person-To-Person** Health Care Apparel
Oriflame U.S.A.	4630 Cerritos Avenue Los Alamitos, CA 90720 **Phone: (800) 959-0699**	**Person-To-Person** Skincare, Cosmetics, Fragrances, Nutritional Products
Oxyfresh Worldwide, Inc.	East 12928 Indiana Avenue PO Box 3723 Spokane, WA 99220 **Phone: (509) 924-4999**	**Person-To-Person** Dental Hygiene, Skincare, Animalcare Products/Food Nutritional Products, Haircare, Homecare Products, Personal Care Products
Oxygen For Life, Inc.	1290 San Marcos Blvd. San Marcos, CA 92069 **Phone: (800) 619-6994**	**Person-To-Person** Stabilized Oxygen, Weight Management Products, Nutritional Products
The Pampered Chef, Ltd.	350 South Rohlwing Road Addison, IL 60101-3079 **Phone: (709) 261-8900**	**Party Plan** House and Kitchen- wares, Cookware

PartyLite Gifts, Inc.	PO Box 976 Plymouth, MA 02362-0976 **Phone: (508) 830-3100**	**Party Plan** Candles, Candle Accessories
Personal Creations Gift Shows, Inc.	530 Executive Drive Willowbrook, IL 60521 **Phone: (630) 655-3200**	**Party Plan** Personalized Gifts
Petra Fashions, Inc.	35 Cherry Hill Park Danvers, MA 01923 **Phone: (508) 777-5853**	**Party Plan** Lingerie/Sleepwear
Pfaltzgraff/Flemington Outlet Corporation	140 East Market Street York, PA 17401 **Phone: (717) 848-5500**	**Party Plan and Person-To-Person** Tableware
Pola U.S.A., Inc.	251 East Victoria Street Carson, CA 90746 **Phone: (310) 527-9696**	**Party Plan and Person-To-Person** Skincare, Cosmetics, Haircare, Fragrances
Premier Designs, Inc.	1551 Corporate Drive Irving, TX 75038-2431 **Phone: (800) 486-SERV**	**Party Plan and Person-To-Person** Jewelry
Primerica Financial Services	3120 Breckenridge Boulevard Duluth, GA 30199-0001 **Phone: (770) 381-1000**	**Person-To-Person** Financial/Investment Services, Insurance
Princess House, Inc.	455 Somerset Avenue North Dighton, MA 02754 **Phone: (800) 622-0039**	**Party Plan** Decorative Accessories, Crystal/ China, Jewelry
PRP Wine International, Inc.	1701 Howard Street Elk Grove Village, IL 60007 **Phone: (847) 290-7800**	**Person-To-Person** Wine
RACHAeL International	1706 East Semoran Blvd. Suite 114 Apopka, FL 32703 **Phone: (800) 366-3806**	**Party Plan and Person-To-Person** Skincare, Haircare, Cosmetics, Nutritional Products
Regal Ware, Inc.	1675 Reigle Drive Kewaskum, WI 53040 **Phone: (414) 626-2121**	**Party Plan and Person-To-Person** Cookware, Cutlery, Tableware, Water Treatment Systems

Reliv', Inc.	PO Box 405 Chesterfield, MO 63006-0405 **Phone: (314) 537-9715**	**Person-To-Person** Nutritional Products, Personal Care Products
Rena-Ware Distributors, Inc.	PO Box 97050 Redmond, WA 98073-9750 **Phone: (206) 881-6171**	**Party Plan and** **Person-To-Person** Cookware
Rexair, Inc.	3221 W. Big Beaver Road Suite 200 Troy, MI 48084 **Phone: (810) 643-7222**	**Person-To-Person** Vacuum Cleaners, Homecare Products
Rexall Showcase **International**	853 Broken Sound Pkway, NW Boca Raton, FL 33487-3694 **Phone: (561) 994-2090**	**Person-To-Person** Health/Fitness Products, Nutritional Products, Water Treatment Systems, Personal Care Products
Rich Plan Corporation	4981 Commercial Drive Yorkville, NY 13495 **Phone: (800) 243-1358**	**Person-To-Person** Food/Beverage Products, Home Appliances
RMC Group, Inc.	2969 Interstate Street Charlotte, NC 28208 **Phone: (704) 393-1860**	**Party Plan and** **Person-To-Person** Skincare, Nutritional Products, Fragrances, Cosmetics
Saladmaster, Inc. **(Regal Ware, Inc.)**	912 113th Street Arlington, TX 76011-5407 **Phone: (817) 633-3555**	**Party Plan and** **Person-To-Person** Cookware, Tableware
Seaborne, Inc.	6200 Windward Parkway Alpharetta, GA 30202 **Phone: (770) 663-6633**	**Party Plan and** **Person-To-Person** Nutritional Products
Shaklee Corporation	Shaklee Terraces 444 Market Street San Francisco, CA 94111 **Phone: (415) 954-3000**	**Person-To-Person** Nutritional Products, Personal Care Products, Homecare Products, Water Treatment Systems
Shaperite	9850 South 300 West Sandy, UT 84070 **Phone: (800) 562-3600**	**Person-To-Person** Weight Management Products, Personal Care Products

Society Corporation	1515 W. Kilgore Avenue Muncie, IN 47304 **Phone: (317) 289-3318**	**Person-To-Person** Cookware, Crystal/ China, Cutlery, Tableware, Water Treatment Systems
The Southwestern Company	PO Box 305140 Nashville, TN 37230-5140 **Phone: (615) 391-2500**	**Person-To-Person** Books, Educational Materials
Sportron International, Inc.	1249 Commerce Richardson, TX 75081 **Phone: (800) 843-1202**	**Person-To-Person** Nutritional Products, Weight Management Products, Skincare, Homecare Products
Stanley Home Products	50 Payson Avenue East Hampton, MA 01027 **Phone: (413) 527-4001**	**Party Plan and** **Person-To-Person** Homecare Products, Personal Care Products
Stef International Corporation	6870 Goreway Drive Mississauga, Ontario L4V 1P1 Canada **Phone: (905) 672-3212**	**Person-To-Person** Personal Care Products, Nutritional Products
The Story Teller	308 East 800 South PO Box 921 Salem, UT 84653 **Phone: (801) 423-2560**	**Party Plan** Books, Educational Materials, Cassettes, Toys/Games
Success Motivation Institute	1600 Lake Air Drive Waco, TX 76710 **Phone: (817) 776-1230**	**Person-To-Person** Self-improvement Program, Time Management Programs
Sunrider International	1625 Abalone Avenue Torrance, CA 90501 **Phone: (310) 781-3808**	**Party Plan and** **Person-To-Person** Nutritional Products, Skincare, Personal Care Products, Cosmetics, Homecare Products
Symmetry Corporation	420 South Hillview Drive Milpitas, CA 95035 **Phone: (408) 942-7700**	**Party Plan and** **Person-To-Person** Nutritional Products, Weight Management Products

Table Charm Corporation	248 Steelcase Road East Markham, Ontario L3R 1G2 Canada **Phone: (905) 470-7861**	**Person-To-Person** Cookware, Tableware
Tiara Exclusives	717 E. Street Dunkirk, IN 47336 **Phone: (317) 768-7821**	**Party Plan** Decorative Accessories, Tableware
Totally Tropical Interiors, Ltd.	4310-12th Street, NE Suite 100 Calgary, Alberta T2E 6K9 Canada **Phone: (403) 291-9366**	**Party Plan** Plants/Foliage, Decorative Accessories
Tri-Chem, Inc.	One Cape May Street Harrison, NJ 07029 **Phone: (201) 482-5500**	**Party Plan** Crafts
Tupperware Corporation	PO Box 2353 Orlando, FL 32802-2353 **Phone: (407) 826-5050**	**Party Plan and Person-To-Person** House and Kitchen- wares, Toys/Games
United Consumers Club, Inc.	8450 South Broadway Merrillville, IN 46410 **Phone: (219) 736-1100**	**Party Plan** Group Buying Services
U.S. Safety & Engineering Corporation	2365 El Camino Avenue Sacramento, CA 95821 **Phone: (916) 482-8888**	**Person-To-Person** Security Systems/ Devices
USANA, Inc.	3838 West Parkway Blvd. West Valley City, UT 84120 **Phone: (801) 954-7200**	**Party Plan and Person-To-Person** Nutritional Products, Skincare
Usborne Books at Home	10302 East 55 Place Tulsa, OK 74146 **Phone: (800) 475-4522**	**Party Plan and Person-To-Person** Books
Vita Craft Corporation	11100 West 58 Street PO Box 3129 Shawnee, KS 66203 **Phone: (913) 631-6265**	**Party Plan and Person-To-Person** Cookware, Crystal/ China, Cutlery, Table- ware, Water Treatment Systems

Viva America Marketing, Inc.	1239 Victoria Street Costa Mesa, CA 92627 **Phone: (800) 243-8482**	**Party Plan and Person-To-Person** Nutritional Products, Skincare, Weight Management Products, Fitness Products
Watkins Incorporated	150 Liberty Street Winona, MN 55987-0570 **Phone: (507) 457-3300**	**Party Plan and Person-To-Person** Food/Beverage Products, Health/Fitness Products
Weekender Casual Wear, Inc.	1485 Busch Parkway Buffalo Grove, IL 60089 **Phone: (847) 465-1666**	**Party Plan** Clothing
The West Bend Company	400 Washington Street West Bend, WI 53095 **Phone: (414) 334-6935**	**Party Plan and Person-To-Person** Cookware, Water Treatment Systems
Wicker Plus, Ltd.	N112 W 14600 Mequon Road Germantown, WI 53022 **Phone: (414) 255-7377**	**Party Plan** Decorative Accessories
The Workshops of Gerald E. Henn	1001 Country Way Warren, OH 44481 **Phone: (330) 824-2575**	**Party Plan** Decorative Accessories
World Book, Inc.	525 West Monroe Street 20th Floor Chicago, IL 60661 **Phone: (312) 258-3933**	**Person-To-Person** Encyclopedias, Educational Materials
Youngevity, Inc.	4951 Airport Pkwy. Dallas, TX 75248 **Phone: (800) 469-6864**	**Person-To-Person** Nutritional Products

22

IF IT'S BROKEN, FIX IT FOR MONEY

Repair-Related Home Businesses

R epair-related services offer some of the more lucrative homebased opportunities. Many items are too valuable to discard and people are always seeking out convenient and reliable local repair services. Where special skills are required, hourly fees charged can be as high as forty dollars.

Four types of repair services have a good success record in home operation—furniture repair, restoration, and refinishing; equipment repair; fix-it shops; and a variety of auto services. Entrepreneurs going into these businesses should prefer physical, hands-on work and possess the necessary technical aptitude. Affordable advertising and promotional techniques include house signs, if legal; neighborhood door-to-door distribution of fliers or fliers placed under auto wiper blades; telephone directory listings; posters in the windows of retail stores and supermarkets; and classified advertising in the appropriate classifications.

FURNITURE REPAIR, RESTORATION, AND REFINISHING SERVICES

Furniture today is not inexpensive and most consumers are willing to pay reasonable amounts to have items repaired. Providing such a service can be a profitable home business for a skilled craftsman with a large basement or garage. Repairing and restoring old furniture, especially antiques, is very popular. This entails stripping off the old finish, sanding, refinishing, regluing chairs, replacing hinges, and so forth. Chair caning and upholstery services are also in demand. Charges are based on an estimate of the number of hours to complete the job. Additional business revenue can come from buying used furniture at house auctions and flea markets, restoring the items, and reselling them retail or to antique stores.

EQUIPMENT REPAIR SERVICES

Many homeowners have engine-powered equipment—lawn mowers, snow blowers, chain saws—that requires regular maintenance and periodic repairs. Services should include—in addition to repairs and annual seasonal maintenance—cleaning and lubrication, oil change, spark plug replacement, blade sharpening for mowers, and so forth. Rebuilding and reselling used items is another source of revenue. While dealing direct with the consumer is the primary sales method, contacts may also be made with retailers, such as hardware stores, which sell the products but prefer to job out the service work. They can serve as convenient drop-off points for consumers with defective equipment, and can be paid a commission of 20 percent to 30 percent.

FIX-IT SHOP

For a small investment in basic tools plus a workbench and shelving located in a basement, garage, or spare room, an entrepreneur can provide a local fix-it service. Special technical talents may not be needed. General handyman mechanical and electrical skills, combined with service manuals, can be adequate. Small appliances, telephones, bicycles, video games, lamps, typewriters, leather products, and toys are the most frequently repaired. Other services can include assembly of products, such as bicycles and toys, for consumers without the time or aptitude. Sharpening knives, scissors, mower blades, skates, and so forth is another service that can add revenue. Some entrepreneurs specialize. Home businesses servicing antique clocks and restoring porcelain have been quite successful. These services also supplement income by buying, repairing, and reselling items. Other repair services suitable for home operation are jewelry, watches, musical instruments, and electronic components. Hourly rates charged for conventional repair services generally must be in the low range, since the products themselves sell for less than one hundred dollars new and consumers will not pay more than 40 percent of the new price on repairs. Antique item repairs command higher prices.

AUTO SERVICES

People are always spending money on automobiles, and a number of home business options are available to entrepreneurs who have garages or driveways. Handling consumers on a by-appointment-only basis often permits this activity to go on in residential areas.

An *oil change service* is a business that can be done by home entrepreneurs without special skills. Customers would schedule appointments in advance so the right oil filter would be on hand when the car is brought in for service. *Winterizing*—radiator flush, antifreeze change, hose and battery check—can be another income add-on. Gas stations no longer perform many services to keep cars running and few gas pump attendants are qualified mechanics. This opens up opportunities for skilled home entrepreneurs.

Tune-up services, brake services, and *general auto repair* are the most popular home operations and justify high hourly billing rates. Less popular auto-related businesses, but still suitable for home operation, are tire sales and service, air-conditioning service, security system installation and service, tape players, stereo systems, and CB radio sales, installations, and service, carburetor rebuilding, and engine overhaul. Some individuals also add to profits by buying used cars, doing the necessary repair work, and reselling them. In addition to autos, services might include motorcycles and minibikes.

DOLLARS FOR LESSONS

Educating/Instructing Work-at-Home Business Opportunities

23

Having students come in after school for help in math or holding small group classes is a popular and profitable home business and can be started by anyone who has knowledge of a special subject, has an ability to communicate, and can turn a room of his or her apartment or house into a classroom. Formal training or credentials are rarely needed for providing education from the home. The business does require enthusiasm and patience on the part of the entrepreneur.

Teaching can take three forms: (1) one-on-one tutoring, such as working with slow learners; (2) group instruction (a group of up to eight people is appropriate for most subjects); and (3) running clinics, for example, for weight loss or to quit smoking. Individual instruction brings in $8 to $15 an hour while group pricing goes from $5 to $10 per student hour. Clinics charge $5 to $7 for each visit. Fees vary by subject and location. Material costs for classes are usually minimal—pads, pencils, some reproduced handouts. Books and course supplies should be provided but charged for separately. Taking courses given by others is a good way to get acquainted with what's required to get started in the teaching business. Instructional techniques and the materials used can provide entrepreneurs with ideas for preparing their own course.

MEGASUCCESS—EDUCATION: STANLEY H. KAPLAN EDUCATIONAL CENTERS

Many people consider the Stanley H. Kaplan Educational Centers the Harvard Business School of test preparation. Few, however, are aware of the company's modest beginnings. The founder and present CEO, Stan Kaplan, started the school in the basement of his Brooklyn home.

Stan's love for teaching goes back to his youth. While attending high school he tutored students, charging them twenty-five cents an hour. The Stanley H. Kaplan Educational Centers started in 1938, after Stan graduated from college, and the operation remained in his home until the end of World War II. The glut of returning veterans going to school under the G.I. Bill forced most colleges to rely on the Scholastic Aptitude Test (SAT) as one of the criteria for admission. The tutoring business boomed and Stan's company expanded nationally. In addition to college admissions testing, the firm offers preparation courses for licensing examinations and self-improvement, such as speed reading.

Every year more than 150,000 students attend the school's 150 permanent and 600 satellite centers, paying several hundred dollars each. The firm operates from an extensive office complex in midtown Manhattan and is now owned by The Washington Post Company.

The types of courses that will attract sufficient numbers of students will vary by population region. Here are the general categories and some examples of the subjects that lend themselves to home instruction:

◆ *Individual tutoring:* For slow learners (e.g., remedial reading), specialized subjects (e.g., math, English), for students with emotional or psychological problems, for the disabled, foreign languages (e.g., for businesspeople going overseas, students, vacationers), religious instruction, musical instruments, vocal, acting, dancing.

◆ *Personal growth instruction:* Public speaking, speed reading, assertiveness training, self-hypnosis, increasing your vocabulary, getting organized, how to meet people and carry on a conversation, how to look beautiful, memory improvement.

◆ *Career orientation:* Finding a better job, career success, how-to courses in any career subject (e.g., computer programming, typing, word processing, office skills, how to run a retail store), managing people, how to get into a top school.

- *Leisure time activity instruction:* Food preparation, arts and crafts, hobbies, bridge, chess, yoga, introduction to the personal computer, winning at blackjack, photography.
- *Special subject teaching:* How to invest, how to make money in real estate, first aid, gun safety, exam preparation, licensing preparation.

Making people aware of the courses being offered can sometimes be difficult. Posters in high-traffic locations help get the word out. Sharply focused promotions will probably be the most effective. A mailing to senior citizen groups, for example, would likely attract a number of individuals to leisure-time activity instruction.

PART FOUR

Profitable Cybermarketing: Using the Internet to Launch and Grow Your Home Business

MAKE YOUR HOME OPERATION A GLOBAL COMPANY 24

How to Establish a Presence on The Web

America is going on-line and creating new and exciting opportunities for those seeking a home business career, as well as for entrepreneurs already working from home. On-line technology—the Internet—is making it possible for small-time ventures, operating out of spare rooms and garages, to reach customers in the global marketplace. But while opening a business on the Internet is relatively easy, turning a profit isn't. Many businesses have discovered that success requires more than simply hanging out a shingle in cyberspace. The Internet isn't just a new twist in marketing, but a completely new medium following its own set of rules.

Covered in this new section of *Home Business ◆ Big Business* are ways the Internet can be used to start a new home venture, or enhance an existing one. Emphasis is on the three areas most critical to success.

Creating a distinctive Web site.

Choosing the right on-line business.

Making money on the Internet.

WHAT BEING ON-LINE MEANS TO A HOME BUSINESS

- Makes reaching a huge audience affordable.
- Gives customers direct access to sales literature at no incremental cost to the seller.
- Permits the business to serve customers 24 hours a day, 7 days a week, without staffing.
- Allows marketing materials and product pricing to be instantaneously updated at almost no expense.

MEGASUCCESS—INTERNET PIONEER MARC ANDREESSEN AND MOSAIC

For about thirty years the Internet linked government agencies, universities, and research centers with software only those well-versed in computer technology could master. In the early 1990s University of Illinois undergraduate student, Marc Andreessen and some associates, developed a much simpler program. They called it a browser and gave it the name *Mosaic*. It enabled any computer user to navigate the Internet. Millions of hobbyists started tying onto the network. Businesses, seeing the situation as an unprecedented marketing opportunity, joined the "gold rush." That was the beginning of the World Wide Web. Marc later designed a much-improved Web browser, *Navigator*, and formed a company, *Netscape*, to market the software. When the firm went public, Marc's shares were worth $100 million. He had just turned 25.

◆ *What is the Internet and how does it differ from the World Wide Web?*

The Internet is an interconnected global network of millions of computers. The World Wide Web, The Web for short, is the commercial segment of the Internet and consists of a mix of text, graphics, sound, and electronic data-file transfer capability—all of which operate under a common language umbrella. To keep things simple, think of the Internet as the hardware and The Web as the software. While the Internet and Web are technically different, the terms are very often used interchangeably to describe a system of electronic commerce.

◆ *What can the Internet do for a home-based business?*

Possibly the best answer comes from entrepreneur Alycia Carmin, owner of *Jake and Me*, a tiny children's clothing manufacturer located in Kersey, Colorado—population 1,200. "I'm out here in Nowheresville and have contact with people all over the world."

In the past, money-factors such as real estate, bricks and mortar, and sophisticated marketing gave big business significant competitive advantages over small business. These capital-driven elements are now being replaced by the Internet's personal computer and interactive electronic marketing network—a system readily affordable even to solo operators working from home on shoestring budgets. The experience of a company named *HOT HOT HOT* well illustrates how the playing field between big and small business is being leveled. Prior to

going on-line, this 300-square-foot Pasadena, California–based spicy chili merchant sold to a mostly local market. But after the firm invested a few thousand dollars for a professionally produced Web site, sales jumped. Orders started to come in from as far away as New Zealand. In just two years, the Internet made this husband-and-wife micro-business an international company.

THE STORE NEVER CLOSES

Technology permits cyberstores to accept orders 24 hours a day. But not everyone yet completely trusts electronic transmission of their credit card number and may prefer to call in the order. The problem is that a 9 PM call from Honolulu arrives on the east coast at 2 AM. Solo-operated home businesses can get around this problem—or any inconvenience created by phone calls—by using the services of a phone center. They usually work with toll-free (e.g. 800, 888) numbers. When a call comes in, the telephone operator using a computer screen provides information and processes the order following a client-prepared script. The order or message is then E-mailed or faxed to the client. The cost depends on the level of service and there's a minimum, but the average is $1.00–$1.50 per call, plus the cost of the call.

So in answer to the question, "What does the Internet do for home-based business?"—it makes entrepreneurial creativity count more than size and resources.

◆ *Who uses the Internet?*

Tens of millions of people are now on-line, but only about a quarter of them do any purchasing. The rest are just browsers. Demographically, Internet users very much differ from the U.S. population as a whole: they are overwhelmingly male, two-thirds are in the 18 to 54 age range and are generally better educated. If your business is selling books and records, the Internet has a good chance of working for you. But if you're peddling factory work clothes, don't expect to see any sales miracles. At least not right now. But as technology links The Web to the television set, electronic commerce will become much more mainstream. The real revolution in marketing is still a few years off.

◆ *What's a typical transaction like on the Internet?*

It begins with a file of information called a Web site. This is nothing more than digitized text and graphics, though some sites also have sound. A site can consist of one or more pages. The pages are digitally linked so they can easily be "flipped through"—sort of the way you would thumb through a mail-order catalog. Internet users who know the Web-site address, called a Universal Resource Locator, or URL for short, keyboard it into their terminal. If the exact address is not known, the user can refer to various types of Internet indices. Up pops the Web site's first page, commonly known as the Home page. The information displayed on the screen can be viewed and usually, but not always, copied. Downloading is the technical term for copying. If the Web site is programmed to accept orders or linked to an E-mail ordering system, an on-line form will guide users through the process. Shipping charges and taxes are usually shown on the order form. Payment over the Internet is by credit-card number and most systems are capable of encoding the data for transmission security. A click of the mouse sends the order on its way.

HOW COMPUTER USERS LOCATE A WEB SITE

People familiar with a company can bring it up on the screen by simply inputting the Internet address—the URL. If the exact address is not known, it can be looked up in one of the business-locating databases—essentially the Internet's telephone White Pages. Infoseek, Four11, and Switchboard are the most frequently used databases.

Surfers seeking a product, service, or information supplier without having any particular company in mind have to do a search by keyword or phrase. There are two types of search sites. Directories are indices sorted by humans into category and subcategory formats. They're the Internet's Yellow Pages and Yahoo is used the most. Search engines, the other type of index, utilize computers to digitally comb through site pages for the keyword or phrase. Alta Vista, Excite, HotBot, and Infoseek are the major search engines. Search engines have been criticized for producing too many irrelevant matches, forcing surfers to sift through volumes of useless listings before finding what they want.

POPULAR
WEB PAGE—
CREATING
SOFTWARE

Home Page (by Claris)
Pagemill (by Adobe)
FrontPage (by Microsoft)
Compose (by Netscape)
Internet Creator (by
   Forman Interactive)
Web Designer (by Corel)

◆ *So to get my business on-line all I have to do is create some Web-site pages, right?*

That's the first step and it can be accomplished in a number of ways. If you possess a reasonable amount of computer expertise and don't mind borrowing ideas from other Web sites, try creating the pages yourself. Greatly improved and very affordable off-the-shelf software has reduced the amount of specialized coding—known as hypertext markup language, HTML, for short—that's needed to build a Web site. This software writes in most of the necessary codes and allows novices to create and edit text, import and manipulate graphics, and add links to other pages as well as other Web sites. The manuals supplied with the software aren't all that helpful, so site creators may need to shell out a few more dollars for a nuts-and-bolts applications book. A scanner is needed to digitize any graphics you may want. If your computer system doesn't include one, the digitizing process can be handled quite inexpensively by computer stores and graphic-design shops. Store scanners electronically transfer images to a disk which then gets inserted into your computer's CD-ROM player. Sometimes you may even find appropriate graphics available on The Web itself. If so, download the images directly onto your system's disk.

A do-it-yourself Web presence can cost as little as $300. More importantly, it allows design originality that can make the site more appealing to shoppers. Frequent page changes to freshen up the site can be made without incurring additional cost as stale content discourages return traffic.

◆ *Suppose I decide creating my own Web site is not for me. What other choices are there?*

Probably the least difficult way for a home business to get on the Internet is to rent space on a cybermall. There are hundreds of malls available and they provide standard design templates that makes it easy for just about anyone to customize their own Web pages. The problem is the templates very much restrict design creativity and that's why so many sites on the Internet look as though they came off a cookie cutter.

If the product or service doesn't fit the template mold, or requires a site that's technically more challenging, the design work will have to be outsourced. Expect to pay several hundred dollars a page, plus extra for interactive features. A typical multipage Web site is likely to cost a minimum of $2,000.

SETTING UP SHOP IN CYBERSPACE THE EASY WAY— RENTING SPACE ON A CYBERMALL

Cybermalls are collections of businesses operating on the Internet in a sort of land-lord-tenant arrangement. The merchants pay a monthly rental to an on-line host who provides a range of Web-site services. Malls fall into three categories. Some malls host a mixed bag of businesses. Specialized malls only rent to retailers with related products and services, such as Civil War memorabilia, or stamps and coins. The third type of cybermall actually attempts to mirror the experience a shopper would have walking down the center aisle of a store-filled conventional retail mall. Some of these malls even have "anchor" stores—well-known retailers—to help build traffic for the smaller mall tenants. Rents in this type of mall are generally on the high side—$10,000 a year and up—and they have not lived up to sales expectations. A number have closed in the past several years.

Cybermall hosts provide a package of services that make it very easy for a business to establish a Web site. Usually it includes:

1. Space on the Internet for a Web site. Space is measured in megabytes—roughly one million bytes of information—which determines the number of site pages. Mall landlords charge a monthly rental and sometimes a commission on site sales. A few also assess a setup fee. Site maintenance is included in the monthly rental.
2. Standard templates for mall tenants to customize their own Web site pages. Some landlords offer design assistance for $50 to $75 per hour.
3. Help in obtaining a domain name (an Internet address registered to your business).
4. Assistance in registering the site with Internet directories and search engines.
5. Interactive site capability—shopping systems, membership systems, forms handling, etc.—technically referred to as CGI.
6. Twenty-four-hours-a-day sales transactions with secured credit-card payment.
7. Marketing advice.

Some of the more popular general malls for small businesses are:

Primehost (America Online): $199 monthly rental, $149 one-time setup.
Live Store (Viaweb): $100 basic charge for up to 100 items sold.
Alphagraphics.com: Monthly rental starts at $150, setup is $250. Company provides customized design service for $150 a Web page.

Welcome to the finest shopping on the web! This is where you'll find thousands of products and services for yourself, plus fantastic gift ideas for others, from the best shopping sites on the web. Take a stroll through our gourmet mall, or flip through our online classifieds... You'll find fantastic products, free catalogs, free contests, free samples, fun newsletters, hot specials, and lots more!

- **Mall Entrance**
- **Sales & Specials**
- **Enter Free Contest**
- **Send a Free Postcard**
- **Top 10 Lists**
- **Join Marketplace**

[   ] (SEARCH)

Featured Shoppe

Hammonds Hand Made Pretzels
The Oldest Continuously
Family Operated Hand-Made
Pretzel Bakery in America!
Find out about their famous
pretzel tins, their pretzel making process, & their history - then order their products for yourself, or as a gift for someone you care about.

MALL departments

GOURMET FOODS AND DELICACIES
Herbs/Spices . Baked/Sweets .
Ethnic/Regional
Health Food . Hot & Spicy . Meat/Game
Pot-Pouri of Items . Seafood . Snacks
Specialty Foods . Special Diets
Sauces/Condiments . Vegetarian .
Wholesale
BEVERAGES AND LIBATIONS
Coffee & Tea . Beer . Clubs . Wine/Spirits
NA Beverages . Accompaniments
PUBLICATIONS
Books . Bookstores . Newsletters/Mags
On Disk/CD-Rom
HOME, KITCHEN AND FAMILY
Appliances . Table & Cookware
Computer/Electronics . Computer Software
Pets
FLORAL AND GARDEN
Flowers Delivered . Seeds & Materials
Gardening Information

HEALTH, BEAUTY AND FITNESS
Diet Related . Vitamins/Supplements
Exercise Equipment & Accessories
Cosmetics

HOBBIES AND COLLECTIBLES
Antiques . Crafts

JEWELRY AND CLOTHING
Kids Clothes . Mens/Womens

LEISURE, TRAVEL AND HOSPITALITY
Dining Out . Tourism . Travel Accessories
Biking/Hiking Tours . Cigars

UNIQUE TREASURES AND GIFTS
Baskets . Corporate Gifts

Putting a Web site on a specialized cybermall can result in "foot traffic" from other mall tenants.

Acme Consulting
8615 Westwood Center Drive
Vienna, VA 22182
Phone: 1-888-AOL-1111
E-mail: acme@primehost.com

The nation's premier consulting service, Acme Consulting provides: systems integration service; hardware and software recommendations and sales; Internet consulting services; and business solution technical advice.

| Products/Services | Success Stories | Resource Library |
| Customer Service | What's New | About |

Typical template provided by cybermall hosts.

♦ *How important is Web site design?*

Since the Web site is your storefront, your brochure, your product catalog in electronic format, you certainly want it to stand out. It should catch the surfer's eye, keep them interested enough to stay with the site and, hopefully, buy what you're selling—and, if appropriate, return to your site for future purchases. Neither amateurish-looking site pages nor a site that simply reflects a throw-together of some of your print catalog pages will accomplish all your sales goals. How glitzy you make the site depends on what it takes to tip the decision scale in your favor. Remember, it takes only one click of the mouse for a visitor to jump to a competitor. When designing a Web site keep in mind the following:

1. Make the site professional in appearance. On the Internet, the only perception viewers frequently get of a company comes from the quality of the Web site. *HOT HOT HOT*'s Madison Avenue–look pages made the two-person, postage stamp–size company appear like a giant food conglomerate. Customers felt comfortable.

Welcome to Hot Hot Hot, the Net's original hot sauce shop!

We want to welcome you to the Internet's first "Culinary Headshop"! Here you'll find fiery foodstuffs you never thought existed. Please come in and browse!

We have MOVED! You are invited to drop by <u>our NEW Pasadena location</u> if you are in Southern California.

Our featured sauce this month is

<u>DOA - Cyanide Hot Sauce:</u>

If you're a first time user of this catalog, you may be interested in taking a look at.

- · <u>catalog instructions</u> or
- · <u>an introduction from the founders</u>

And now,

<u>To the Catalog!</u>

Check out some of our featured products.

2. Web pages have to be consistent in design, well-organized, and easy to navigate. Search engines, the Internet's site-locating mechanism, can bring visitors onto any Web page containing specific keywords or phases, not always the Home page first, as most people think. Visitors must be told where they are in the site and the choices available to them.

3. Don't overdose viewers with graphics. Downloading of nontext material can be painfully slow. Surfers are not known for their patience.

4. Make sure the HTML coding smoothly connects viewers to other pages. Haphazard links will cause surfers to abandon the site.
5. The inclusion of keywords and phrases—things that help the indices categorize your site—is a must if you expect the search engines to locate your site. Failure to use them properly can result in your site being overlooked.

Home-business entrepreneurs going on-line should first view a variety of Web sites that creatively blend typefaces, images, layout, and color into page structure, and learn from them how to incorporate the best elements into their own Web-site design.

♦ *How do I connect my site to The Web?*

Once the pages are composed, they have to be uploaded onto a server—usually a souped-up personal computer hooked to the Internet. While it's possible for a small business to acquire a server of their own and install a high-speed communication line, running and maintaining such a system requires too much in technical expertise. A better option for most small businesses is to let an Internet service provider—ISP, for short—provide the link to The Web. This can be one of the national commercial services, such as America Online, Prodigy, or Microsoft. Telephone companies and local ISPs also provide connections. Expect to pay $20 a month for basic service, and about $70 a month for higher-speed lines. In choosing an ISP, look for reliability first, followed by the availability of hosting services. These services can range from space for Web pages to the ISP acting as "Webmaster," handling site maintenance. When shopping around for an ISP, also consider access to a local telephone exchange. These calls are part of your basic monthly service, and free. Out-of-area calls have a charge.

♦ *Am I now ready to go live?*

Just about, but let's first check out the Web site to make sure it functions the way you intended. Call up the pages off-line with a Web browser, such as Netscape Navigator or Microsoft Explorer, and let someone unfamiliar with the site test it by selecting a product and placing an order, or for whatever other business the site is being used. If the process proves user-friendly, you're ready for cybermarketing.

Welcome to Joan & Annie's Brownies!

Hello Internet shoppers and welcome to our cybershop which features our gourmet, ultra-rich, deliciously fudgy brownies. Tucked midway between the shores of beautiful Lake Champlain and the Green Mountains of Vermont, Joan & Annie's is a small company whose fans include not only local Vermonters and New Englanders but Internet customers from all over the world.

We now use encrypted order forms to provide secure and private transaction via the internet

Who are Joan & Annie?

Joan and I are sisters. We started baking our brownies in 1988 and selling them from a pushcart at fairs and festivals around Vermont. Vermont is famous for its numerous summer and fall festivals and before long our brownies became quite well-known.

Today, Joan & Annie's Brownies are shipped all over the country, but they are still made the old-fashioned way-from scratch- just as we made them as kids growing up on a farm in rural Vermont. We use only the finest ingredients including creamy Vermont butter, farm fresh eggs and a premium grade chocolate. This makes our brownies rich, ultra-fudgy and very chocolaty- the way homemade brownies should be!

● **Need a quick, delicious, GIFT? Send a Brownie-Gram**

Husband's Birthday? Need to thank a client? Click to view our famous Brownie-Grams! We ship them all over the USA and positively guarantee them to arrive fresh and delicious.

ISP reliability important: Joan & Annie's Brownies started in a Vermont kitchen. In 1995 they contracted with an Internet service provider to host their Web site. For six months everything went fine, and media attention helped them sell their eight varieties of brownies all over the world. Then the ISP went out of business, taking with it the Joan & Annie's Brownies Web site and E-mail capacities. It took the company three months to get back up speed.

YOUR OWN WEB SITE—FREE

Most Internet service providers give subscribers some Web digital storage space—usually a minimum of two megabytes—for a personal home page. The number of Web-site pages a megabyte translates to depends on the mix of text and graphics. A home-business entrepreneur can use the personal Web site to promote products or services. The cost is nothing—it's covered by the subscriber fee. While such sites will not have all the interactive bells and whistles of a commercial cybermall, it still can serve as an effective promotional tool for a small business merchandiser or service enterprise just providing general information. Most sites will permit viewers to download E-mail forms, which can be used for ordering or inquiries.

In addition to the free Internet service-provider sites, home-based entrepreneurs should also check out no-charge sites offered by various cybercommunities. The major ones are:

www.tripod.com
www.geocities.com
www.angelfire.com
townsquare.usr.com

While the sites don't allow much in creativity, have strict guidelines for commercial promotion, and may have ads posted to your pages by the site host, it should be viewed as additional Web exposure at the right price.

25 CYBERMARKETING BUSINESS OPPORTUNITIES

♦ *What types of Internet businesses are suitable for home operation?*

Generally, the businesses fall into one of five categories. The most dominant, by far, is PRODUCT SELLING. Just about everything, with the possible exception of big-ticket items, can be sold on-line. Many products are sold by Internet merchants working from home. The Web also does well as an ELECTRONIC MARKETPLACE where buyers and sellers "meet" and transact business. More than a few auctions, classified ad sites, and special-interest cybermalls are hosted by home-based entrepreneurs. SERVICES, by their nature, don't easily lend themselves to electronic commerce. For a few types of businesses, such as job search and employee screening, being on-line has advantages. But for most service-type enterprises The Web only provides information on the business—essentially digital advertising. Providing INFORMATION is a popular Internet business, but revenues mostly come from advertising or the sale of site-related products, not from fees for content. The final category is CYBERACCESS, enterprises that help others use the Internet or set up a shop commercially. Web-site design, ideally suited for home operation, is included here.

What follows is a sampling of businesses operating on-line. Many were home-started. They reflect the diversity of commercial activity

> ## MEGASUCCESS—CYBERMARKETER: AMAZON.COM
>
> While there are tens of thousands of firms doing business solely on the Internet, few have achieved the success of *Amazon.com.* The company, started in a Seattle garage in 1994 by Jeff Bezos and four employees, created the concept and wrote the interactive software for the on-line mass merchandising of books. In only a few years the electronic retailer became a major competitor of long-established bookchains, such as *Barnes & Noble, Borders,* and *Books-A-Million.*
>
> *Amazon.com* customers who bring up the Web site on their computer screen are able to romp through a database of millions of books. Inquiries can be by title, author, subject, or even keyword. Ordering, also done on-line, only requires the completion of a simple form. Credit-card payments are accepted, with the transaction safeguarded by encryption. As one customer commented, "They don't make shopping any easier."
>
> The on-line book retailer keeps overhead low by inventorying only popular, fast-moving titles. Orders for nonstocked books are relayed to wholesalers and distributors for fulfillment. This allows *Amazon.com* to offer a very large selection of books from limited warehouse space and pass on the savings in the form of discounts to customers.
>
> Beating the competition by being the first super-cyberstore to mass market books has advantages, especially when it's done close to perfection. In a few years, *Amazon.com* was serving over half a million customers in 100 countries. Annual sales approached the $100 million–mark and a public stock offering gave the company a market value of $200 million. The firm's success, of course, has not gone unnoticed. The major chains have set up their own Web sites and are using sales promotion techniques pioneered by *Amazon.com.*

on the Internet, and, in some instances, exceptional entrepreneurial innovation.

PRODUCT SELLING

Music Superstore

CDnow was started by two brothers from the basement of their parents' Pennsylvania home. Initially, the cyberstore specialized only in jazz albums, offering just about every compact disc produced anywhere in the world. No inventory was stocked. Internet-placed orders were turned over to distributors for fulfillment. In two years the start-from-scratch venture hit $6 million in annual sales. The firm now offers a complete selection of CDs.

Wine Merchant

Some people say that the success of Internet wine retailer, *Virtual Vineyards*, is its cutting-edge Web site. "You can practically smell the Chardonnay." Also helping is the fact on-line store cofounder, Peter Granoff, is a well-known wine expert. Most of the wines are from smaller vineyards and not readily available in all stores. *VV* also sells specialty food items through the same site.

Novelty Distributor

When Canadian Susanne St. Amants shopped for merchandise associated with the TV cartoon, Sailor Moon, she couldn't find the items in any retail store. She was told the wholesalers stopped handling the products because the volume wasn't sufficient. But Susanne thought a market existed and set up a Web site run from her home. Named *Moon Kingdom*, the site is an order form for T-shirts, notebooks, and other Sailor Moon novelties. Reaching a worldwide audience, sales quickly grew to $10,000 a month. With profit margins at close to 50 percent , *Moon Kingdom* is profitable.

Industrial Product Supplier

World headquarters of *EPM*, Jerry Whitlock's industrial seal and gasket company, is his Stockbridge, Georgia home. The company maintains no inventory. When an order comes in over The Web (or phone, fax, and E-mail), Jerry tracks down a source and orders it for next-day delivery to his house. He then checks and repackages the items with *EPM* labels. Then, they're forwarded to the customer. Low overhead enables the home business to operate at a 60-percent profit margin.

Vintage Apparel

Looking for a 1970s sateen mustard-paisley long-sleeved blouse? You can find it on the *Rusty Zipper* Web site. The three people who founded the

rusty zipper vintage clothing

vintage clothing, books, patterns, & collectables

| all | All Clothing | | browse |

what's new   your order   home   email   about us   i was here   help   links   bulletin board   chat

add items to order

All Clothing (1-10). Total in this Category: 655.

Buy	Item	Product Description	Characteristics	Price
0	3205-M2186	70s -Lee- Dark green ladies leisure suit with jeans-cut flares. qty 1 available.	Womens Leisure Suit 36Bust 29Waist 31Inseam Good Cond.	$50.00
0	3204-M2185	70s -Unwinders, Dallas- Beige leisure suit with flares and white stitch trim. qty 1 available.	Mens Leisure Suit 40Chest 33Waist 31Inseam Good Cond.	$55.00
0	3203-M2184	70s -Levis Panatela- Medium brown leisure suit with flared pants. qty 1 available.	Mens Leisure Suit 40Chest 34Waist 31Inseam Good Cond.	$60.00
0	3201-M2182	60s Black beaded and sequined evening purse with goldtone trim. qty 1 available.	Womens Purse One Size Good Cond.	$24.00
0	3200-M2181	60s -Magid- Saks Fifth Avenue Black beaded and embroidered clutch purse. qty 1 available.	Womens Purse One Size Good Cond.	$16.00
0	3198-M2179	60s Navy blue patent purse with silver and gold bead handles. qty 1 available.	Womens Purse One Size Good Cond.	$14.00
0	3197-M2178	50s -Etra- Red leather clutch purse with convertible handle. qty 1 available.	Womens Purse One Size Good Cond.	$12.00
0	3194-M2175	50s -Smiths- Brown and white with black flocked abstract pattern tie. qty 1 available.	Mens Tie One Size Good Cond.	$8.00
0	3192-M2173	60s -Homespun Tweeds- Square bottom black and white, brown and red striped tie. qty 1 available.	Mens Tie One Size Good Cond.	$8.00

company from a Portland, Oregon, apartment felt there was a market for vintage clothing and various other 60s collectibles. But it was a market impossible to sell profitably—until the Internet came along. In 1995, a site

INTERNET AD EMPORIUM

EARRINGS, by Lisa!

Ordering Information...

NOTICE

Colors used to describe earrings do not reflect materials except: All `Turquoise` is GENUINE. `Sterling` and `14K` are used to describe precious metals, `Stones` used to describe real rock materials, `Beads` used to describe glass, clay and plastic, and non-precious metal objects.

Click on the description to see a picture of the product.

ITEM#--DESCRIPTION and PHOTO

More earrings coming soon!

IN16--Black and Silver Beads, Turquoise stones$6.00 **SOLD**

IN17--Turquoise stones flanked by silver$5.00 **SOLD**

IN18--Turquoise stones with gold$6.00 **SOLD**

IN19--Turquoise and pink stones$6.00**SOLD**

IN20--Green marbled glass with gold**SOLD**

IN21--Blue and Gold Beads in Gold Triangle$6.00 **SOLD**

IN22--COLORFUL Translucent Beads$4.00 **SOLD**

IN23--Black and Silver with Silver Medallion$5.00 **SOLD**

The Internet provides even the smallest home-based business with marketing opportunities previously available only to big business.

was developed for less than $1000. Service-provider monthly operating costs came only to $130. With expenses that low, *Rusty Zipper* made money almost immediately.

Up   **Show Order**   amnesty international usa   **Info**

Documents on Demand

Use this form to order many of the publications listed in the publications catalogue or under the online publications page. The file of the document(s) will be sent to your email address in text format within 48 hours. When you click the "order" button you will be taken to the Secure Order form. Under Section 4 of the the Secure Order form, please place the email address you wish the documents sent to. In the "Comments" blank of Section 4, please place the Country Name, Report Title, and AI Index Number for each document. If the document you requested is not available, you will be notified. Your credit card will not be charged until after the documents are sent.

Document   10.00   [Order]

Two Documents   20.00   [Order]

Three Documents   30.00   [Order]

Four Documents   40.00   [Order]

Five Documents   50.00   [Order]

Nonprofit organizations use the Internet to promote their cause and sell products to raise funds.

ELECTRONIC MARKETPLACE

Cyberauctioneer

Going once, going twice . . . sold. The sound of the gavel coming down may be missing from *Onsale* auctions conducted over the Internet, but the excitement of competitive bidding is still there. *Onsale* plays to The Web's strengths—real-time communication and interaction. Users can view the bidding on screen. Jerry Kaplan, *Onsale*'s founder, had failed with a previous Silicon Valley startup. True entrepreneurs don't discourage easily and he began again, this time with an on-line auction of computer goods and electronic items—mostly excess inventories of major suppliers. Within two years annual sales were approaching $80 million. *Onsale* went public in 1997 and Jerry's stock is worth $140 million.

Classified Ads

Aircraft Shopper Online provides a classified ad marketplace for corporate airplanes. Site visitors are able to download specification sheets. There are 800 to 1,000 ads listed daily and it takes an average of four months to sell an aircraft.

Real Estate

Owner's Network is a national home-listing service for people selling their own home. Users don't have to slog through lists of ads. They define the search parameters and receive matches via E-mail.

Wholesale Merchandise Broker

International Commerce Exchange Systems provides an on-line place where buyers and sellers can get together and negotiate for mostly closeout and wholesale merchandise. The Web site contains graphics and text describing 5,000 or so products. Sellers pay an annual fee to use the service.

SERVICES ON-LINE

People Finding

Old Friends Information Services of San Francisco, was founded as a hobby by someone experiencing difficulty locating a buddy. The firm uses electronic databases ranging from telephone books to state motor-vehicle records, and charges a $70 fee to begin the search. If the person is found, there's an additional charge of $50.

Consulting

Newport News, Virginia, psychologist Leonard Holmes does mental-health counseling on-line. Anxieties, marital problems, sexual difficulties—just about anything else bothering people—receive professional insight. The charge is $1.50 a minute and people are asked to pay only if they feel some benefits were received. About half do.

MEGASUCCESS—ON-LINE BROKER SERVICES: AUTO-BY-TEL

Auto-By-Tel (ABT) founder, Peter Ellis, was just recovering from the bankruptcy of his automobile dealership (he had 16 at one time), when he came up with the idea of selling cars via the rapidly growing Internet. The business concept wasn't exactly high-tech. In fact, it was rather simple. Car buyers complete a Web-site form specifying the car they want. The information then gets routed to a participating dealer close by. Within 48 hours the dealer has to contact the customer with a firm and fair price. Ellis launched his program on the Prodigy network in March 1995. He figured on 500 requests a week. On the fourth day 1,348 were received.

ABT now handles three-quarters of a million inquiries a year and feeds them off to 2,000 auto dealers who pay a subscription fee to belong to the system. Even with only $20 million in sales, ABT is now a major player in the trillion-dollar auto industry. General Motors is copying ABT's techniques. Almost $24 million has been invested by insurance and lending companies who want "a piece of the action."

In just two years the Internet has revolutionized a century-old business.

Leonard Holmes, Ph.D.

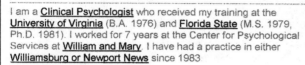
Behavioral Medicine Institute
640 Denbigh Blvd.
Newport News, VA 23608
(757) 872-8303
len@visi.net (Click to send email)

I am a Clinical Psychologist who received my training at the
University of Virginia (B.A. 1976) and Florida State (M.S. 1979,
Ph.D. 1981). I worked for 7 years at the Center for Psychological
Services at William and Mary. I have had a practice in either
Williamsburg or Newport News since 1983.

click here Internet Consultation Available--Pay if it helps **click here**

- Services Provided:

Individual and Couples Therapy, Stress Management, Biofeedback, Hypnosis, Eye
Movement Desensitization and Reprocessing (EMDR), Psychological Assessment, Divorce
Mediation.

- I work with:

Anxiety, Depression, Trauma & Incest Survivors, Eating Disorders, Substance Abuse,
Chronic Pain, Marriage and Family problems, Dissociative Disorders. Ages 13-up

Leonard Holmes is able to take advantage of the Internet's interactive feature to provide on-line consulting services. However, for most service-type businesses, The Web serves only as advertising—an electronic brochure.

Personal Matchmaking

Rosalind Resnick runs *Love Search.com*, an Internet personal-listing service, out of a Brooklyn brownstone. There is no membership fee, but users have to buy units of "playing time"—called lovebeads—to interact with the system.

Education

Legal aide Kathie Lachance and teacher Maureen Robinson founded the *Legal Services Institute*, which provides training material for scopists—people who proofread and edit court transcripts. In less than a year the educational firm hit $100,000 in sales.

Employment Services

In Pursuit, of Warrenton, Virginia, is a regional résumé preparation and job-search service. For a $40 fee, job seekers can have résumés posted on-line. Employers are charged $5 to list job openings.

INFORMATION PROVIDER

Entertainment News

Entertainment Drive—eDrive, for short—was started in 1994 by Michael Bolanos and Jeffrey King from an Astoria, New York apartment. The company, an entertainment forum hosted by *CompuServe*, was self-supporting almost immediately. *CompuServe* paid them a percentage of the time users were on-line reading the latest showbiz gossip, chatting, and downloading pictures of movie stars. The five-cents-a-minute they received has built a million-dollar business supporting a staff of thirty. *eDrive* is now on its own and an on-line store has been added to sell entertainment-oriented merchandise. Revenue-generating ad banners are displayed along with the entertainment news.

Investment Newsletter

In 1994, when two brothers, David and Tom Gardner, decided to go on-line with their financial newsletter, *The Motley Fool*, they could only boast 300 print subscribers. Setting up two server computers, the brothers contracted with America Online to publish a newsletter and conduct an interactive forum. AOL paid them a commission for member activity and the site became very popular. *The Motley Fool* is now available on the Internet and receives half-a-million "readers" a day. Advertisers pay well for the exposure.

Golf Library

GolfWeb primarily is an information service that posts everything anyone would want to know about golf—35,000 Web pages. A large viewer following attracts Fortune 500 advertisers who pay $30 to $40 for each thousand hits (Web surfers who key into the site). Premier membership and merchandise sales add to revenue.

Insurance Resource

A former financial journalist runs an insurance news site called *Insurance News Network*. Commercial arrangements with auto, home, and life insurance firms enable the site to sell insurance.

On-Line Magazine

A bunch of journalists decided they had had enough of the corporate rat-race and job uncertainty. They started their own on-line magazine, an E-zine, which is short for electronic magazine. The digital,

<u>bylines</u>
A gallery of fine writing

Table of Contents
To preview stories, click on titles

If I Die in the Service of Science	by Jon Franklin and Dr. John Sutherland, M.D. -- *The strange and sometimes tragic stories of medical scientists who experimented on themselves. This tour de force of the nonfiction short story explores the idiosyncratic ego and ambition that often drive medical history.-- 85,000-word nonfiction short story collection. $1.99*
The Mark	by Jacques Leslie -- *A war correspondent's memoir of Vietnam and Cambodia. In this lucid narrative a young Los Angeles Times reporter searches for truth in a land of lies and discovers the dark obsessions hidden in all of us. -- 101.000-word book. $2.50*

Getting a book published has always been difficult, but now even more so for publications with only modest sales expectations. Some authors are offering their books in digital format over the Internet. Customers pay by credit card and for about one-tenth the price of a retail store–sold print version, they can download the publication onto their disk. On-line publication offers no-risk publication opportunities for home-based entrepreneurs with knowledge of specific subjects that appeal to limited audiences.

advertiser-supported publication is called *Salon,* and it contains print-quality editorial content.

Cyber-Columnists

Working out of a cramped Los Angeles apartment, Matt Drudge provides a digest of newspapers, wire services, and journalist columns in a Hollywood gossip format, which is E-mailed to 85,000 subscribers. Support comes from America Online and $10 voluntarily donated by subscribers. Texas home-based Harry Jay Knowles also covers the Hollywood beat with his column, *Ain't-It-Cool-News.* Revenues come from the on-line sale of movie collectibles.

▆ RAINWATER PRESS

home | who we are | CHAT | CONNECT
titles | FAQs | glossary | guestbook

Rainwater Press Books

CHAT
by Nan McCarthy,
$7.95 (2nd edition) / $8.99 (1st edition)
First published by Rainwater Press in the
fall of 1995, this modern-day epistolary
novel is now available in bookstores
throughout North America as a 2nd
edition co-published by Rainwater Press
and Peachpit Press. Click here to read a
synopsis of CHAT, to read a sample
chapter of the book, to read what people
are saying about CHAT, or to go directly
to the order form.

CONNECT
by Nan McCarthy, $8.99
The wild ride continues in the second
book of the cybernovel trilogy,
CONNECT, which was published by
Rainwater Press at the end of 1996.
Everyone wants to know what will
happen next to Beverly and Max, two
lovers who met in cyberspace. Click here
to read a synopsis of CONNECT, to read
a sample chapter of the book, to read
what people are saying about
CONNECT, or to go directly to the
order form.

CRASH
by Nan McCarthy, $8.99
Don't let the title fool you! In the third
and final book in the series, CRASH, Bev
and Max's relationship takes some
breathtaking turns. If you've ever
wondered how to push the envelope in
an e-mail relationship, CRASH shows

Books can be effectively promoted on The Web by authors.

Just about every business is buying into the theory the World Wide Web will grow into a giant cyberbazaar. At first, Web sites were viewed as billboards, created once and then forgotten. Now they're recognized as continuing enterprises needing constant updating. Consequently, not only has setting up shop become a high priority, so has the establishment of an organization to maintain the site. But designing digitized pages that combine text, graphics, audio, animation, and video—not to mention product information—using the latest computer tools, isn't something that can be assigned to the secretary to do in spare time. The vast majority of companies lack the in-house technical skills to do the job themselves and have

(Continues)

CYBERACCESS

Internet Directory

In 1994, two trailer-living Stanford PhD candidates, David Filo and Jerry Yank, decided the Internet would be more useful if Web sites could be located in an orderly manner. They wrote a program that indexed the site in library catalog format and gave it the name, *Yahoo*. It was made available free to Web users. Revenues came from advertisers who were charged for the banners that span the top of their reference-site pages. The *Yahoo* directory has become the most popular Internet search index, visited daily by millions of surfers. When *Yahoo* went public, the two Stanford students ended up with stock worth $35 million.

Web Site Design

Meta 4 of Jersey City, New Jersey, began operation in 1995 with four people. Almost immediately they bid on a $4-million *General Electric* contract to develop Web sites for sixty-eight divisions of the global super-conglomerate. They won the bid. In just two years the design firm grew to thirty employees and were commanding fees running into six and seven figures. Cris Swenson founded *BATNET* from a Montclair, New Jersey, bedroom. The firm works almost exclusively for statewide and national associations. It quickly grew to a staff of ten. The *Princeton Internet Group* began designing Web sites as a sideline. It now serves over 100 clients. The New York City–based agency, *Com.Ltd.*, was started by two people in 1995. Two years later the Web-site design firm employs fifty.

Internet Service Provider

Dick St. Peters connects small business and consumers to the Internet from his rural home in Ballston Spa, in upstate New York. For a service-related fee, *Net Heaven* subscribers get access to the Internet, E-mail privileges, Web-site design help, and a one-to-one human response when computer assistance is needed.

CYBERCOMMUNITIES

The Internet has given birth to a completely new business model. Cybercommunities—on-line gatherings of people with common interests—didn't exist a few years ago. The Internet paved the technological way for easier communication and interaction, but it took business people to provide the framework for the human element—the chat rooms, bulletin boards, and discussion forums. Some were home-started. In 1995, Jackie Needleman and David Cohen installed two server computers in their Manhattan apartment. They created an electronic community for parents who wanted to exchange ideas with other parents—a sort of on-line coffee klatch for moms and dads. They called it ParentsPlace.com. Stephan Paternot and Todd Krizelman started Web Genesis in their Cornell University dormitory in 1994. They called their cybercommunity The Globe.

Other cybercommunities sprang up about the same time. Tripod was for young college-to-work adults who wanted a place on the Internet to "hang out." The Web site is anchored by an on-line magazine that provides information of interest to that age group, such as personal finance and career development. Members—now about 400,000—get help creating their own home pages and a forum is provided for "conversation." Joining is free, but requires the supplying of personal information used to attract advertising, their main source of income.

Geocities, a 500,000 "homesteader" cybercommunity, is organized into neighborhood groups. Members pick a "neighborhood"—Wall Street, science fiction, Hollywood—whatever their interest. About 70 percent of the revenues are derived from advertisers who like the neighborhood concept because it makes it easier to target consumers. Other Internet communities include UTNE, described as a hippie Reader's Digest, The Well, with hundreds of discussion groups, Chatty Talk City, Women's Wire, and Parent Soup.

Not every cybercommunity makes it. Mom's On-line was taken over, and, after two years of operation ParentsPlace.com was bought out by the parent of their competitor, Parent Soup and the two founders became employees. Web Genesis had better luck. When The Globe had grown to 600,000 subscribers, Jack Egan, the founder of Alamo Rent-A-Car, invested $20 million. Web Genesis now operates from lower Manhattan with a staff of twenty.

to outsource the work to Web-site design firms. Many of these firms were started by computer hobbyists who learned to use The Web's basic writing tool, HTML, and freelanced services to small business. Providing Web-site design and maintenance services to the business community offers better than average profit opportunities for those seeking to work from home.

VIP version

NEWS ROOM

GRAB BAG

CHAT
Atomic Café
Box Music Zone
TV Chat
Rapture Café
Singles Bar
Original Globe Chat
Private Rooms
The Crypt
Club K-Swiss Chat

ORBIT
Globe Mail
VIP Directory
Dear Livewire

SPARK
Singles Bar
Forums
Flirt Personals
Lola

RAPTURE
Rapture Café
Box Music
Ink
Tainted
Flicker

HI JINX
Blackjack
GlobeComics
Flip

Welcome to The Globe! With more than 650,000 members, The Globe is **the premier community on the Internet**. Members of The Globe have their own websites, launchpads, and they engage in live chat and discussion forums twenty-four hours a day, seven days a week.

Make friends while chatting in The Globe's live chat with your choice of four interface types, including auto-scroll Java.

Want your own website? Try the easy-to-use HomePage Builder!

Discuss anything from politics to relationships with thousands of other Globe Members in BabbleOn..., or get News Headlines automatically. |F|L|I|C|K|E|R| and Mute are your sources for the latest in movies and music

Join the premier community on the 'Net! Just Register for FREE! Then, upload your **Personal Chat Icon**, set up your **Globe Personal Homepage** and your **Launch Pad**! It's free! Register today!

LIGHT AT THE END OF THE CYBERTUNNEL

26

Making Money on the Internet

♦ *Now that I've established a presence on The Web, how do I get people to visit?*

If I build it, will they come, is a question every marketer asks. Once the pages have been uploaded to a server and a URL assigned, the Web site is accessible to tens of millions in the global marketplace. That's where the technology ends and the management talent begins. Marketing is no less a challenge in cyberspace than it is in the traditional business world. Start out by letting surfers know you're out there. Write a brief, but attention-getting announcement describing your product or service and register the site with Web directories and search engines—indices that help surfers locate sites by category or keywords. This is the Internet equivalent of the Yellow Pages. The fastest listing method is to use "Submit It," an Internet marketing service that has links to all of the indices. They offer various registration and new site announcement options for a fee. Internet service providers and cybermalls hosting Web sites also offer listing services. But if you have the time and want to save some money, you can handle the registration process yourself by bringing up each directory and search engine on your computer screen and just following their listing instructions. After you've gone through the process don't automatically assume you're registered. Mistakes happen. Take the time to

NEWSGROUPS

Newsgroups, also known as forums, consist of numbers of Internet users interested in a particular subject. Information on the subject is exchanged through the posting of E-mail messages on "bulletin boards." There are over 15,000 newsgroups across The Web.

verify it using your business category and key words. If a search doesn't produce a listing, find out why.

◆ *Is registration alone sufficient to attract enough site visitors to make the business profitable?*

Some people, no doubt, will stumble onto your Web site by accident. Directories and search engines contribute to building traffic, but inquiries usually produce a staggering number of matches. Without some name recognition, the odds are against your site being selected. So while registration puts your site into play, that alone won't attract enough visitors to keep the business afloat. You'll have to do more.

One proven traffic builder is the posting of E-mail notices with appropriate newsgroups—ones that might appeal to the same type of audience. That's what LaVerne and George Ferguson did and it paid off. The husband-and-wife team operate *Rail Pass Express*—a company that sells Brit Rail and Eurail train passes from a Columbus, Ohio location. In 1994 they began posting information on train travel to America Online's travel forum message board, only mentioning in a sort of by-the-way fashion that the firm also sold train passes. The first year they took in $60,000. The following year a Web site was established in addition to the postings, and revenues jumped to $300,000.

An Arizona law firm also used E-mail for promotion, but less discreetly. They posted a 170-word message (i.e., advertisement) for immigration legal services to the members of 6,000 discussion groups. In Internet jargon, this is known as *spamming*. The process, which only took a few hours and cost less than $100, reached a million people. Close to 25,000 verified inquiries were received (along with an abundance of hate mail) and the promotion produced over $100,000 in billing.

Overt selling should be avoided when dealing with newsgroups. While some groups accept advertising, most do not, and resent the commercializing of their forum and retaliate in the form of bombarding the E-mail address of the intruder with derogatory messages. It's called *flaming*. Internet etiquette requires you to first check the newsgroup's "Frequently Asked Questions" section to see what's acceptable. Obtain permission if you're not sure. However, some group members may have previously signed up for product and service offerings and it's okay to target them with E-mail pitch letters. E-mail lists are sold by Internet marketing firms.

♦ *What about using conventional promotional techniques?*

Going on the Internet doesn't eliminate the need for nonelectronic advertising. The Web should be viewed only as a component of a comprehensive marketing-mix program. All your customers may not yet be on the Internet, and the only way to reach them is the old-fashioned way—print. In addition, a high percentage of traffic will come from people who see an ad or mailing piece, and then go to the Web site for more information. That's why it's important to continue with some traditional promotion, though possibly reduced. One more thing. *Don't forget to list the Web site address on all company communications.* This includes letterheads, business cards, and fax cover sheets.

♦ *Some Internet businesses seem to have done better than others. What can we learn from their experiences that might help those just coming onto The Web to turn the profit corner faster?*

There are two ways the Internet can improve a company's bottom line. Generating a profitable level of sales is, of course, the most obvious. What follows are some steps a business can take to make this happen. But it would be a mistake to ignore the cost benefits of marketing on The Web. Case-in-point: Ursula Kuehn, owner of *She Sails*, used to spend $20,000 a year to print and mail 12,000 catalogs promoting her company's line of clothing for women sailors. She now gets the same customer response on-line, but the cost is only $300 a month to maintain the electronic catalog. And there are ancillary benefits, such as instantaneous merchandise availability and price adjustments. Timely information updating is a major advantage of catalog marketing on the Internet.

Now for some solid advice from the Internet-savvy.

1. Stay flexible in your business planning and be prepared to go with the flow of the market. The Internet is still developing and hard and fast rules don't always apply. Even well thought-out business plans may fail to produce expected results. Some business-plan

She Sails
Product Catalog

Section: Off-shore/On-shore Clothing

To see a larger picture, click on any graphic.
Select Size, Color (if needed) and Add item to your shopping cart.

On-Shore/Off-Shore Clothing

Clothes that both fit a woman's body and are specifically designed for sailing are still fairly hard to come by, but we've found some for you.

NEW! Sailing Shorts

Made of supple, breathable and quick drying Supplex® with a super tough Cordura® double seat. PACKED With useful design amenities like deep side pockets, non-corroding zippers and waist adjustment straps that adjust down 2", these shorts can't wait to go sailing. The fanny fender®, an insertible 1/2" closed cell foam protector, distinguishes this functional short from all others as it offers buttocks and thigh protection at your option. Offered in two leg lengths -- Breaker Bermudas ... just above the knee, Breaker Midlengths ... three inches shorter

No:		Size:	Color:	Price:	
No: 085-034	Sailing Angles Breaker Bermudas	6	Khaki	$65.00	Add
No: 085-035	Sailing Angles Breaker Midlengths	6	Khaki	$65.00	Add

tinkering may be necessary and, occasionally, a complete change of direction. For example, take the experience of *InfoSeek*. They started out as a search engine and anticipated profits would come from the selling of subscriptions to a variety of databases. Millions used their free Internet search services, but few subscribed to the databases. They quickly altered their business strategy and began to promote the Web site as an advertising medium. It's now their major source of revenue.

2. Utilize The Web's interactive features. Creative use of the Internet's two-way communication can give cybermerchants competitive advantages over non–on-line businesses. *Virtual Vineyards* doesn't just sell wine over the Internet, but entices wine buffs into an informative, interactive world where they can tour the Web site and get questions intelligently answered. In another example of interactive creativity, *Amazon.com* and a number of other on-line book retailers post personal critiques of publications and keep customers informed via E-mail of new books on their favorite subjects and by their favorite authors. These are the kinds of services that are making the Internet the first stop for an increasing number of shoppers.

3. Offer a broad selection of merchandise, or specialize. Two of the most successful pioneer cybermerchants, *Amazon.com* and *CDnow*, are nothing short of on-line superstores. Viewers choose from a vast digital inventory—far more product than they would physically find at most local retailers. But bigness isn't the only way to make it on the Internet. There's also success on the other end of the electronic commerce spectrum. Small, specialty businesses such as the Ferguson's *Rail Pass Express*, which sells European train passes, have carved out profitable niches in much larger markets.

4. Develop multiple revenue sources. While the numbers of people using The Web to acquire goods and services is growing, many businesses have found pursuing a hybrid strategy helps them break-even faster and widen profit margins. *GolfWeb*'s revenues come from a combination of advertising, merchandise sales, and fee-charged premier memberships. Seventy percent of on-line community *GeoCities* is from advertising, but the remaining 30 percent

Niche marketing offers most home-business entrepreneurs the best opportunities for succeeding on-line.

comes from premium services, merchandise sales, and pay-to-play gaming. Auctioneer Jerry Kaplan's *Onsale* has begun to accept advertising. Jerry says, "It's money from heaven."

5. Link up with other cybermerchants. *Amazon.com* has signed up 10,000 associate Web sites. Mostly mom-and-pop on-line businesses, they programmed their Web site to refer customers to the book retailer and receive commissions on the sales made. All that the users have to do is click on highlighted areas—called hot links—and they are automatically moved to the new site. The referral arrangement is called syndicated selling and practiced in one form or another by the more successful cybermerchants. An Internet marketing firm, *Link-Exchange*, has a membership program that allows small-time Web-site operators to swap advertising space on their own site for space on others.

SMALL BUSINESS RESOURCES ON THE INTERNET

There are lots of helpful information on The Web for aspiring entrepreneurs. To save you time, I've listed below the Internet addresses of some of the better sites. The site sponsors are all selling something, but the resource material accompanying the commercial message will help start you off on the right foot. Each address begins with http://www.

> smalloffice.com
> wilsonweb.com
> lowe.org
> inc.com
> workingsolo.com
> viaweb.com

In addition, check out yahoo.com. Their small- and home-business listings are well-organized and easy to use. The Small Business Administration is also worth a look. Their Web address is http://www.sba.gov/.

---

6. Create businesses unique to the Internet. Some ventures on The Web are not just replications of traditional businesses, but new commercial concepts. *Tripod* is an Internet "virtual community" that allows its members to "hang out"—communicate with and share ideas and thoughts with other members. Members are also encouraged to create site content and programs. The Web site has become the cyberspace equivalent of the local bar.

7. Offer bargains. Surfers seem to flock to Web sites that save them money. Cyberauctioneer *Onsale* provides computer and electronic items that can be purchased at prices way off list. The site attracted a large following almost from day one. Electronic investment brokering is growing at a dazzling pace because the fees charged are even lower than that of discount brokers. *Auto-By-Tel's* "no haggle" pricing appeals to car buyers who don't like the take-no-prisoners sales tactics of some auto dealers.

8. If the product is information, get businesses to pay if possible. Internet surfers, spoiled by the abundance of free material on The Web, don't readily shell out dollars, even for popular services. The most successful information sites—directories, search engines, and on-line communities sites—derive most of their revenues from advertisers. *Auto-By-Tel* is funded by the auto dealers

NEW LIFE FOR AN OLD BUSINESS

After *Jetstream,* a traditional mail-order catalog company for aviation products, went bankrupt, Marc Coan, an individual associated with the firm, decided to offer the same merchandise through a catalog published only on-line. That saved almost $3 million in printing and mailing costs. He changed the company's name to *The Aviation Shopping Network* and had Viaweb host the thousand-item catalog Web site for $300 a month. Orders received are immediately E-mailed to suppliers who drop-ship to Network customers.

who pick up sales leads. Participating companies looking for business support *Life Quote*, a Web site listing life-insurance rates.

9. Make transactions easy. Whether it be ordering merchandise, auction bidding, receiving services, or making payments, cybermerchants who make doing business on-line a snap for users are rewarded with repeat sales. Some have even gone further in making the process customer-friendly. *RoweCom*, a firm that sells publications to libraries, uses a debit-card payment concept. When a magazine is ordered, the cost is automatically deducted from the library's bank account, eliminating bills, checkwriting, and credit-card approvals.

10. Cybermerchandise. Web surfers return to sites that offer periodic super-sale specials, contests, and giveaways. *Smart Games*, an on-line game retailer, promotes cash prizes to high scorers. *Amazon.com* has regular drawings for free books, but to be eligible to win surfers have to register and answer some questions on their marketing preferences. The companies use this information to attract advertisers and in promoting sale of their own merchandise.

The Internet is changing the face of entrepreneurial opportunity. New avenues to attain financial independence are being created. Here are some on-line business models. Match them up with specific products and services and it is possible you'll have the seeds of the next *Amazon.com*, *Yahoo*, or *Auto-By-Tel*.

◆ No-Inventory Merchandising: Increasing numbers of manufacturers, wholesalers, and distributors are willing to work with home-based businesses to drop-ship orders directly to customers. They provide the warehousing and fulfillment while the home business provides the on-line marketing and billing.

◆ Referral Partnerships: Create Web site-linked partnerships with electronic commerce merchants willing to pay commissions for referrals leading to sales. Internet technology makes it easy to track.

◆ Information Micromarketing: Text and graphics can be delivered over the Internet at almost no cost. Provide user-pay, on-line niche newsletters with information not easily available elsewhere and you'll be able to turn a profit with just a few thousand subscribers.

Punk Rock Prize Package Giveaway

This week 5 people will win prizes from:

SUB POP + LOOKOUT records

Are You Feeling Lucky?

You could be the proud owner of this week's prize, a package filled with goodies from
two of todays premiere independent labels, Sub Pop and Lookout Records!

Your prize package will include:

- Limited edition Sub Pop Records catalog poster
- Sebadoh poster
- Sebadoh notepad
- Sebadoh suntan lotion
- Sebadoh stickers.
- Lookout Records postcards
- Lookout Records stickers
- Auntie Christ CD
- Mr. T Experience CD
- Groovie Ghoulies CD

There's no purchase necessary, so what do you have to lose?
Just fill in the entry form below and cross your fingers!
Only one (1) entry per person.

We will choose five (5) winners from the entries received by 1 PM EST July 29, 1997.
We always have a new contest in the works, so be sure to check out this page regularly!

<u>Click Here For Official Rules of This Week's Cool Contest</u>

Contests and prizes return shoppers to the Web site.

Contests and prizes return shoppers to the Web site.

This announcement is neither an offer to sell nor
a solicitation of an offer to buy these securities.
The offer is made only by the prospectus.

850,000 Shares

JAVELIN
SYSTEMS INC.

Common Stock

Meridian Capital Group, Inc.
Sharpe Capital, Inc.

$5.00 Per Share

Copies of the Prospectus may be obtained
in any State in which this announcement is
circulated only from such of the undersigned
as may be legally offer these securities in such State.

You may view the prospectus of the completed offering by double-clicking the tombstone.

If you are not a member of IPOnet, please check the QUALIFIED INVESTOR definition and REGISTER.

W.J. Gallagher & Company, Inc., is not an underwriter of the securities of Javelin Systems Inc.
but is authorized to accept customer orders for the purchase of the securities.

PLEASE REVIEW THE STATES LIST BELOW.

As of 10-21-96, the Javelin Systems Inc. offering may be circulated in the following States;

CA. CO. FL. GA. HI. NV. NJ. NY. OR. VA. UT. WA.

As of 10-21-96, the Javelin Systems Inc. offering is pending in the following states;

None

Securities Offered Through
W.J. Gallagher & Company, Inc.
Which Conducts it's Investment Banking & Securities Business at
747 East Green Street, Pasadena, California 91101
Securities may also be offered by other Broker/Dealers
(Please see individual offering)

" W.J. Gallagher & Company, Inc. is not registered in the following states, therefore residents of these states may
not receive sales material or, make indications through W.J. Gallagher & Company, Inc. or its representatives."

AR. AZ. DE. ID. MA. MN. ND. NH. RI. TN. VT. WV.

Prospectus published on-line. There's increased use of the Internet by business to raise investment capital.

RAISING CAPITAL ON THE INTERNET

Not only does the Internet offer moneymaking business opportunities, it also is providing entrepreneurs with a new tool in their search for small amounts of capital through public stock offerings. When Jim Webb of *U.S. Abalone* wanted to add tanks that would expand his firm's fish farm capacity, he chose the Internet to promote the stock offering. Instead of spending $160,000 for the printing and mailing of circulars, he got the SEC and California to approve publication of the prospectus on a Web site. Within a few months 400,000 shares were sold at $5 a share. New York's *Spring Street Brewery* had difficulty getting a bank loan for expansion. They didn't turn to the public-offering brokers who take sizable commissions, but chose instead to go to the World Wide Web. Approximately $1.5 million was raised from 3,500 investors. Connecticut-based *Annie's Homegrown* used their existing product-merchandising Web site to describe the offering. It was promoted to the public by stuffing announcements as to the availability of the stock issue into one million macaroni-and-cheese boxes, the firm's food product. Underwriting costs only came to 5 percent of the $3 million raised, instead of the usual 13 percent.

Raising money on the Internet requires companies to follow the same Federal public offering regulations as those who use conventional methods of raising capital. Five million dollars is the limit under the simplified SEC program created for small business, but direct public offerings of one million dollars or less are exempt from Federal regulations.

♦ Regional Resources: It's only a matter of time before most people will make the Internet their primary local information source for sale items, classified ads, and entertainment. Advertising-supported, regionally focused Web sites have promising growth potential.

Technology is moving at a blinding pace and The Web's future ability to deliver quality sound, video, and animation will give it increasing mass-audience appeal. In the next few years purchases on The Web are expected to go from $1 billion to $8 billion. For home-based entrepreneurs who take the time to learn the craft of cybermarketing, the future will not be disappointing.

PART FIVE

Special Information Chapters

READY-TO-RUN HOME BUSINESSES

27

Business Opportunities

F or those who feel comfortable running a business but prefer to avoid some uncertainties as well as minimize the bumps and grinds of starting one there are business opportunities. Some can be run out of the home.

A business opportunity is a licensing agreement to sell products or services. It can take two forms—a franchised or nonfranchised business opportunity arrangement. With a franchise comes a protected territory, use of the seller's trade name, trademark, business systems, and procedures, extensive training, materials, and continuing support. For this the franchisee pays an initial fee, monthly royalties on sales, and often an advertising surcharge.

A nonfranchise business opportunity is generally less expensive than a franchise, the support provided by the seller is usually (but not always) limited to manuals and telephone assistance, it does not permit use of a trade name, and there are no protected territories. Nonfranchised business opportunity arrangements are far less restrictive and allow entrepreneurs much more operating freedom. Most important, royalties are not required. While franchise sellers make most of their money by taking a percentage of the monthly sales of the buyer, nonfranchise business opportunity sellers generate earnings through the initial fee and the sale of equipment and supplies.

Entrepreneurs who are thinking about going the franchise route should be aware of what to expect from a turnkey package, as well as what not to expect.

◆ While the franchisor provides marketing support in the form of advertising and promotional material, the responsibility for acquiring customers still rests with the franchisee. This usually means hard work and long hours—no different from any other type of business venture.

◆ Some franchisors tend to inflate statements of earnings potential, leading buyers to anticipate more profit than the business is likely to deliver. For the earnings claim to have any validity, it has to be written in the disclosure document or more comprehensive "Uniform Franchise Offering Circular." Profit representations made verbally by salesmen mean nothing legally. A prospective franchise buyer should carefully investigate revenue claims by contacting other franchisees *not* selected by the franchisor. A personal visit to several operating units is recommended.

◆ Don't overestimate the value of protected territories. All this means is that the franchisor will not license someone else in the designated area. It won't, however, keep out competitors licensed by other franchisors.

◆ Beware of scams. While the majority of franchisors are legitimate, rip-off artists are everywhere. It's against the law to require up-front fees and no payment is allowed until ten days after receiving the disclosure information. A dishonest franchisor will use the services of "singers"—people paid to pose as successful franchisees. Some fraudulent operators provide little more than training courses. Others set up phone offices, take the money, and disappear. A call to the Better Business Bureau can help identify disreputable franchisors.

The most difficult task for an entrepreneur is selecting a franchisor who is new, and therefore, doesn't yet have a successful track record. Will it live up to the agreement and be around in a year or two to provide support? If the franchisor has been operating for years on a nonfranchise basis, chances are it will remain in business. If not, the risk is, of course, greater. Also, always have a franchise attorney look over the agreement.

Nonfranchise business opportunity sellers operate under fewer legal regulations than franchise providers. For example, only a 5- to 10-page contract is needed for a sale to take place, compared to the 75- to 100-page "Uniform Franchise Offering Circular" that franchise transactions require. This, however, puts more of a "buyer beware" responsibility on the non-franchise business opportunity purchaser and certain precautions should be taken.

♦ Don't accept the seller's profit figures without checking with others who have bought business opportunities.
♦ Read the contract and get everything in writing. If you are not sure, consult a lawyer.
♦ Check out the company. How long has it been in business? Is the company willing to provide a financial statement? Does the Better Business Bureau list any complaints or the state attorney general any legal violations?
♦ Don't readily accept purchase terms—negotiate. Some payments may be deferred until delivery of equipment or supplies or even later.

Included in this chapter is a selected list of both franchise and non-franchise business opportunities that can be run from the home and brief descriptions of some typical operations. These listings are in no way an endorsement, and they are not the only business opportunities available in each category. A complete listing of franchises can be found in the annual franchise issue of *Entrepreneur* magazine, which comes out in January, and the *Franchise Annual* published every year by Franchise News. Lynie Arden's *Franchises You Can Run from the Home*, published by John Wiley, contains in-depth descriptions of 101 franchises. Nonfranchise business opportunities are included in the annual July issue of *Entrepreneur* magazine.

FRANCHISES: BUSINESS SERVICES

Franchisor trains franchisee to provide payroll, bookkeeping, and tax services to small business owners. Franchisee then markets the services in a designated territory and works with clients gathering data. The information is entered into a computer terminal and processed on the franchisee's

computer or transmitted to the franchisor's mainframe. Completed reports
are then delivered to the client by the franchisee.

◆ *AFTE Business Analysts*

2180 North Loop West
Houston, TX 77040
713-957-1592

◆ *Advantage Payroll Services*

800 Center Street
P.O. Box 1330
Auburn, ME 04211
207-783-2068

◆ *Binex-Automated Business Systems*

6324 Marshall Drive
Sacramento, CA 95842
916-483-8080

◆ *Padgett Business Services USA*

160 Hawthorne Park
Athens, GA 30606
800-323-7292

FRANCHISES: ADVERTISING SERVICES

Franchisors in this business are direct-mail marketers of advertising material, while franchisees are essentially sales representatives who call on
local businesses to solicit advertising for a mailing with other advertisers
to a designated area. The franchisee roughs out the ad and forwards it to
the franchiser, who does the typesetting, artwork, printing, and mailing.

◆ *Coupon—Cash Saver*

1020 North Milwaukee Ave.
Deerfield, IL 60015
708-537-6428

- *Money Mailer*

  14271 Corporate Drive
  Garden Grove, CA 92843
  800-624-5371

- *TriMark, Inc.*

  184 Quigley Boulevard
  New Castle, DE 19720
  800-874-6275

- *Val Pak Direct Marketing Systems*

  8605 Largo Lakes Drive
  Largo, FL 33773
  813-393-1270

FRANCHISES: TAX SERVICES

Franchise sellers train franchisees in personal income tax preparation. Franchisee markets service, meets with clients, and obtains relevant tax data. A worksheet is prepared by the franchisee, which is processed by a computer and checked for accuracy by the franchisor. Tax data may be electronically filed with the IRS. Some franchisors allow clients to borrow money on refunds claimed.

- *H&R Block*

  4410 Main Street
  Kansas City, MO 64111
  800-829-2000

- *Jackson Hewitt Tax Service*

  4575 Bonney Road
  Virginia Beach, VA 23462
  800-277-3278

- *Triple Check Income Tax Service*

  727 South Main Street
  Burbank, CA 91506
  818-840-9077

FRANCHISES: REFERRAL SERVICES

Franchisor instructs franchisee in program administration. In pet and house care service this instruction might cover number of visits, feeding techniques, special pet medication, and other house sitting–related duties. Franchisee recruits local personnel to carry out service and receives a percentage of the charge. In some referral services, such as home improvement, franchisee screens and lists tradesmen, who pay monthly for listing and also a fee per lead.

◆ *Child-sitting service*

Sitters Unlimited
23015 Del Largo Dr.
Laguna Hills, CA 92653
714-752-2366

◆ *Family day-care services*

Monday Morning Moms
276 White Oak Ridge Road
Bridgewater, NJ 08807
800-335-4666

◆ *Domestic help search*

TGIF Peopleworks
P.O. Box 828
Old Lyme, CT 06371
203-434-1262

◆ *In-home pet care*

Pet Nanny of America
340 Morgan Lane
Lansing, MI 48912
517-336-8622

◆ *Pet boarding at private homes*

Pets Are Inn
27 North 4th Street, #500
Minneapolis, MN 55401
800-248-7387

FRANCHISES: MISCELLANEOUS

◆ *Newborn announcement products and services*

Stork News of America
5075 Morganton Road, #1214
Fayetteville, NC 28304
919-868-3065

◆ *Dining and shopping guide*

Buying & Dining Guide/TV News
80 Eighth Avenue
New York, NY 10011
212-243-6800

◆ *Balloon decorating*

Balloon Bouquets
69 Killburn Road
Belmont, MA 02178
617-484-5907

NONFRANCHISE BUSINESS OPPORTUNITIES

◆ *Monogramming and embroidery service*

Meistergram
3517 West Wendover Avenue
Greensboro, NC 27407
919-854-6200

◆ *Personalized children's books*

Create-A-Book/Presto Personalized Books
1232 Paula Circle
Gulf Breeze, FL 32561
800-732-3009

Best Personalized Books
4201 Airborn
Dallas, TX 75428
800-275-7770

NONFRANCHISE BUSINESS OPPORTUNITIES COME WITH HIGH RISK

Franchised business opportunities have a reasonably good track record. Nonfranchised business opportunities don't. Too often the only ones making money are those selling the dream. Unfortunately, it's an industry with more than a fair share of con men who move from scam to scam. A million dollars here, a million dollars there, adds up to a comfortable lifestyle. Those buying into the "low investment–high profit potential–no experience necessary" sales pitch will usually end up as victims. The fast-talking, high-pressure peddlers of business opportunities have even given them a name—"moochies." Of course, not all nonfranchise business opportunities are dishonest. Many have been around a long time and provide the investor with realistic expectations. But if you're in the market for a business opportunity, just don't move too fast and keep your guard up.

◆ *Home-sitting referral service*

Homewatch
2865 South Colorado Boulevard
Denver, CO 80222
303-758-7290

◆ *Business billing services*

Bluejay Systems
2579 Clematis S.
Sarasota, FL 34235
813-325-3357

◆ *Gift baskets*

Gift Basket Connection
3 Juniper Court
Schenectady, NY 12309
800-437-3237

◆ *Photo business cards*

Color-Fast Marketing Systems
9522 Topanga Canyon Boulevard
Chatsworth, CA 91311
818-407-1881

Kustom Cards International
1018 E. Willow Grove Avenue
Wyndmoor, PA 10938
800-207-1678

◆ *Sewing instruction for children*

Kids Can Sew
P.O. Box 1710
St. George, UT 84771
800-KIDS-SEW

28 THERE'S A BUSINESS FOR EVERYONE

Work-at-Home Opportunities for Retirees and the Disabled

There are a number of similarities between retirees and the disabled, and for that reason both groups are covered in this chapter.

♦ Often retirees and the disabled have no choice other than home-based work for health reasons. Commuting can be too strenuous, and for some, an impossibility.

♦ Both groups, more often than not, are faced with limited work-at-home opportunities—the handicapped because of physical or mental problems and retirees because of self-imposed restrictions (avoiding stress, for example), as well as health factors for some.

♦ Both retirees and the disabled generally have limited capital to invest in home ventures. Banks hesitate to make loans to members of either group, and retirees who have savings will generally not risk their nest egg.

♦ Both retirees and the disabled will usually choose to limit earnings, since government benefits are reduced when reportable income reaches certain levels.

Here are a number of work-at-home opportunities that easily fit into lifestyles that are different.

MCADOO RUGS

McAdoo Rugs was started in 1975 as a home retirement activity by Preston McAdoo's parents. Six years later Preston took over and with his wife, Cynthia, built it into the largest suppliers of hand-hooked rugs in the country.

Ideas for rug designs come from the McAdoo family's creative imagination. Grandmother McAdoo came up with the primitive drawing of a house, a barnyard, and a pair of red long johns hanging from a clothesline. The most famous design came from the McAdoo's daughter, then eight years old, who created a black-and-white holstein cow with starry eyelashes.

As the firm grew, it had to move out of the McAdoo barn to a 200-year-old mill across the street. Here employees do the wool color dyeing and some of the rug hooking. The firm also jobs out rug hooking to three dozen home-based craftspeople, many Laotian refugees, who were trained in hand hooking by Preston. The company supplies the yarn and design.

Rugs are priced about $70 to $80 a square foot. About one-third of the orders from the North Bennington, Vermont, company are for custom designs, such as customers' pets and houses, which cost up to $500 extra. Over a thousand rugs are sold every year, some through retailers, but mostly mail order. It is, and is likely to remain, a family business.

CRAFTS

Craft activities offer the opportunity for retirees and the disabled to engage in creative and stress-free work as well as earn money to maintain their standard of living. A wide range of craft products are marketable, but obviously the workmanship has to be at quality levels that would appeal to people other than family and friends.

Selling crafts presents more of a problem to the disabled than to retirees. Most craft items are sold at craft fairs, something many retirees enjoy doing. For example, retired former schoolteacher Ken Cassie and his wife, Shelly, have turned a pottery hobby into a $20,000-a-year business. They do about twenty shows a year—all within four hours' driving time of their New Jersey home—and sell everything from tiny $5 vases to $150 birdbaths.

Many disabled persons would have difficulty doing shows and must depend upon retailers—boutiques and gift stores—to sell their creations. Direct sales are sometimes possible by mail order. Displaying consignment merchandise at church bazaars is another selling opportunity. Product displays in lobbies of government buildings and in libraries provide recognition and can result in some revenue.

TELEMARKETING

Telephone-related activities can be done at home by just about anyone with the ability to communicate verbally. The work may include making appointments for professionals and home-service businesses, market surveys, fund-raising for charities, and product selling. Charges can be by the hour, on a per-call basis, or solely a commission on sales.

HOUSE SITTING

An increasing number of vacationers prefer to leave their pets—dogs, cats, birds, fish—in the hands of a reliable house-sitter who will make one to two visits each day for feeding and caring for pets, watering plants, and taking in the mail and newspapers. Generally this type of service is limited to fifteen miles from the sitter's home and charges are in the eight-dollar-per-visit range with add-ons for extra pets.

CHILD AND ELDERLY CARE

Many people feel more comfortable with older sitters than with teenagers. While five-day-a-week care activities can fray the nerves of some, special services may be especially rewarding financially and not tie down an individual to a daily routine. These services might include baby-sitting for hotel-stayers, weekend sitting for vacationers, and conventional evening sitting.

WORD PROCESSING

Many businesses, students, and professional people have typing needs that can be easily filled by retirees and some physically challenged people.

Transcription services—medical, legal, etc.—offer additional work-at-home opportunities. (The Hadley School for the Blind, 700 Elm Street, Winnetka, IL 60093, offers tuition-free courses in medical transcriptions). Data entry and typesetting are also frequently outsourced, and offer the disabled money-making activities that can be done at home. Social service agencies in major cities (The Federation of the Handicapped in New York City, for example) provide training for disabled using Federal funds, and in some instances utilize the homebound in a telecommunication-linked dictation system.

COMPUTER PROGRAMMING

Possibly the most interesting opportunities for those restricted to the home are in computer-related businesses. Major corporations, both out of need and to comply with the Americans With Disabilities Act, have increased their use of retirees and the disabled in programming. Federal and sometimes state money is available for training. Pennsylvania-based *Abilitech* sells programming and system analysis services to industry. About 75 percent of their staff are disabled trained under a grant project. Some of the trainees have gone on to freelance careers. Check with the local rehabilitation and employment services offices as to what training funds might be available.

BED-AND-BREAKFAST

More than a few retirees have added to income by running a bed-and-breakfast establishment, either in the house they've lived in for years or in a new home in an area in which they choose to spend their senior years. What tourists look for is an old, elegant house with some history—something Grandma might have lived in. Extra income can come from a willingness of the owners to move into the basement or enclosed porch during peak seasons. Meeting new people can be fun, but retirees should be aware that servicing them isn't. It's a round-the-clock activity.

PET BOARDING

Many pet owners would choose to leave animals with someone who could give them the tender loving care the pets get at home. An ideal money-making business for homeowner retirees and disabled persons who have a fenced-in backyard.

INCOME TAX AND MEDICAL FORMS PREPARATION

Retirees and even wheelchair-bound handicapped persons can assist others in simplified tax preparation four months out of the year and in medical-form submissions to health insurers.

TUTORING

One-on-one instruction in a variety of academic or special subjects can produce sideline income with practically no investment. All it usually takes to get started is a small classified ad.

HOME BUSINESS STARTUP FUNDS AVAILABLE FOR DISABLED

Edith Quarles, of Wyandanch, New York, had lupus and was unable to work outside her home. In 1989 she applied for and received an $11,000 not-to-be-repaid grant from a state agency that passes through Federal funds for the disabled. With the money, which was used to build a separate kitchen—a health-department requirement—she opened a home catering business specializing in sweet potato pie. Pathmark Supermarkets was her first major customer. To handle the increased business volume, Edith received a $60,000—3-percent interest—handicap assistance loan from the SBA and moved the operation out of her kitchen and into a 5,000-square-foot factory building. The company, "Q's," produces 2,000 sweet potato pies each week.

TELECOMMUTING

Some firms use the handicapped in jobs that have a home computer linked to a processing center in the home office. JCPenney has been using home-bound disabled people for catalog sales since 1987.

◆ ◆ ◆

Retirees and the disabled need not necessarily be restricted to small-scale activities. Some have built substantial businesses.

- ◆ June Griswold, who has multiple sclerosis, turned Special Care, a referral service that provides aides to the elderly, chronically ill, and disabled, into a business with multimillion-dollar revenues.
- ◆ At age sixty-nine, Richard Ellis of Annapolis, Maryland, started Senior Services, a referral service that helps older people find contractors for home-improvement jobs. The fee is 10 percent to 20 percent of the labor charges.
- ◆ Sixty-nine-year-old Bernice Seiden operates Executive Research Associates, a human resource management firm, out of her Baltimore home.
- ◆ Former IRS agent Myron Gold started MG Tax Consultants at the age of fifty-five from his Monsey, New York, home. The firm assists companies and individuals who have dealings with the IRS.

Those with special circumstances should focus on capabilities, not on their limitations. Remember, some of the world's greatest people—Roosevelt, Beethoven, Stienmetz, Edison—had difficulties to overcome, and someone by the name of Harlan Sanders, known as the Colonel, started Kentucky Fried Chicken with a Social Security check at age sixty-five.

29 LEGALESE MADE EASY

Home Business Legal Advisor

L ike it or not, if you go into business, even a small home venture, it
means dealing with the law. Home-based entrepreneurs should become familiar with some fundamental legal concepts as well as specialized
problems that relate to working from home.

CONTRACTS

In simple terms, a contract is an exchange of promises between two or
more parties that is enforceable by law. Contracts require that there be an
offer and an acceptance of the offer for some consideration (compensation), that the people who sign it be competent (mentally competent and of
legal age), and that the transaction be legal, that is, not in conflict with the
law. When merchandise or services are ordered by you or from you using
a purchase or sales order, those documents are legally binding contracts.
If you don't pay, you can be sued, and if you don't get paid, you have the
right to sue. In the event a favorable judgment is entered but the debt is not
paid, a lien—a legal device that holds property for satisfaction of the
debt—can be placed against some asset. This asset can be sold to satisfy
the debt.

IMPLIED WARRANTY

When you buy or sell a product or service, certain conditions are implied even though they are not stated in writing. The first condition is that the seller has the right to transfer the goods, that is, owns them. The second implied warranty is that the merchandise is fit for ordinary purposes for which such goods are used, or if sold for a special purpose, that it can be used for that purpose. For example, if you sell someone a watch, it's expected to keep accurate time or the law can make you refund the money. These implied warranties can only be avoided if the goods are sold "as is" or a defect exists that is clearly evident upon inspection.

PRODUCT LIABILITY

A business is responsible for any product or service manufactured or provided or sold by it that, because of defect, causes injury. Generally the law is on the side of the injured party. The first line of defense is to make certain the product or service created or purchased for resale is safe, and written materials warn against potential hazards. Product liability insurance is available to protect against lawsuits.

ADVERTISING—GENERAL

False advertising, whether intended or through a misunderstanding, is a violation of the law and is subject to a penalty. Moderate degrees of exaggeration are acceptable but not claims that fool the public. That is considered deceptive advertising intended to mislead the purchaser. For example, you can't offer something free and then increase the original price to make up the cost. You also cannot decrease the price of a ten-dollar item a few cents and legally advertise it as a sale. Advertising claims must be backed up in the event they are challenged, or you can end up in court—and sometimes jail.

Displayed advertising, such as signs outside places of business, are restricted by zoning laws in many communities. Local laws should first be checked.

Distribution of advertising fliers, such as handouts or door-to-door delivery, may require permits from local governmental agencies. Also, you can't put any advertising material in mail boxes. It's against USPS regulations.

MAIL-ORDER ADVERTISING

Fraud, that is, taking money under false pretenses, is illegal and postal authorities are always on the lookout for mail-order offers that promise a return that far exceeds the norm. The penalties can be quite severe. Superior Worm Brokers Exchange advertised that they would set up investors in earthworm farming and provide them with a ready market for the worms. They collected $6.5 million before the postal service forced the company to suspend operations. The president was sentenced to twelve years in federal prison. In another instance 28,000 investors lost almost $80 million from a yogurtlike culture that "unlocked beauty secrets." The Kansas-based firm claimed there was a commercial market for the product, which could only be grown in six-ounce glasses. The operators pleaded guilty to fraud-related charges and are now serving prison time.

The law also specifies delivery requirements. Mail-order merchandise has to be delivered in a thirty-day period unless a longer time is stated conspicuously in the advertisement. If the thirty-day period can't be met, the seller must send an "option notice" indicating a new shipping date and give the buyer the opportunity of either canceling the order and receiving a full refund or agreeing to the new shipping date. The refund must be paid within seven business days, or on a charged purchase, within one billing cycle.

PATENTS, COPYRIGHTS, AND TRADEMARKS

A patent provides a seventeen-year exclusive right to make, use, and sell an invention in the United States. It will only be issued for new or improved useful products, processes, and machines. While it takes several years to obtain, inventors can still obtain some protection by documenting developments in a dated, stitched (not looseleaf) notebook or prepare a disclosure letter describing the invention in detail, signed by two witnesses, notarized, and mailed to themselves. Entrepreneurs should be cautious about spending several thousand dollars for protection because some patents can easily be circumvented by anyone who wishes to steal the idea. A reputable patent attorney is the best source of information on whether any worthwhile protection can be obtained.

Copyrights protect artistic creations, literary writings, graphic illustrations, musical scores, computer programs, and published material such as newsletters. Ideas and concepts cannot be copyrighted. The process is simple and inexpensive. All that has to be done is to print a copyright notice somewhere visible on the work, followed by year of publication and the name of the originator. Then make application to the U.S. Copyright office.

Trademarks are words, names, illustrations, or a combination of these used to identify products or services to distinguish them from items of other firms. A trademark doesn't prevent anyone from selling similar products or services, just from using similar names and illustrations.

To avoid using trademarks already licensed, first check with the *Trademark Register of the United States*, found in major libraries. Full legal protection is available by registering the trademark with the U.S. Patent and Trademark Office.

EMPLOYING LABOR (NONHOMEWORKER)

Home businesses employing individuals must abide by federal and state wage laws that include:

- ◆ The minimum wage—federal or state, whichever is higher—must be paid.
- ◆ Overtime must be paid at one-and-one-half times the regular hourly rate for all hours in a week beyond forty.
- ◆ Excluded from the minimum wage and overtime requirements are spouses, children under the age of twenty-one, executive, administrative, and professional employees, and salespeople who work off premises on commission.
- Accurate records on wages and hours must be kept for three years.

Employing Homeworkers

With the exception of certain products prohibited by the federal and state regulations, businesses may employ people over the age of eighteen to work out of their homes. In addition to the usual employee information—name, address, Social Security number, hours worked, wages earned, overtime pay, and deductions for Social Security and withholding taxes—specific records must be kept on the type of work, operations performed, dates work is assigned and returned, piece rates paid, and the hours and wages paid for each batch of work. The purpose of this data is so the governmental labor agencies can verify minimum wage levels are at least being met.

Laws Restricting Homework

Industrial homework laws, both federal and state, regulate the farming out of work by employers to home-based employees. The laws are intended to eliminate sweatshop-type conditions and the use of underage workers in the home. They do not restrict individual entrepreneurs from manufacturing products that they sell themselves, or the right of legitimate independent contractors to produce items. While federal restrictions on homework have recently been modified, some states still prohibit the manufacture of specific products and require employer or homeworker registration, or both. The restricted products are:

- ◆ *Food and drink:* California, Illinois, New Jersey, Pennsylvania.
- ◆ *Wearing apparel:* California, Hawaii, Indiana (certain items), Maryland, Massachusetts (certain items), Michigan, Missouri, New Jersey (certain items), Ohio.
- ◆ *Toys and dolls:* California, Illinois.
- ◆ *Artificial flowers:* Maryland, Missouri.
- ◆ *Purses:* Indiana, Michigan.
- ◆ *Feathers:* Missouri.
- ◆ *Note:* New York has a general restriction on all homework in all industries, but with many exceptions. Certain types of apparel, gloves, artificial flowers, and feathers are covered under special provisions. Contact the regional office of the Department of Labor for a copy of the regulations.

◆ *States with employer or homemaker registration requirements, or both:* California, Connecticut, Hawaii, Illinois, Indiana, Maryland, Massachusetts, Michigan, New Jersey, New York, Pennsylvania, Rhode Island, Tennessee, Texas, West Virginia, Wisconsin.

◆ *Federal regulations:* Employers must obtain licenses, which are renewable every two years, and also keep a log of hours worked and products made so inspectors can judge whether wage laws are being met.

◆ *Occupational safety and health:* If you employ people, they must be provided with a work situation that does not expose them to risk of harm. While all businesses are covered by Occupational Safety and Health Act regulations in concept, companies with ten or fewer employees are exempt from the record-keeping requirements or inspection unless in response to a complaint.

SALES AGENTS

If people are to be used to sell a product or service, all terms should be spelled out in a formal agreement that includes the following:

◆ A clear description of the products or services to be sold.
◆ Limitations preventing the agent from selling or representing competing products or services.
◆ Territory assigned and exclusivity if intended.
◆ A stipulation that sales will be made at designated prices and that orders are subject to acceptance.
◆ Commission rate and when payments will be made.
◆ Responsibility for expenses.
◆ Method for terminating contract.

CONSIGNMENT

Home entrepreneurs who produce items such as crafts and works of art often market them through retailers on a consignment basis. To make certain the consigned merchandise legally remains the property of the consignor an agreement should be drawn up that clearly spells out the conditions of the sale. It should include:

◆ Specific items consigned.
◆ Length of time the merchandise can remain unsold before the consignor can demand their return.
◆ The retail price and percentage of the selling price to go to the consignor.
◆ When payment of sold products is due.
◆ Responsibility for loss.

RESOURCE GUIDE

Gathering information on a business before startup can help would-be entrepreneurs avoid some of the pitfalls of inexperience and channel efforts down the right path from the outset. Resource material in this book covers valuable references of a more general business nature and items related more or less to specific subjects.

RECOMMENDED BOOKS

The following selection of books will be found in most libraries and well-stocked book stores.

Two excellent resource publications are *Working Solo Sourcebook*, by Terri Lonier, and Lynie Arden's *Work-At-Home Sourcebook*. They both list all the general business books relating to home operation, as well as publications that go into somewhat more detail on specialized work-at-home topics. For general books on home entrepreneurship, there's the Paul and Sarah Edwards series. Start with *Working from Home. Homemade Money*, by Barbara Brebec, is one of the more popular guides to a home-based business career. Barbara is especially knowledgeable in crafts, so check out her *Creative Cash*. Also worth a look is *Small Business Advisor*, published by *Entrepreneur Magazine*. Two classic books in their respective fields are Bob Stone's *Successful Marketing Methods*, and *Tested Advertising Methods*, by John Caples. John's book has been around for half a century and is still considered to be the advertising copywriter's "bible."

HELP ORGANIZATIONS

Startup assistance can come from the variety of organizations. All provide information of sorts, some conduct seminars and workshops and also publish newsletters. The membership associations are good for idea networking and may be able to put you in touch with someone who is already operating a home business similar to the one you are contemplating.

◆ *Small Business Administration:* Provides a range of services, including technical and financial, from its regional offices. It also assists entrepreneurs in their information search. Call the Small Business Answer Desk at (800) 827-5722. They are open 9:00 A.M. to 5:00 P.M. On The Web, the address is www.sba.gov.

◆ *Service Corps of Retired Executives (SCORE):* Has a group of more than 10,000 business executives who volunteer free counseling to startups and going businesses. It is sponsored by the Small Business Administration. Their Web address is www.scn.org/civic/score-online.

◆ *American Association of Home-Based Business*, P.O. Box 10023, Rockville, MD 20849. (202) 310-3130 or (800) 447-9710. www.aahbb.org.

◆ *Small Office Home Office Association*, 1767 Business Drive, Reston, VA 22090. (703) 438-3060 or (888) SOHOA-11. www.sohoa.com.

◆ *Home Business Association*, 4505 S. Wasatch Blvd., Salt Lake City, UT 84124. (800) 664-2422. www.homebusiness.com.

◆ *National Association for the Self-Employed*, 2316 Gravel Road, Fort Worth, TX 76133. (800) 443-8004. www.nase.org.

◆ *Home Office Association of America*, 909 Third Ave., New York, NY 10022. (800) 809-4622. www.hoaa.com.

SMALL BUSINESS MAGAZINES

Business Week, Fortune, Nations Business, and *Forbes* are fine publications for keeping up with general business news but they don't usually cover small business topics particularly well. What follows are magazines especially targeted at "little guys" who want to become entrepreneurs of bigger businesses.

- ♦ *Entrepreneur Magazine*, 2392 Morse Avenue, Irvine, CA 92714. This is an excellent magazine for the small business entrepreneur.
- ♦ *Inc.*, 38 Commercial Wharf, Boston, MA 02110. A quality publication for the larger small business.
- ♦ *Home Office Computing*, 730 Broadway, New York, NY 10003. Provides valuable information for computer-related home entrepreneurs.
- ♦ *Income Opportunities*, 1500 Broadway, New York, NY 10036. Monthly magazine focusing on home-based business and companies with five employees and under.

LIBRARY REFERENCE BOOKS

Reference books can provide information or direct you to sources where help is available. Here is a list of the general reference guides most used by those engaged in operating a small business. They are almost always available in larger public or college libraries.

- ♦ *Books:* Check the subject heading of *Books in Print* (R.R. Bowker) and you'll find the titles available, publisher, and ordering information. Aside from publishers and local libraries, books can sometimes be found through regional library systems and trade associations.
- ♦ *Publications:* More likely than not there will be one or more publications covering the subject of your interest. *The Gale Directory of Publications* (Gale Research Co.) contains 23,000 publication listings. The *Standard Periodicals Directory* (Oxbridge Communications, Inc.) is another source for publications on specific subjects. A listing of 5,000 newsletters in 150 areas will be found in the *Oxbridge Directory of Newsletters* (Oxbridge Communications, Inc.).

◆ *Magazine articles:* Magazine articles can provide helpful information of more recent doings. A listing of what's been published is available in the *Business Periodicals Index* (H. W. Wilson).

◆ *Associations:* If there is a group functioning in a specific field, it will be listed in the *Encyclopedia of Associations* (Gale Research Co.). These organizations also often have available publications related to their specialty that are not easily obtainable elsewhere.

◆ *Local industrial firms:* The *State Industrial Directories* (State Industrial Directories Corp.) are excellent guides for data on manufacturing firms. Each directory covers a single state and lists businesses by county, city, and type of business. Also listed are sales volume, employees, and company officers. Almost every public library will have this or a similar publication available.

◆ *Products and services:* The *Thomas Register* (Thomas Publishing Company) is a multivolume reference series that provides information on American manufacturers categorized by products and services, brand names, alphabetical listings, and detailed product data. If you want to find where products, parts, and materials can be purchased, this reference is the bible.

◆ *Media information for advertising:* The *Standard Rate and Data Service* (Standard Rate and Data Service, Inc.) provides all you need to know about data and advertising rates for magazines, newspapers, radio, TV, direct mail, community publications, and card-deck mailings.

◆ *Trade shows:* Possibly the quickest way to gather business information is to attend a trade show. When and where they are held will be found in *Trade Show and Professional Exhibits Directory* (Gale Research Co.), *Directory of Conventions* (Successful Meetings magazine) and *Tradeshow Week Data Book*. (Trade show listings on The Web are at www.expoguide.com.)

◆ *Publicity:* The most comprehensive reference source on what media editors want is *Bacon's Publicity Checker* (Bacon's Publishing Company). Another source of publicity information is *Working Press of the Nation* (National Research Bureau). For an easy-to-use guide on the media, try *Gebbie Press All in One Directory* (Gebbie Press, Box 1000, New Paltz, NY 12561). It is inexpensive enough to be considered for a small-business home reference library.

GOVERNMENT PUBLICATIONS

Available free or at nominal cost are a number of government publications helpful to small entrepreneurs.

Internal Revenue Service Publications: These are free—check with the local IRS office, or write to IRS Technical Publications Branch, 1111 Constitution Avenue, N.W., Washington, D.C. They also can be ordered from the Government Printing Office (800) 424-3676, or downloaded from The Web: www.irs.ustreas.gov.

- Tax Guide for Small Business (No. 334).
- Business Use of Your Home (No. 587).
- Record Keeping for Small Business (No. 583).
- Self-Employment Tax (No. 533).

Small Business Administration: The SBA publishes a series of helpful booklets and useful bibliographies on different subjects. They may be available at the local SBA office, or you can write to Small Business Administration Publications, P.O. Box 46521, Denver, CO 80201, and ask for SBA 115A (free publications) and 115B (low-cost booklets). They also may be ordered by phone—(202) 783-3238—using charge cards, and also over the Internet: www.sba.gov.

THE FIFTY MOST USEFUL WEB SITES FOR HOME-BASED BUSINESS

While there are many good sites on The Web containing information for starting and operating businesses run out of the home, a number stand out as being exceptional from the standpoint of regularly updated content, ease of use, and an acceptable level of commercial intrusion. They offer a mixed bag of solid advice, business-opportunity ideas, real-life success stories, downloadable articles, links to other small business-related sites, and some also serve as a forum for communicating electronically with other entrepreneurs. Here are the sites, by category, but in no particular value order (all addresses begin with http://).

Home/Small Business—General Reference

On-line magazines/newsletters:

◆ *Inc.* Online: www.inc.com
◆ *Small Office Computing/Home Office Computing*: www.smalloffice.com
◆ *Entrepreneur Magazine* Small Business Square: www.entrepreneurmag.com
◆ *Business@Home*: www.gohome.com
◆ *Entrepreneurial Edge* Online: www.edgeonline.com
◆ *Income Opportunities* Online: www.incomeops.com

Major company sites:

◆ Apple Small Business: www.smallbusiness.apple.com
◆ Claris Small Business Central: www.claris.com/smallbiz
◆ Intel: www.intel.com
◆ American Express Small Business Exchange: www.americanexpress.com/smallbusiness
◆ Ideacafe (Costco): www.ideacafe.com
◆ Time Vista Boardroom: www.pathfinder.com/timevista
◆ BellSouth: www.smallbiz.bellsouth.com

Other sites:

◆ Janet Attard's Business Know-How: www.businessknowhow.com
◆ Business Resource Center: www.morebusiness.com
◆ Entrepreneur's Mind (The Benlore Company): www.benlore.com
◆ smallbizNet (The Edward Lowe Foundation): www.lowe.org
◆ The Small Business Advisor: www.isquare.com
◆ Working Solo: www.workingsolo.com

The commercial on-line services also offer home business information. Check America Online's "Workplace" and Prodigy's "Working from Home."

Electronic Commerce

On-line magazines/newsletters:

- Ziff-Davis Publications: www.zdnet.com
- *Computerworld Emmerce*: www.computerworld.com/emmerce
- CMPnet: www.techweb.com/smallbiz
- *NetProfit Magazine*: www.netprofit-mag.com

Major product/service company-sponsored sites:

- IBM: www.ibm.com/e-business. Also pay a visit to IBM's small business center, which is linked to the above.
- Microsoft: www.microsoft.com
- Hewlett-Packard (*E Business Magazine*): www.hp.com/Ebusiness. The company's site also has a link to a general small business section.

Other sites:

- Wilson Internet Services: www.wilsonweb.com/webmarket

Women and Minorities

- BizWomen: www.bizwomen.com
- The Women's Network: www.ivillage.com
- *WAHM* (The Online Magazine for Work At Home Moms): www.wahm.com
- Women in Business, Cyberspace Field of Dreams: www.fodreams.com
- WOW (Woman Owned Workplaces Network): www.womanowned.com
- Online Women's Business Center: www.onlinewbc.org
- *MLM Woman Newsletter* Online: www.mlmwoman.com
- Black Business Web: www.blackbusiness.com
- *Hispanic Business Magazine* Online: www.hispanicbusiness.com

The U.S. Small Business Administration (www.sba.gov) also offers a variety of programs to assist women and minority entrepreneurs.

Franchising and Business Opportunities

◆ American Association of Franchisees and Dealers: www.aafd.org
◆ Be The Boss: www.betheboss.com
◆ Business International Sales & Opportunity Network (BISON): www.bison1.com
◆ FranInfo: www.franinfo.com
◆ Federal Trade Commission Franchises and Business Opportunities: www.ftc.gov/bcp/franchise/netfran.htm

Telecommuting

◆ The Homeworker's Network: www.sktc.net/rjmurphy/index.htm
◆ EscapeArtist: www.escapeartist.com/tele/commute.htm

Some of the general home/small business Web sites previously listed also contain information on telecommuting. *Business@Home* (www.gohome.com) is one with better than average coverage.

Raising Capital

◆ MoneyHunter: www.moneyhunter.com
◆ Venture Associates: www.venturea.com
◆ America's Business Funding Directory: www.businessfinance.com

Two other sites previously listed are also worth a visit by capital-seeking entrepreneurs. They are the *Ideacafe* (www.ideacafe.com) and the *U.S. Small Business Administration* (www.sba.gov).

Miscellaneous

- ◆ Liszt: www.liszt.com. This directory of E-mail lists can help a startup business build a customer base.
- ◆ American Success Institute: www.success.org. An educational Web site especially helpful to first-time-in-the-business-world entrepreneurs.
- ◆ The Canadian Office Products Association (COPA): www.copa.ca
- ◆ Canada/British Columbia Business Service Centre: www.sb.gov.bc.ca/smallbus

The last two entries are Canadian sites providing home and small business information that can be just as useful to American startup entrepreneurs.

INDEX